Kennedy's Kitchen Cabinet
and the Pursuit of Peace

Kennedy's Kitchen Cabinet and the Pursuit of Peace

The Shaping of American Foreign Policy, 1961–1963

PHILIP A. GODUTI, JR.

McFarland & Company, Inc., Publishers
Jefferson, North Carolina, and London

LIBRARY OF CONGRESS CATALOGUING-IN-PUBLICATION DATA

Goduti, Philip A., 1974–
 Kennedy's kitchen cabinet and the pursuit of peace : the shaping of American foreign policy, 1961–1963 / Philip A. Goduti, Jr.
  p.   cm.
 Includes bibliographical references and index.

 ISBN 978-0-7864-4020-7
 softcover : 50# alkaline paper

 1. United States—Foreign relations—1961–1963. 2. Kennedy, John F. (John Fitzgerald), 1917–1963—Friends and associates. 3. Cabinet officers—United Staes—History—20th century. 4. Political consultants—United States—History—20th century. I. Title.
 E841.G576   2009
 973.922—dc22   2009031981

British Library cataloguing data are available

©2009 Philip A. Goduti, Jr. All rights reserved

No part of this book may be reproduced or transmitted in any form or by any means, electronic or mechanical, including photocopying or recording, or by any information storage and retrieval system, without permission in writing from the publisher.

Cover images and art ©2009 Shutterstock

Manufactured in the United States of America

McFarland & Company, Inc., Publishers
 Box 611, Jefferson, North Carolina 28640
  www.mcfarlandpub.com

For Alyssa, Alex and Olivia

Acknowledgments

Many scholars have documented the Kennedy administration, and this book stands on the shoulders of their work. For this book, Arthur Schlesinger's work on Robert Kennedy deserves special mention. His work, *Robert Kennedy and His Times*, uses papers that are not yet available to the public. His study remains instrumental in any analysis of RFK's role in the Kennedy administration. Additionally, Ernest May and Philip Zelikow's work, *The Kennedy Tapes*, provides a one-volume resource for Kennedy scholars that sheds light on the drama within the cabinet room those thirteen days in October.

The first six chapters of this book could not have been done without the help of Dr. J. Garry Clifford and Dr. Shirley Roe of the University of Connecticut. Both of these professors provided feedback that was essential for the book's completion. I am very grateful for their time and suggestions.

The first six chapters of this book served as my master's thesis, entitled "To Khrushchev, with Love: Kennedy's Soviet Policy, 1961." The thesis looked at McGeorge Bundy, Ambassador Llewellyn Thompson, Secretary of State Dean Rusk, and others who counseled JFK in that first year. This study was done under the guidance of Dr. Frank Costigliola of the History Department of the University of Connecticut. Dr. Costigliola read several drafts of the manuscript and gave advice on the scope and nature of these times. He has been a wonderful mentor in understanding the complex issues surrounding the Berlin crisis. Indeed, his instruction endured helping me finish the manuscript into this final product, covering the entire Kennedy administration.

Special thanks goes to the Arnold Bernhard Quinnipiac University Library. The interlibrary loan department housed Robert Kennedy's oral histories for me in the summer of 2008. Also, Stephen Plotkin and the staff at the John F. Kennedy Library were very helpful in bringing together the vast sources related to the Kennedy administration. Special thanks to Santo Galatioto for accompanying me to the Kennedy Library and sifting through documents—we had a great time.

This book would not have been possible without the encouragement of Dr. Ronald Heiferman at Quinnipiac University. Professor Heiferman has been an advisor, mentor and friend for fifteen years. He was one of my first college history professors and also the man who gave me my first class to teach. In more ways than one, he started my career in teaching and studying history. His guidance over the past fifteen years has helped me a great deal, and for that I am very grateful.

I also want to thank my family. My parents, Philip and Rosemarie Goduti, have always encouraged me in my pursuits. Thank you for giving me the gift of dreaming. My Uncle John and Aunt Sharon have been instrumental in my growth, and I am thankful for their positive influence and constant support. My grandparents, John and Rose Mendes, who are no longer with us, were also instrumental in this book. Their support of my education gave me the drive to explore history. Indeed, their story is inspirational.

Finally, I want to thank my wife Alyssa and our children Alex and Olivia, to whom this book is dedicated. I started writing this book nearly five years ago, holding my then-infant son in the early morning hours. I finished it with my two-year-old daughter playing at my feet. This project took a great deal of time and Alyssa was very committed to helping me achieve this goal. For that I am eternally grateful. She always told me to write from the heart and stay true to my passion for history. I hope I have succeeded in that endeavor. The three of you are my greatest inspirations.

Table of Contents

Acknowledgments — vii
Preface — 1
Introduction — 5

Part One. The First One Hundred Days: Crafting Foreign Policy in the Kennedy White House

1. The Over-Cautious Approach — 12
2. Germany and Cuba — 26

Part Two. Mission to Vienna: The Preparation of the Commander in Chief and the Impact of a Summit

3. The Art of Diplomacy — 40
4. "A very sober two days" — 54

Part Three. "Once more unto the breach": Constructing the Wall Between America and the Soviets

5. The Vienna Effect — 70
6. "Perhaps a wall" — 85

Part Four. Brother's Keeper: Robert F. Kennedy's Role in Presidential Decision-making

7. Jack and Bobby — 106
8. RFK and the CIA — 119

Part Five. "Dogs of War": McNamara, the Joint Chiefs and the American Military Complex

9. Whiz Kid and War Hero …… 132
10. The Joint Chiefs of Staff …… 145

Part Six. Waiting for the Enemy to Blink: Perspectives on the Cuban Missile Crisis

11. Preparing for a Storm …… 158
12. Brinkmanship in the Kennedy White House …… 176

Part Seven. "No man is an island, entire of itself": Leading to Peace and Cooperation

13. "A Strategy of Peace" …… 198
14. "Ich bin ein Berliner" …… 212

Epilogue …… 223
Chapter Notes …… 225
Bibliography …… 235
Index …… 237

Preface

In the spring of 2003, America prepared to wage war on Iraq. Less than two years after 11 September 2001, George W. Bush and his advisors laid the groundwork for an invasion. At the time, I was working on a master of arts in history at the University of Connecticut. For my thesis, I wanted to explore the Kennedy years, but was unsure how to approach the topic. On the brink of the Iraq war, the media depicted very able and intelligent people leading America. After all, Richard Cheney and Colin Powell were very influential in George H.W. Bush's presidency, leading a successful war in the Persian Gulf. The events of 2003 led me to ask what role these advisors played in history. Would the war in Iraq be portrayed as Bush's war or as belonging to those who led him there? Indeed, these advisors shaped that war. John F. Kennedy was presented with similar crisis-driven situations. Contrary to Bush, his team of advisors was untested and young. Presidential advisors have been at the heart of the some of the most important decisions in United States history. Seeing the Iraq War unfold brought my research back to Kennedy's advisors and the perilous Cold War.

This is a book about presidential leadership and decision-making. It is a book that explores a president's willingness to use all available resources in an effort to make decisions that positively affected the United States. John F. Kennedy was not always successful in that endeavor. There are many historians who see the "New Frontier" as a vain attempt at peace, failing to change the course of the Cold War. The fact that the United States went to the brink of nuclear war twice during Kennedy's short presidency begs historians to question his leadership. That being said, his presidency serves as a reminder for leaders to take time in finding their voices. Kennedy's leadership and success in the latter part of his presidency is largely due to the strength of his advisors. His ability to establish a rapport with these men gave him the forbearance to successfully navigate one of the darkest periods in the Cold War.

The Kennedy years were arguably the most crisis-driven period in the history of the United States. John F. Kennedy and Nikita S. Khrushchev squared off with nuclear arsenals capable of destroying the world. The Cold War drove domestic as well as foreign policy. Since there was the potential for large consequences from these policies, it is vitally important to understand how Kennedy's advisors shaped their response to Cold War posturing. Both George W. Bush and John F. Kennedy had limited experience in the area of foreign affairs, yet it defined both presidencies. They both came from political dynasties and had fathers who served their government in times of war and peace. After 1961, Kennedy sought out close advisors to help him attack the critical issues of the Cold War. At the start of the administration, *New York Times* reporter Sidney Hyman called some of these advisors "Kennedy's Kitchen Cabinet," as JFK looked to establish his own leadership style.[1] After the Bay of Pigs, Kennedy created a very personal, trusting relationship with a core group, which included McGeorge Bundy, Robert McNamara, Maxwell Taylor, Theodore Sorensen, and his brother, Robert Kennedy. This kitchen cabinet affected Kennedy's decisions, helping him avoid nuclear catastrophe and establishing his doctrine of peace.

This book assesses how Kennedy realized that he needed this kitchen cabinet. Furthermore, it evaluates any direct impact they had on history. Unlike George W. Bush, Kennedy did not send American soldiers to war. JFK chose to embrace a new approach of flexible response instead of massive retaliation, utilize covert methods of counter-insurgency instead of military strikes in Cuba, use a back-channel communication instead of posturing at Checkpoint Charlie in Berlin, send a group of advisors instead of troops to Vietnam, and use quarantine instead of a nuclear exchange when missiles threatened the United States. These are all examples where Kennedy listened to trusted advisors, staving off calamity.

Beginning with George Washington, it was clear that the office of the president was larger than the person who held it. Indeed presidents' choices for key cabinet posts have shaped history. Doris Kearns Goodwin's book, *Team of Rivals: The Political Genius of Abraham Lincoln,* is an excellent comment on how Abraham Lincoln's choice for cabinet positions helped the Union win the Civil War. Additionally, Goodwin's book demonstrates that when these selections do not prove fruitful, a president must reexamine the choices made. John F. Kennedy realized that he needed to make changes in government after the failure of the Bay of Pigs. Indeed, that failure shaped the success of the Cuban Missile Crisis. From the Bay of Pigs emerged his own kitchen cabinet. Those advisors saw him through many predicaments that could have changed the world.

National Security Advisor McGeorge Bundy played an important role at the start of the administration. The National Security Files at the John F. Kennedy Library helped determine Bundy's impact on JFK's presidency. Memoranda, letters and position papers show a trusted and loyal advisor to Kennedy. Bundy's advice brought Kennedy from the depths of the Bay of Pigs to his position as the leader who confronted the Soviets on Berlin and Cuba. Bundy was an important person to JFK when the young president faltered in 1961.

After 1961 John Kennedy looked to regroup and form a better system of advisement. While Attorney General Robert Kennedy played a limited role in the first one hundred days of the administration, after the Bay of Pigs he slowly became the heart of Kennedy's kitchen cabinet. Arthur Schlesinger's *Robert Kennedy and His Times* is the best volume to determine RFK's role in his brother's presidency. Schlesinger used sources still unavailable to the public, offering insight from inside the administration. His contribution is invaluable. In addition, RFK did a series of oral histories available at the John F. Kennedy Library and through interlibrary loan; these allowed me to appreciate the scope this person played in his brother's legacy. Indeed, there is no other historical precedent.

Since the Bay of Pigs led to JFK's suspicion of the military establishment, the roles played by Robert McNamara and Maxwell Taylor were important to explore. In an effort to infuse New Frontier ideology into the Joint Chiefs of Staff, JFK welcomed Taylor's philosophies and leadership. Taylor's Bay of Pigs inquiry impressed RFK and the president. Subsequent to that role, Taylor was brought on as a military representative to the president. Kennedy embraced his notion of flexible response and eventually appointed Taylor chairman of the Joint Chiefs of Staff, replacing the truculent Lyman Lemnitzer. Memoranda and meeting notes at the John F. Kennedy Library, the *Foreign Relations of the United States* series, and Taylor's memoir *Swords and Plowshares* were used as a basis to gauge his involvement. Indeed, from these sources, there is evidence that Taylor cared for Kennedy and established a strong rapport with him.

Robert McNamara, secretary of defense, was an advisor that had been a part of the administration from the beginning. He was considered one of the brightest among the Kennedy advisors, utilizing new methods of analysis to determine the effectiveness of the armed forces. His approach to the Defense Department scared the stalwart military men, while at the same time it ingratiated him to Kennedy. After his time in office, McNamara wrote and spoke about his decisions and how they affected history. The Academy Award-winning documentary by Errol Morris, *The Fog of War*, highlights McNamara's role in the Cuban Missile Crisis and Southeast Asia. Indeed, McNamara became a polarizing figure, especially after John Kennedy's death. This book uses sources from the John F. Kennedy Library, the *Foreign Relations of the United States* series, McNamara's oral history, and his memoir to ascertain his role in decision-making. Since the military was such a concern and there were many on the Joint Chiefs of Staff pushing for war during Kennedy's presidency, McNamara's and Taylor's roles are important perspectives to evaluate JFK's relationship with the military.

Special Counsel to the President Theodore Sorensen was another New Frontiersman who shaped Kennedy's presidency. While Sorensen was undoubtedly a core advisor, his contribution came mostly from his pen. His American University and Berlin speeches from 1963 proved to be culminating comments in Kennedy's quest for peace. An examination of Sorensen's speeches and his many works on the administration paint a clear picture of the path JFK envisioned for his presidency. Indeed, Sorensen's philosophy on speech writing helped foster a clear message to the world and the United States.

Covering the many facets of the Kennedy administration is not possible without the secondary source material that offers precious insight. Aleksandr Fursenko and Timothy Naftali's works on Kennedy and Khrushchev are essential in determining the complexities of the Soviet-American relationship. Their books *One Hell of a Gamble: Khrushchev, Kennedy and Castro 1958—1964* and *Khrushchev's Cold War: The Inside Story of an American Adversary* break down the history of this necessary association. In addition, Michael Beschloss's book, *Crisis Years: Kennedy and Khrushchev, 1960–1963*, served as a valuable resource for exploring the background of these two leaders. When looking at the Cuban missile crisis I found that *The Kennedy Tapes: Inside the White House during the Cuban Missile Crisis*, edited by Ernest R. May and Philip D. Zelikow, provided raw material to clearly see the role these men played in advising Kennedy. These are only a few sources that have laid the groundwork for my research. Indeed, this book stands on the shoulders of historians who have explored these times. In addition, the men examined in this book have had an opportunity to comment on their roles on several occasions.

John F. Kennedy was not a perfect leader. Much like George W. Bush, he responded to the times thrust upon him. JFK struggled in his first year, hampered by inadequate advice from typical Cold Warriors. His second and third years in office left a legacy of strong leadership and resolve in the face of pressure from abroad and at home. This evolution was chiefly owed to his kitchen cabinet. Kennedy served as the center of decision-making, utilizing people he trusted for guidance. His forbearance in these situations sets him above other presidents who had similar stressors, and whose response was to defer to their advisors rather than seeing them as appointed counsel and not officials elected by the people.

Introduction

"Preserve peace on earth"

Sergei Khrushchev, son of the late Nikita Khrushchev, wrote an article for *American Heritage* on the fortieth anniversary of the Cuban Missile Crisis. Entitled "How My Father and President Kennedy Saved the World," the article concluded that mankind might have disappeared from the face of the earth if both countries had failed to keep the peace. "The fact that this did not happen," he wrote, "is the greatest achievement of those Cold War warriors President John F. Kennedy and my father, the premier of the Soviet Union, Nikita Khrushchev." He goes on to quote his father saying of Kennedy, "Both he and I did everything we could to preserve peace on earth."[1] If these two men had such an impact on the current state of the world, it is clear that we should study how they persevered under such pressure. John F. Kennedy and Nikita Khrushchev squared off during one of the most crisis-driven periods in history. In an effort to understand the impact these two leaders had on history, this study focuses on how the Kennedy administration approached Cold War problems. Also, what level of influence did JFK's advisors have on presidential decision-making? If these two countries had the ability to destroy the world, then one should understand how Kennedy, with the guidance of others, faced this challenge.

The purpose of this study is to explore three themes in presidential history. First, what role do presidential advisors play in establishing policy? In light of the growing power of the executive, it seems appropriate to understand how men and women in the White House assist in the development of United States foreign policy. Second, how do presidents use this advice? Kennedy may have had many perspectives and differing opinions, but did he use all of them? How did he determine what was the best advice? Finally, when foreign policy leads America into harm's way, who is responsible? Is the president ultimately the person who should bear the burden? On the other hand, should all the people involved in decision-making be liable? If the latter is true, it is especially important that historians scrutinize those perspectives.

John Kennedy had many advisors that helped him with foreign policy. This was an aspect of the administration that was considered crucial for both national security and world prestige. These advisors had varied views and experiences. On occasion, one of these men was George Kennan. On 22 October 1963, Kennedy received a letter in which Kennan wrote: "I am now fully retired and a candidate for neither elective nor appointive office. I think therefore that my sincerity may be credited if I take this means to speak a word of encouragement." Kennan wrote to Kennedy that he was "in full admiration, both as a historian and as a person with diplomatic experience, for the manner in which you have addressed yourself at the problems of foreign policy with which I am familiar."[2]

Kennan went on to say, "I don't think we have seen a better understanding of statesmanship in the White House in the present century." In the handwritten letter Kennan also said, "I hope you will continue to be of good heart and allow yourself to be discouraged neither by the appalling pressures of your office nor by the obtuseness and obstruction you encounter in other branches of government." He finished by writing, "Please know that I and many others are deeply grateful for the courage and patience and perception with which you carry on."[3] While it is unclear if Kennan was vying for another post in the administration, this is a clear example of how one person saw the Kennedy White House and its approach to foreign affairs. Near the end of 1963 it seemed that Kennedy was successful, according to Kennan. The diplomat did not always feel this way about Kennedy. Kennedy's first year in office was arguably his most difficult. He was trying to adjust to the new stresses as well as create a leadership style. In that first year he stumbled, but as he moved on found himself. His second year in office was equally difficult, leading almost to nuclear war. By 1963, the hardened JFK had foreign policy experience and a vision for peace. Kennan was commenting on the journey Kennedy took to get to that point in his presidency.

Kennedy wrote back to Kennan on 28 October 1963. "Your handwritten note of October 22 is a letter I will keep nearby for reference on hard days. It is a great encouragement to have the support of a diplomat and historian of your quality, and it was uncommonly thoughtful for you to write me in this personal way."[4] The one thing that Kennedy wanted most for his presidency was to leave his mark on history. The area of foreign affairs had interested him since his days at Choate and Harvard. Before the war, Kennedy had traveled the world, gaining deeper insight into other governments. While this journey was from the perspective of a privileged youth, it is evidence of how Kennedy valued foreign policy as a part of his legacy.

This letter was an example of how one of Kennedy's contemporaries saw his foreign policy in 1963. In 1961, after the Bay of Pigs and the Vienna Summit, many believed that Kennedy was inexperienced and out of his element in the Oval Office. JFK's first large test occurred in Berlin later in the first year of his presidency. If Kennedy was unable to maintain prestige in Berlin, he would lose credibility abroad as well as at home. Therefore, he sought advice from many people to aid him in that endeavor. However, Kennedy was always sure to be at the center of foreign policy decision-making. His approach was to get information from many sources and then make a decision on his own.

By 1962, Kennedy intimately employed the help of his brother in foreign affairs. He went even further by restructuring the Joint Chiefs of Staff to include Maxwell Taylor; first as military representative, then as chairman. The Cuban Missile Crisis demonstrated how effective the restructured Kennedy team approached problems. Finally, that crisis paved the way for the new vision of peace and cooperation in the subsequent year. By June 1963, JFK outlined his doctrine of peace in his American University commencement address.

This study examines how a president received and utilized information in foreign policy making. It was clear that Kennedy planned to design his own foreign policy. Part one examines the first one hundred days of the administration and how Kennedy and his advisors started their relationship with the Soviet Union. Chapter 1, "The Over-Cautious Approach," begins with examination of White House memoranda, meeting notes, and secondary source material. Through this approach one can see to some extent the role Kennedy's advisors played during his crucial period in the cold war. This chapter focuses on Ambassador Llewellyn Thompson's role in policy making with a close examination of his telegrams to the president. Chapter 2, "Germany and Cuba," examines McGeorge Bundy's role in those first few months. While there were many individuals who assisted in policy making, Bundy and Thompson had Kennedy's attention; therefore, they become an integral aspect of seeing this perspective. Part 1 deals with the foundation of the United States response to the Soviet Union threat. Kennedy had major problems in those first hundred days that included the Bay of Pigs fiasco. Equally important, as result of the disaster, was the Vienna summit in June.

While part one introduces the players in the Kennedy circle, part two closely examines how JFK digested their advice. Further, it attempts to give some explanation of how that advice was applied in a diplomatic situation. Again using similar sources from the first part and focusing on key White House advisors, chapter 3, "The Art of Diplomacy," attempts to understand the extent to which JFK prepared for the Vienna conference. This chapter delves into the meeting notes from many advisors in an attempt to explore the varied perspectives on dealing with Khrushchev. This approach may prove useful in establishing how independent JFK was from his advisors in determining foreign policy. It may also prove useful in determining how both governments came closer to a crisis in Berlin that year. Chapter 4, "A very sober two days," explores the many levels of the meeting between JFK and Khrushchev. This chapter examines transcripts of this exchange while secondary source material aids in understanding the tone. In addition, video footage from these two days offers another element. In an effort to gain insight into the meeting between these two leaders, this study examines all aspects of the Vienna conference.

Finally, while part two examines diplomacy, part three examines how these individuals advised the president in a crisis situation. Chapter 5, "The Vienna Effect," examines a link between the summit and the Berlin crisis. How was JFK advised in this situation? How was the advice different in a crisis situation than in a diplomatic one? While this part uses similar source material, it also looks at how a back-channel correspondence may have assisted in solving this perplexing problem that led to a wall between East and West Berlin. Chapter 6, "Perhaps a wall," analyzes how JFK and Khrushchev came to a solution. What role did the correspondence between the two leaders play in this crisis? In this chapter the letters exchanged between Khrushchev and Kennedy are explored for their impact and validity. Additionally, it studies the role JFK's advisors had in developing that back channel.

Part four examines the role Robert Kennedy had in presidential decision-making. No advisor was closer to JFK than his brother. At first, however, RFK was not included in high-level foreign policy decision-making. Chapter 7, entitled "Jack and Bobby," explores the relationship of JFK and RFK and how it evolved after the Bay of Pigs. This book uses the oral histories Robert Kennedy provided the library before his death in 1968 and secondary source material to analyze this relationship. Chapter 8, "RFK and the CIA," takes this analysis further by looking at the record of Robert Kennedy's involvement with counterinsurgency and other projects on which President Kennedy wanted his oversight.

On the heels of examining RFK's role, part five focuses on the military's role in foreign policy. A thorough analysis of primary sources involving Robert McNamara and Maxwell Taylor reveals their roles at the center of American foreign policy. Chapter 9, "Whiz Kid and War Hero," delves into the issues inherent in America's relationship with Cuba and Southeast Asia and how McNamara and Taylor played a role shaping that association. Chapter 10, "The Joint Chiefs of Staff," investigates JFK's vision for the military in the wake of the Bay of Pigs. The transition in military advice from Lemnitzer to Taylor is explored through memoirs, oral histories, and memoranda.

Part six traverses the Cuban Missile Crisis by examining how Kennedy's advisors counseled the president before and during the predicament. Chapter 11, "Preparing for a Storm," explores the period before Kennedy realized that there were offensive weapons in Cuba. Was this an oversight on the part of Kennedy's team and, upon the weapons' discovery, did they provide a successful response to the nuclear threat? This chapter investigates memoranda and statements given by Kennedy regarding weapons in Cuba. Chapter 12, "Brinkmanship in the Kennedy White House," centers on critical periods in the crisis. By looking at these important junctures, this study hopes to illuminate the role these men played in decision-making, Kennedy's forbearance in the face of American militarism, and the strategy this administration used in a crisis situation.

Finally, part seven looks at Kennedy's vision for peace in the wake of the crisis. By dissecting two important speeches from this period, it becomes clear that Kennedy had a pointed philosophy for peace with the Soviets. Chapter 13, "A Strategy of Peace," looks to bring into focus the importance of the American University speech and the role it was intended to play in Kennedy's future foreign policy. Ted Sorensen, the speech's chief architect, chose specific words that exuded the imagery Kennedy wanted to give off to the world. In the wake of nuclear confrontation, Kennedy sought peace. In contrast, Chapter 14, "Ich bin ein Berliner," brings the issue of the Western alliance to the forefront. Kennedy endeavored to strengthen his alliances with Europe as a part of his scheme to foster peace. His trips to Germany and Berlin are evidence of this attempt, and the main focus of the chapter. While Kennedy highlighted his "strategy of peace" at American University, he looked to sharpen its focus at Berlin, attain solidarity with Europe, and entwine them with that vision.

Each part of this study investigates critical themes in American foreign policy during the Kennedy years. Since there have been countless studies of this administration, this book hopes to offer a new perspective by looking from the point of view of several Kennedy advisors. Instead of one memoir, the hope is to entwine these "best and brightest" to see how they collaboratively shaped what would be called "Camelot." Sidney Hyman, a *New York Times* reporter, called some of these men "Kennedy's Kitchen Cabinet." In a 5 March 1961 article, Hyman wrote, "President Kennedy has been trying to grow extra hands that can help him grip the vast work of his office." The article went on to say, "These now constitute his Kitchen Cabinet, whose form directly reflects Mr. Kennedy's wish to be a President in Franklin D. Roosevelt's style." Hyman argued that Kennedy believed that a "President must be the political leader of the nation; he must be free to use every permissible tool in any permissible way to advance the national interest."[5] Kennedy took his relationships with his advisors very seriously. He needed to establish a rapport with them before he fully trusted their counsel. Indeed, Kennedy sought advice in an unorthodox manner. He did not have a chief of staff and instead relied on several members, whose relationships he held close, for advice. Kennedy's use of these varied advisors illustrates that the executive is at the center of all foreign policy decision-making. While many members can offer him advice, the president ultimately makes the decisions. With that in mind, this book endeavors to examine the people who brought Kennedy to those conclusions and how important trust was in this intimate, world-changing relationship.

Part One.

The First One Hundred Days: Crafting Foreign Policy in the Kennedy White House

1

The Over-Cautious Approach

"The best job in the world if it weren't for the Russians"

Historians have made many conclusions on the Kennedy administration. These conclusions vary, but each harks back to a time of grand expectations from the senator from Massachusetts. Historian Thomas Paterson writes that John Kennedy appeared "as both confrontationist and conciliator, hawk and dove, decisive leader and hesitant improviser, hyperbolic politician and prudent diplomat, idealist and pragmatist, glorious hero and flawed man of dubious character."[1] This characterization points to Kennedy's many facets in politics and history.

Arthur Schlesinger writes, "The Presidency itself would show how national vitality could in fact be released — not in an existential orgasm but in the halting progression of ideas and actions which make up the fabric of history."[2] Schlesinger's point of view is from the inside of the administration. For years, his book *A Thousand Days* was the Kennedy administration's standard history. David Halberstam writes, "It was a glittering time. They literally swept into office, ready, moving, generating their style, their confidence — they were going to get America moving again."[3] While this description exuded excitement, there was also arrogance. Kennedy, in many ways, did not wait his turn. The young and privileged senator from Massachusetts took his seat in history as the youngest president elected. The Kennedy mystique was something that every historian since Schlesinger has tried to unlock. In contrast to the above, Anna Kasten Nelson wrote, "In general, Kennedy's national security policy was not marked by a surge of innovation but by forces of continuity; not by radical policies, but by conservative assumptions; not by the unique nature of that administration but by its similarity to other modern presidential administrations."[4] With her ideas in mind, this analysis looks at the people who crafted Kennedy's White House and attempts to consider not only Kennedy's public policy but also the debate behind his actions. Were these men truly the *Best and the Brightest*, as David Halberstam called them, or did this administration, as Nelson writes, merely consist of "forces of continuity?"

This book focuses mostly on Kennedy's foreign relationship with the Soviet Union. This aspect of the administration was an important factor in defining Cold War America. It was, arguably, the most dangerous time in the history of the Cold War. After all, Kennedy commented that being president was "the best job in the world if it weren't for the Russians.... You never know what those bastards are up to."[5] The unpredictability and volatility of this time is evident in such a frustrated remark. Kennedy spent a great deal of time trying to understand and respond to the Soviets, respecting that these two countries had the ability to destroy the world if they were not careful. Kennedy was also aware that his relationship with the Soviet Union could make his presidency or wreck it. With that in mind, Kennedy was very careful in crafting his foreign policy team.

While many historians focus on the actions of the administration it is equally important to examine how JFK determined those actions. An analysis of how his advisors assisted in his creation of policy offers a unique perspective and provides insight into high-level decision-making. How was the president briefed on issues such as the Soviet Union, Cuba, and Germany? Did Kennedy take the advice of these people, or did he follow his own instinct when dealing with foreign policy? Through an examination of the documents that assisted in Kennedy's foreign policy making, one can realize the impact advisors had on presidential politics.

Since the Soviet Union was a major problem in the administration, Kennedy took great care in his approach to Nikita Khrushchev, the Soviet premier. While he had a very capable secretary of state, evidence shows that Kennedy himself planned to make decisions regarding diplomacy. Robert Dallek writes, "Since [JFK] intended to keep tight control over foreign policy, finding a secretary of state was a lower priority."[6] Dean Rusk, the president of the Rockefeller Foundation, was one of the many choices for the State position. After meeting with Rusk, Kennedy determined that he was very qualified to head the State Department. Robert Dallek argues that "it was clear to Kennedy from their one meeting in December 1960 that Rusk would be a sort of faceless, faithful bureaucrat who would serve rather than attempt to lead."[7] A good example of Rusk's ability to implement JFK's wishes was when he persuaded Adlai Stevenson to take the post as Ambassador to the United Nations. "I am going to be a soldier," Rusk said. "I think this is necessary. We need you, the country needs you. I hope you will serve as he has asked you to serve."[8] David Halberstam writes, "The Kennedy's were looking for someone who made very small waves."[9] There was a businesslike relationship between these two men. "There was no intimacy; the President never called him by his first name as he did other senior officials."[10] In the role of secretary of state, it was apparent that Kennedy wanted someone who would not contradict him in matters of foreign policy. This person, rather, would implement Kennedy's ideas; he would not try to leave a legacy. Kennedy wanted a soldier, not a general.

Kennedy had been interested in world affairs since Choate and Harvard. Robert Dallek writes, "During his years at Choate, Jack remained more interested in contemporary affairs than his classes.... he became a regular subscriber to the *New York Times*, reading it, or at least glancing at it, every morning."[11] Another example of Kennedy's curiosity with world affairs was his book *Why England Slept*. His Harvard thesis, originally entitled "Appeasement at Munich," was a clear indication of two things. First, this paper highlighted his disdain toward the policy of appeasement. While it was a common position for many thinkers, including his father, before the Second World War, it is evidence that Kennedy contemplated these issues. The book "emphasizes the need for unsentimental realism about world affairs."[12] Realism in world affairs was the backbone to the Kennedy presidency. Kennedy realized that the Soviet Union and the United States needed to find a common ground. He was a lot like FDR as he fostered relationships with the Soviets and other nations in the hopes to create a better post-war world. Indeed, FDR had learned from Woodrow Wilson that peace could not be brokered without considering other nations' objectives, not just those of the United States. Some of Kennedy's realism is evident in both the Berlin and the Cuban crisis. It seems that JFK tried to surround himself with similar people who could make tough decisions while understanding the grand scheme of the world. Secondly, the book demonstrated that along with this interest, Kennedy also wanted to play a role in world affairs.

In the summer of 1937, Kennedy and a friend went on a tour of Europe. The diary Kennedy kept "on the two months [he] spent abroad [was] largely a running commentary on public events and national character."[13] Kennedy visited communist Russia and fascist Germany. Robert Dallek argues, "Questions about international relations and Europe's future intrigued Jack."[14] Much of this trip was spent gathering information for his thesis at Harvard. Most importantly, it brought Kennedy into the realm of world affairs. When Kennedy became president, he knew that foreign policy was something he could control. He also knew that he could make a mark on history if he made the right decisions, which was why Kennedy remained very careful about whom he picked to advise him in this venture.

If Dean Rusk was the face to the State Department, then McGeorge Bundy was the mind Kennedy utilized when making important foreign policy decisions. Appointed national security advisor, Bundy would play a large role in the Kennedy presidency. Bundy was a dean at Harvard when he was offered the position on Kennedy's staff. David Halberstam writes that after turning down the post of deputy undersecretary of state for administration, Bundy was offered the national security advisor position, "where by the force of his personality, intelligence, and great and almost relentless instinct for power, he was to create a domain which by the end of the decade would first rival and then surpass the State Department in influence."[15] Bundy's father, Harvey, graduated from Yale in 1909 and was first in his class at Harvard Law. He went on to clerk for

1. The Over-Cautious Approach

Oliver Wendell Holmes and was a close aide to Henry Stimson.[16] Kennedy and Bundy shared a privileged upbringing and their fathers' involvement in politics. McGeorge Bundy went to Yale and was a junior fellow at Harvard. He left Harvard and went to war, as did Kennedy. He was involved in various assignments that included the Marshall Plan after the war.[17] After the war he went back to Harvard where he worked with undergraduates. Halberstam argues that "though Bundy was a good teacher, he was not in the classic sense a great expert in foreign affairs, since he had not come up through the discipline."[18] Bundy's addition to the White House staff was a brilliant choice. His tenacious and relentless pursuit at his post gave Kennedy the person he needed to make tough decisions.

Halberstam writes, "Bundy and Kennedy got on well from the start, both were quick and bright, both hating to be bored and to bore.... each anxious to show to the other that he was just a little different from the knee jerk reactions of both his background and his party."[19] JFK was careful to be bi-partisan while picking a cabinet. Bundy, a Republican, was an important figure for his politics and his vision. "[Bundy] had to sense Kennedy's moves, his whims, his nuances. To an uncommon degree Bundy possessed that capacity to sense what others wanted and what they were thinking and it would serve him well."[20] From their privileged background to their relentless pursuit for United States dominance, these two men worked well together. Bundy's analysis and approach to foreign policy was a mainstay for Kennedy. JFK relied on his advice and sought it often.

It was Bundy who briefed the president about nuclear missiles in Cuba. He was told about the missiles in Cuba while Kennedy was at a dinner with French diplomats and a reporter on 15 October.[21] He waited to call his boss about the incident. The next day, Bundy took the elevator to the residence to brief JFK. Michael Beschloss quotes Bundy saying that he "decided that a quiet evening and a night of sleep were the best preparation [Kennedy] could have in light of what would face [him] in the next days."[22] This was an example of how Bundy would shape the presidency. He had his hands in many aspects of the president's relationship with the Soviet Union and was not afraid to use that influence. While Bundy was a key figure in decision-making, there were many others who made a difference in Kennedy's thinking.

Llewellyn Thompson was another key figure in the early days of the administration. Thompson worked his way through the University of Colorado by washing dishes. He was sent to Moscow by the Foreign Service and withstood the firebombs during the siege at Moscow.[23] He was involved in almost every diplomatic situation that involved the West and the Soviet Union after the war. Thompson took over as ambassador to the Soviet Union from Charles Bohlen in 1957. He fostered a relationship with Khrushchev after the chairman consolidated power in 1958.[24] Khrushchev and Thompson also shared the fact that they came from humble roots. They spent personal time together and had a strong, frank relationship. Since Thompson had such a strong background with the Soviet Union, Kennedy sought his advice on how to foster a relationship with Khrushchev. After Kennedy's inaugural address, Khrushchev telephoned Thompson at the American embassy. "You'll never guess who just called me," Thompson said to an aide.[25] Michael Beschloss describes Thompson as "something of a diplomatic Gary Cooper. He had ulcers and usually kept a glass of milk and graham crackers within easy reach."[26] Due to their personal interactions and shared background, it can be argued that while Khrushchev was apprehensive with other diplomats, he felt at ease with Thompson. This relationship would have an effect on the outcome of the Cuban Missile Crisis in October 1962.

Rusk, Bundy and Thompson were integral people in this early stage of the new administration. Indeed, they played essential roles in the crises that shaped 1961. They would work independently as well as together in advising the president regarding foreign affairs. Rusk was the presenter, Bundy the mind and Thompson the insider. Together, they would not have to wait for the inauguration before making an impact on history.

"Return to the warmth of Franklin Roosevelt's time"

On 13 January 1961 President-elect John Kennedy had a phone conversation with Adlai Stevenson. During this phone call, Stevenson stressed the importance of understanding the Soviet Premier: "What seems to me the most important first thing that this administration has to do is to discover what is in [Khrushchev's] mind, if possible."[27] Stevenson suggested that someone meet with Khrushchev. This, he argued, was the only way to truly understand Khrushchev's thinking. Stevenson said he thought that Kennedy needed someone "who would go there after the inauguration as your emissary to review the situation and exploit what opportunities there may be."[28] Kennedy was very cautious in those first few months and wanted to be careful what they "exploited." However, Stevenson stressed something that would be a topic in the beginning of this relationship between the Soviet Union and the United States: "What we want to do is discover some means of creating a favorable world order and we must explore the kind of thing we could do—for example, if they would make a gesture of releasing the B-47 pilots we could with grace make a gesture in their direction."[29] These fliers were taken captive after the Soviets intercepted a spy plane during the Eisenhower administration. This became an issue during the 1960 election, and JFK inherited it when he took office.

Kennedy did not want Stevenson too involved with his presidency. JFK spoke to Stevenson about the need to bring back Ambassador Thompson to report on the Soviet Union. Here is good evidence of how Kennedy relied on Thompson's inside information with regard to Khrushchev's state of mind. Stevenson, however, wanted to be the person to speak with Khrushchev, having a hand in foreign policy. He spoke of exploiting the release of these pilots in any way possible. Stevenson also wanted a foreign policy feather in his cap. After two failed presidential bids and hopes of a secretary of state post in the Kennedy White House vanished, Stevenson saw his political end in sight. Releasing the fliers, however, was something that both sides felt they could exploit.

Nikita Khrushchev made several overtures to the president-elect from the moment he accepted victory in Hyannis Port. Khrushchev wanted to establish some sort of relationship with the new president. Kennedy received a telegram in Hyannis Port from Khrushchev that expressed "hope that Soviet-American relations would return to the warmth of Franklin Roosevelt's time."[30] Khrushchev asked through many channels what he could do for Kennedy. Soviet Ambassador Mikhail Menshikov had told Averell Harriman, former Soviet ambassador and longtime diplomat, that Khrushchev wanted someone to act as a secret informal emissary between the two leaders.[31] Khrushchev even suggested a summit meeting with the president-elect. Michael Beschloss argues, "Never before had a Soviet leader badgered an American President for a summit meeting before his inauguration."[32] Was Khrushchev trying to take advantage of the new president? Some believed that Kennedy's inexperience would hurt his ability to defend the nation from the communist threat. In addition, did Khrushchev see an opportunity to make history himself?

Khrushchev's hardliners in the government were pressing for action against the West. In addition, there were major problems in the Sino-Soviet relationship. Khrushchev remarked in his memoirs, "I believe that if Kennedy had lived, relations between the United States would be much better than they are."[33] Khrushchev's biographer, William Taubman, writes that "Khrushchev was so delighted by Kennedy's victory on November 4 ... that he positively beamed with satisfaction."[34] Taubman, however, also argues that Khrushchev's attitude toward Kennedy was never simple. Taubman speculates that Khrushchev "must have particularly relished the thought of trouncing a rich man's boy who was 'younger than my own son.'"[35] However, it seems clear from the written record that Khrushchev initiated contact with the Kennedy administration. These overtures are evident of the dangerous times these leaders faced. Khrushchev's pragmatic approach is evidence that he wanted to explore other avenues toward fostering a relationship with the new president. Indeed, his actions clearly demonstrate that Khrushchev was ready for a dialogue. Kennedy's response, therefore, was important.

Michael Beschloss writes that Khrushchev was having other troubles that may have prompted such an overture to the new president. "The Soviet Union's 'unshakable' alliance with China was breaking apart." Mao Zedong was challenging Soviet power with the development of nuclear missiles.[36] The Chinese were not happy with Khrushchev's overtures to the West. William Taubman writes, "Chinese sources indicate that Mao took the Sino-Soviet conflict quite personally, that he did not have a high regard (to say the least) for Khrushchev, and that he even tried deliberately to demean the Soviet leader." Here is a good indicator that the rift was a contest of personalities as well as ideology. Furthering that point, Taubman writes, "As for Khrushchev, his own memoirs indicate quite clearly that Mao got under his skin."[37] The situation was even more complicated.

According to Hope Harrison, Khrushchev was also having issues with the German Democratic Republic (GDR). The GDR opened up relations with the Chinese in an attempt to gain independence from the Soviets and rid Berlin of Western influence. Khrushchev attempted to foster new economic policies in the GDR that opened up relations with the West. In addition, Khrushchev made a secret speech to the Twentieth Congress in 1956 denouncing Stalin's purges when he attained power. Harrison writes, "China's leader, Mao Zedong, criticized Khrushchev's denunciation of Stalin and his calls for reform in domestic and foreign policy. These criticisms contributed to the rift between Khrushchev and Mao and were a great aid in [Walter] Ulbricht's efforts to resist Khrushchev's reform."[38] Kennedy could potentially take advantage of this issue.

Gordon Chang argues that JFK "and his closest advisors, in their quest for a nuclear test ban, not only seriously discussed but also actively pursued the possibility of taking military action with the Soviet Union against China's nuclear installations."[39] Chang's article emphasizes that Russia was worried about a nuclear China. This was something that JFK could use to bring them closer to détente. Additionally, the Soviet Union could have been looking for an ally against the Chinese. Chang argues that Kennedy's advisors, while preparing Kennedy for Vienna, "recommended that the president exploit Sino-Soviet tensions and seek a common understanding with Khrushchev about China."[40] Kennedy's response to Khrushchev was important in that it could bring in other elements of the Sino-Soviet tension. Therefore, the language and tone of the response were critical.

George Kennan, lifelong diplomat and historian, had told the president-elect to make no reply to Menshikov or Khrushchev. Kennan believed that the president-elect should take his time and maybe send a private message to Khrushchev after the inaugural.[41] JFK used Charles Bohlen and Llewellyn Thompson, Soviet experts from the FDR administration, to help him write his response. While Kennedy stalled, Khrushchev offered to release RB-47 fliers that had been caught during the previous administration. In addition, Khrushchev overlooked another incident involving a reconnaissance plane in the Karsk Sea near Vise Island.[42] The pre-inaugural opportunity to establish relations was slipping away. Ironically, it would be a speech made to appease the Chinese that would fracture this budding relationship.

In a very heated speech on 6 January 1961 outlining "Wars of Liberation," Khrushchev made it clear that the Soviet Union would oppose Western ideas. The Chinese were calling Khrushchev soft on the Americans. This act of strength for the benefit of the Chinese may have been construed by the Kennedy administration as a sign to the new administration of Soviet thinking. As a response, Kennedy's inaugural address directly opposed Khrushchev's stance. Richard Reeves argues that it was a speech "meant to inspire an anxious country, a call to national action."[43] Kennedy's use of fear, much like FDR's, permeated the speech, sending a message to Khrushchev and garnering the support of the American people. After Kennedy read the 6 January speech from Khrushchev he sent copies to the National Security Council with a memo that read "Read, mark, learn and inwardly digest.... Our actions, our steps should be tailored to meet these kinds of problems."[44] Kennedy may have missed an opportunity to begin a new relationship with the Soviet Union. Khrushchev could also have wanted to exploit this new relationship to solve his problems with the Chinese. Nevertheless, it seems that this period in American history was ushered in with an already missed chance for peace.

"declaration of cold war"

In a 19 January 1961 memo to the president, Ambassador Thompson outlined the speech that Khrushchev made regarding wars of liberation and the issues with the Chinese. This speech, he wrote, highlighted that wars among imperialist nations are very likely — rekindling a 1952 Stalin thesis. Thompson writes, "I believe the entire speech should be read in its entirety by everyone having to do with Soviet affairs as it brings together in one place Khrushchev's point of view as communist and propagandist.... If taken literally, [the] statement is declaration of cold war."[45] He went on to write that he did not have "any firm view explaining the timing of publication of such [a] stark statement of communist aims."[46] The speech itself represented Khrushchev's issues within his own party as well as the strain in the Chinese-Soviet relationship. Further it is evidence of Khrushchev's own stubborn positions that would become even more evident at Vienna.

In a 26 January 1961 Intelligence weekly review, the president was briefed on what Khrushchev tried to state in the speech. "In effect, Khrushchev defended the validity of his foreign policy and reaffirmed that the only correct and prudent course under conditions of a nuclear stalemate is a policy of limited risks to achieve political gains." According to the document Khrushchev said, "We always seek to direct the development of events in a way which ensures that, while defending the interests of the socialist camp, we do not provide the imperialist provocateurs with a chance to unleash a new world war."[47]

By implying that the United States and its allies were "imperialist provocateurs" Khrushchev satisfied both the hardliners in his government as well as the Chinese. This was especially necessary since Khrushchev was getting pressure from both Mao Zedong and the Ulbricht regime in East Germany. After all, an estimate of Khrushchev's power in the Soviet Union by the United States showed that he had weakened. The same document for the president stated, "Despite Khrushchev's clear-cut victory over a potent combination of enemies in 1957, when he carried out a sharp reorganization of the Soviet Union's top political command, there have been persistent doubts about the essential strength of his authority."[48] With these doubts and his 6 January 1961 speech in mind, it can be argued that Khrushchev may have been trying to win back support with his own party and appease the Chinese. Nevertheless, this proclamation points toward Khrushchev's trying to make a strong stance in the realm of international affairs.

On 21 January 1961, Thompson reported to the White House that the Soviet government would release the RB-47 fliers. Thompson's telegram pointed to statements made during the campaign. JFK said that he did not approve of spy flight over Russia. Additionally, he even thought an apology from Eisenhower was valid. Khrushchev wrote, "We proceed from [the] fact that [the] new U.S. government, which is now led by Mr. Kennedy, will act in practice in spirit of these statements. With this there would be removed a serious obstacle to improvement of Soviet-American relations."[49] Khrushchev wanted to use the RB-47 fliers as a bargaining tool to get a response from the new administration. The statement went on to say, "We should like to put an end to [the] past and open a new page in relations between our countries. ... Let bad past not interfere with our joint work in name of good future."[50] The statement also referred to charges that the Soviets brought to the United Nations regarding U.S. actions. Khrushchev said he would disregard those charges. In addition, it reiterated the Soviet position regarding the flights and asked that the president acknowledge it. Khrushchev's position was a condemnation of future flights, an echo of Kennedy's position in the campaign. Did Khrushchev want a response from the new administration to aid him in gaining more prestige abroad and at home?

Kennedy asked Thompson to come to Washington and advise him in an 11 February 1961 meeting regarding the Soviets. Thompson recommended that

> [The United States] reply accepting Soviet proposal [regarding the] fliers and state that UN agenda items will be subject [to] further discussion. Somewhat difficult define precisely what Soviet proposal is but I understand two factors involved. (1) We accept in some form their interpretation new President's position [regarding] overflights; (2) we give at least oral assurance to endeavor not exploit release of men against them.[51]

There are two themes in this advice that are characteristic of the Kennedy administration in this first year. First was Thompson's advice accepting the

Soviet interpretation of the overflights. While this was a subtle gesture, Thompson's advice could result in Kennedy looking weak before the "communist threat." It was a clear example, however, that some elements of the administration were seeking détente in the first one hundred days. Moreover, it criticizes the previous administration. Second, the assurance not to exploit the release expressed that there was a relationship developing between these countries that was not there previously. Khrushchev himself commented to Thompson that he did not want to let the fliers go during the election, as it would assist in Nixon's campaign.[52] If anything, these telegrams in the early part of the administration prove that Thompson advised the president on these things. It is also evidence that this diplomat had a place in the Kennedy circle. Thompson would eventually attend a meeting at the White House with other people who shaped foreign policy.

"more fruitful life for all mankind"

Dean Rusk assisted in implementing Kennedy's policy. In a 23 January 1961 memo to the Soviet Embassy, Rusk wrote that he wanted "assure the Soviet Government that we have no intention of exploiting the release of the Air Force officers to the detriment of Soviet-American relations."[53] Rusk seemed to be orchestrating the exchange between the governments rather than being a part of the decision-making. The memo goes on to state, "We would hope that release can be arranged prior to President's press conference scheduled for 6 P.M. Jan 25. Arrangements should be made for them to be accompanied out of the Soviet Union by Air Attaché or representative and Embassy doctor." These arrangements were necessary. They were a part of the diplomacy and a perfect example of Rusk acting in the role of presenter. Rusk went to great lengths to ensure the transfer of the pilots as well as state the steps Kennedy would take to announce it.

Rusk went on in this telegram to address the Soviet charges at the United Nations. In this respect, Rusk did an excellent job at communicating the message. He said, "Clearly the nature of the debates at the resumed UN session would reflect the international atmosphere prevailing at that time. It would be our hope that this would be improved over atmosphere characterizing first phase of the current session."[54] Rusk was acting as both presenter and communicator. This is a necessary role of the secretary of state; however, Rusk did not have the same access as Bundy and Thompson did to the president.

In another telegram of the same date to the embassy, Rusk crafted the response of the United States further. In this statement he wrote, "the United States Government shares the hope expressed by the Soviet Government that progress can be made toward improving the relationship between the two countries and toward common efforts of both governments designed to assure a peaceful and more fruitful life for all mankind." He went on to state, "the United States suggests a prompt review through diplomatic channels of proposals presented by either side."[55] In addition to the review, Rusk suggested that the Soviet Union and the United States create consulates in Leningrad and New York respectively. Rusk was the face of the administration. This is another clear example of that role.[56] While it is difficult to see what role Rusk played in crafting foreign policy, he was involved in the major crises of the administration. Regardless of the gaps in the evidence, Rusk was a presence in decision-making.

"The double character of Soviet behavior"

By 1953 Stalin's successors realized that the refugee exodus to the West was a major issue that needed to be resolved. The Soviets attempted to direct the GDR toward a "new course" that would strengthen their economy and keep people in their zone. Walter Ulbricht, who was rooted in Leninism and had actually met the man, was very difficult to control. The Soviets stood by him after the uprising in 1953 and now needed to deal with him to initiate economic reform. Hope Harrison argues that "through [Ulbricht's] capacity to control the local situation, [he] resisted Soviet pressure to change, thus limiting Soviet policy options in Germany."[57] Harrison also wrote, "The GDR's economic problems and their connection to East German instability and viability were made abundantly clear in this period and would play an increasing role in Soviet-East German relations leading to the building of the Berlin wall."[58] The Soviets may have saved the GDR in 1953 by backing Ulbricht, "but in the process promoted the development of a complicated and demanding ally."[59] This relationship experienced further complications as Khrushchev initiated his policies.

The Twentieth Congress played a significant role in relations with the GDR and the Soviet Union. Khrushchev's denunciation of Stalin's policy and his commitment to approach foreign policy with openness to the West led Ulbricht to move further from the Soviet Union. As a matter of fact, as discussed earlier, Ulbricht established stronger relations with China at this juncture. This element further complicated the Soviets' role in East Germany as well as their already strained relationship with the Chinese. Harrison argues that in addition, the upheaval in Poland and Hungary had a "profound impact" on East German leadership. Harrison writes that the events in Hungary "reduced the options for the development of the GDR."[60] Harrison also argues that Khrushchev was growing impatient with Ulbricht, even though he shared his zest for the socialist cause: "After two failed attempts in 1953 and 1956 to

1. The Over-Cautious Approach   23

improve the situation in the GDR by altering domestic and foreign policies, Khrushchev changed strategies in late 1958. He would now focus on compelling the West to reduce its threats to the GDR." Harrison argues, "Maybe it would be easier to change Western policies than it had been to change Ulbricht's policies."[61] It seems that Llewellyn Thompson was aware of these pressures and did his best to convey to Kennedy the essence of Berlin in 1961.

Thompson sent a telegram on 4 February 1961 regarding Berlin. "I believe," he wrote, "Soviet interests as such lie rather in the German problem as whole than Berlin.... Even if Berlin question were settled to Soviet satisfaction, problem of Germany would remain major issue between East and West."[62] With that being said, Thompson stated that Berlin, nevertheless, was still of "great current importance." Thompson argued that Berlin provided leverage for the Soviets in that region. In addition, he argued that Khrushchev's prestige was involved in this issue. Thompson believed that the "present situation in Berlin threatens stability of East German regime because of its use as an escape route, base for espionage and propaganda activities."[63] The German problem was the greatest crisis in the Kennedy administration, especially in that first year. Considering the evidence from the Harrison book, which examines new information from the previously unviewed Russian archives, it seemed that Thompson was giving the president sound advice. Thompson did not know the extent of the pressure from both the GDR and the Chinese, but it seemed that he knew there were unresolved issues with Germany that would come to fruition in the administration.

Khrushchev may have felt that he could push this younger inexperienced leader into a deal on Berlin. Thompson himself argued to the president that Khrushchev "was trying to build up a case for settlement favorable to him this year."[64] Thompson went on to state, "If there is no progress on this specific question and little progress in general situation, Khrushchev will almost certainly proceed with a separate peace treaty."[65] The Kennedy administration wanted to avoid a peace treaty at all costs. This act would put the United States on a collision course with the Federal Republic of Germany. If the United States recognized the East German government then the West Germans would feel betrayed. Thompson argued that the United States must maintain its policy of self-determination and have free elections in Germany to determine the outcome of the situation. "This appears to me," Thompson wrote, "of great importance as it is one of the best cards we have with which to oppose Soviet policies."[66] Berlin had been a debated issue since the Truman administration. JFK knew this coming into office. With that understood, he also needed to define his own policy on how to deal with this issue. How could JFK make a difference with the Soviets to ease the tension?

Kennedy and his advisors met on 11 February 1961 to determine "Soviet thinking." Present at this meeting were Charles Bohlen, Dean Rusk, George Kennan, Lyndon Johnson, Llewellyn Thompson, Averell Harriman and McGeorge Bundy. Bundy, the author of the 13 February 1961 memo on the meeting, stated that the people present established that "Khrushchev would very much like some specific diplomatic successes in 1961.... While Khrushchev's interest in exploiting Berlin continues, he is not likely to bring this situation to a boil unless there is a breakdown of negotiations on disarmament, or perhaps an increase in tension in such a place as Laos."[67] This seemed to contradict Thompson's earlier statement that Khrushchev wanted to press the issue that year. The advisors in Washington may have had a different point of view than the ambassador in Moscow. They also determined that the common enemy of both countries was in fact war itself. Nuclear war, which was the policy of both countries, meant the destruction of both societies. In addition, it described the Soviet government as strong and its economy "formidable." However, agriculture was a weak aspect of this country. The meeting also determined that perhaps the successes of the Soviet Union in places such as Laos, Cuba, and the Congo might result in overconfidence. "Soviet concern over Germany's relation to atomic weapons is real, it is also an example of the duality of Soviet thinking: the German question is not only a real worry, but an excellent crowbar to pry at the seams of the Atlantic alliance."[68] Getting the Allies to accept the U.S. position was another issue.

Marc Trachtenberg argues that Kennedy "had to get the allies to accept what he was trying to accomplish — that is a stabilization of the status quo."[69] The complex circumstances revolving around the Atlantic alliance were among the many issues Kennedy had to face. The Bundy memo stated that Khrushchev wanted to concentrate on economic interests and avoid any large foreign policy issue. With this background of the Soviet Union, the administration crafted its response.

Bundy stated, "Precisely because of the double character of Soviet behavior, American policy must be both rationally stated and evidently strong."[70] U.S. policy, according to Bundy, should exude resolute decisiveness. This meant that the United States needed to avoid "duality" or "double character" in its policies. In short, it had to be clear and direct. This meeting went on to determine that the president and Khrushchev should meet, but not in a formal setting such as a summit. Moreover, there should not be an early meeting at the U.N., because "the Soviet leader can not resist a rostrum, and his speeches in the U.N. would be unlikely to add to the sum of the international good will, or Soviet-American understanding." As a matter of fact, Averell Harriman suggested that the president wait and consult with the other allies before he spoke to Khrushchev. Bundy wrote in his memo that some thought that if the Soviet Union really believed what high officials in the government were saying about the West, then how could America sit down with such cynical people and negotiate?[71]

The Kennedy administration hoped to control Khrushchev. It favored a cautious approach. They wanted to wait before the president met with the chairman. Bundy and others told the president that it would come in due course. Did this policy stall any hope of détente during the Kennedy administration? Khrushchev wanted to talk to the new president. In the 11 February meeting the president asked many questions regarding the Soviet Union. The advisors felt JFK had a very open mind and was willing to hear the whole story in an attempt to gain his own insight into the Soviet Union.[72]

The relationship between Kennedy and Khrushchev deteriorated due to caution and Cold War rhetoric. JFK was hesitant to speak with Khrushchev and the chairman was proclaiming wars of liberation. This exchange tainted Khrushchev's brief overtures, which included releasing the RB-47 fliers and ignoring a plane incident in the interest of peace. In the following months, the Bay of Pigs would lead to larger problems for the administration and threaten any chance Kennedy had to reach peace early in his tenure as commander in chief.

2

Germany and Cuba

"In the area of national security affairs"

McGeorge Bundy had a major impact on the Kennedy administration. He advised the president by distilling information through his office. A good example involved a gesture to Khrushchev and the Soviet people. In a 27 February 1961 memo for the president, Bundy suggested, with others, that Kennedy lift a ban on crab meat from the Soviet Union that had been enacted in 1949. "[Secretary of Treasury] Douglas Dillon," he wrote to the president, "does think the pressure will be very great, but of course in the context of Soviet relations it may take on some slight temperature."[1] This was one of the many actions Bundy undertook to organize his new department.

In an effort to gain confidence from the American people, Bundy also explained certain traits of the Kennedy White House. In a 28 February 1961 memo to Pierre Salinger, press secretary for the president, Bundy suggested that the president was "spending more time on national security affairs than on any other class of problems and he is meeting frequently with those most directly concerned with each specific question." Bundy wrote that Kennedy found "this method on the whole more effective than frequent scheduled meetings of the whole group."[2] This is an example of two themes in the Kennedy White House. One, the president was not as regimented as his predecessor. Many of Kennedy's biographers have commented on Kennedy's loosely organized White House and how it differed from Eisenhower's structured approach to the presidency. Second, and more importantly, while Bundy would not make the important decisions, he did have some control over information to and from the Oval Office. With that in mind, he could influence the center of decision-making at the presidential level.

On the one hand, Bundy told Salinger that JFK had a different yet effective approach to national security. On the other hand, Bundy pushed for a structured approach. In a 10 March 1961 memo to Allen Dulles, the director of Central Intelligence, Bundy wrote that Kennedy had asked him to "start to keep track of directives and requests which he makes in the area of national security affairs." Bundy discussed the various contexts in which these actions would take place, such as phone calls, discussions with other members of the NSC and the administration. "Wherever they come from," Bundy wrote, "[Kennedy] is eager to keep track of the things which he personally initiates."[3] In addition to this action, Bundy explained the series of informational National Security Action Memoranda (NSAM). This memo indicates, once again, Bundy's effort to funnel information though his office. Nothing, it seemed, plagued the National Security Council more in those early months than the situation in Cuba and the Castro regime.

In NSAM number 31, dated 11 March 1961, Bundy argued that certain actions be taken regarding Cuba. After each goal Bundy wrote which office was in charge of the actions to accomplish those goals. According to the memo, first, "Every effort must be made to assist patriotic Cubans in forming a new and strong political organization ... especially those who may be active participants in a military campaign of liberation." At the end of this first part Bundy wrote, "Action: Central Intelligence Agency."[4] In addition to this CIA support of a "campaign of liberation," Arthur Schlesinger, in conjunction with the Department of State, was to prepare a white paper on Cuba. Secondly, Rusk was to "present recommendation with respect to a demarche in the Organization of American States, looking forward toward a united demand for prompt free elections in Cuba, with appropriate safeguards and opportunity for all patriotic Cubans." Finally, "the president," Bundy wrote, "expects to authorize U.S. support for an appropriate number of patriotic Cubans to return to their homeland.... Action: Central Intelligence Agency with appropriate consultation."[5] In this document lay the foundation for the Bay of Pigs. While this invasion was initiated by the previous administration, Kennedy's team was now trying to take hold. Rusk played the diplomat to the Organization of American States and even the American people by assisting in developing a "white paper on Cuba."

Based on this organizational memo, Bundy directed the actions of the administration in this area. Rusk's role, as in the RB-47 exchange, was to communicate the policy of the administration. In addition, the CIA played a role in two very important aspects of dealing with the Cuban situation. With this memo, Bundy funneled the military, intellectual and psychological battle with Cuba through his office.

"renewed pressure by the Soviets"

While Bundy was focusing national security, Thompson had many discussions with Khrushchev regarding the situation in Berlin and Germany. Cuba loomed high in Bundy's priorities, permeating the discussions between the ambassador and the Soviet leader. In a conversation among Kennedy, Heinrich von Brentano, foreign minister of West Germany, and others in the West German and United States governments on 17 February 1961, the president first discussed his desire to meet with West German chancellor Konrad Adenauer and then turned to a very crucial issue in Germany — a peace treaty with the Soviet Union.

If Khrushchev initiated a peace treaty with East Germany it would cause problems with the relationship between the Federal Republic of Germany (FRG) and the United States in addition to altering access rights to Berlin. Due to the overwhelming flow of refugees, Khrushchev needed to do something more than his current policies. He was feeling pressure especially from the GDR. Kennedy said that he "expected renewed pressure by the Soviets in the coming months. He asked the Foreign Minister for his comment and suggestions concerning possible effective means with which to counter the subtle pressures which the Soviets were expected to exert."[6] According to the memo, "The President came back to this point several times, indicating the gradual development of Soviet action, that is, first signing a separate peace treaty — while continuing the status quo in Berlin for a certain length of time — and then resorting to further and more drastic action."[7] It seems from this evidence that Kennedy's advisors were correct. The "subtle pressures" weighed on Kennedy in those first few months. This was clearly a point of both frustration and worry for the president. Therefore, it was not a surprise that Thompson, the insider, would talk about this subject with Khrushchev.

Frank Costigliola outlines what the major issues were in the relationship between the United States, its allies and the FRG. Costigliola writes about the Berlin crisis as seen by Kennedy on two levels: "First was the emergency in East Germany imposed by the attractions of West Berlin."[8] The GDR, he says, suffered a "population exodus." The outflow was about 30,000 in July 1961. "With more than 50 percent of the refugees under the age of twenty-five and many of them skilled workers..., the GDR seemed to be bleeding to death."[9] Costigliola writes, "On a second, more dangerous level, the crisis tested each superpower's toughness and position on Germany."[10] The Kennedy administration tried to strengthen its position with a policy labeled the "grand design," which would "bolster the American position by making Western Europe a unified, faithful helpmate."[11] The plan included easing the British into the common market and increasing exports by reducing transatlantic tariffs. Additionally, the administration hoped to persuade Europe to take more of the defense expenditures and channel European nuclear aspirations into a force controlled by Washington.

This policy went against French President Charles de Gaulle, who expected Paris to have a say in nuclear deterrence. The issue over nuclear arms added another element to this already crowded relationship. If Khrushchev signed a peace treaty with the GDR then the United States would have to formally recognize the GDR in order to maintain access rights to West Berlin. This issue would infuriate Adenauer, who was already moving toward relations with both the Soviet Union and the French. Costigliola argues that a "broad consensus of American leaders feared that if they abandoned that city — or even negotiated directly with East Germany to preserve the Western presence in Berlin — the shock would loosen the Federal Republic of Germany from its mooring in the West."[12] If the GDR gained recognition from the West and the FRG lost Berlin then, many believed, a nationalist would come to power using this resentment to push unification and threatening war.[13] This seems especially rational given what we now know of the relationship between Ulbricht and Khrushchev.

Kennedy probably did not like the opening line in a telegram from Thompson on 10 March 1961 which read, the "USSR would like to sign treaty with Adenauer, Ulbricht, and U.S."[14] Khrushchev understood that Ulbricht and Adenauer could not govern a unified Germany. Therefore, Khrushchev suggested that the two Germanys stay separate. In addition, Khrushchev claimed the socialist camp did not have any ambition to move west. However, Thompson wrote in his telegram that Khrushchev said, "West Berlin is bone in throat of [Soviet]-American relations. If Adenauer wants to fight, West Berlin would be good place to begin conflict."[15] If not taken care of, that "bone in the throat" could suffocate the relationship between the United States and the Soviet Union.

Khrushchev went on to say that his "frank desire ... is not to worsen but to better relations with U.S." Khrushchev had mentioned the same sentiment to Adenauer, but was unsure of his reaction to this treaty. "If Adenauer understands me correctly," Khrushchev said, "this would render it impossible for aggressive forces to use present situation for preparation of aggression, and everyone understands what this would mean with nuclear weapons."[16] William Taubman writes, "The German question too preoccupied Khrushchev.... 'I spent a great deal of time trying to think of a way out,' he later recalled. According to his son, that was putting it mildly: 'He had nightmares about it. The German problem gave him no peace; instead it kept slipping out his hands.'"[17]

The treaty for Khrushchev was an unattainable goal. His simmering frustration was evident when he told Thompson, "If [the] treaty were not signed, American and [Soviet] troops would continue to confront each other, and [the] situation would not be one of peace but one of armistice."[18] Khrushchev's use of the term "armistice" signified the realistic possibility of war. With this in mind the president made some decisions. In a conversation with German ambassador Wilhelm Grewe on the same date of the telegram he said that "he hoped to send a statement to Congress within a matter of days on the strengthening of American military programs and posture."[19] In addition to this measure Kennedy said that "he had been examining the state of our contingency planning with respect to Berlin and that this was a subject which he would want to discuss with Chancellor Adenauer."[20]

Thompson may have had an influence on Kennedy's decision. Until

Kennedy saw the memo, he was hesitant to commit U.S. forces in Berlin. After the 10 March memo, Kennedy received confirmation that Khrushchev was planning the "renewed pressure" Kennedy feared. Therefore it seems logical to deduce that Thompson had a hand in U.S. action. In addition to that, "[Kennedy] also wanted to discuss this with [British] Prime Minister Macmillan and with the French to be sure that [they] are all firmly agreed as to what we would do in case we have a Berlin crisis again this year."[21] Once again, Kennedy was trying to juggle the issues with Russia as well as the complexities of the Atlantic alliance. This was as much an element of decision-making regarding the German issue as was the response to the Soviet Union.

On 13 March 1961, Kennedy met with Willy Brandt, mayor of Berlin. They discussed Soviet insistence on a peace treaty. In what was probably a moment of frustration on the issue Kennedy remarked to Brandt that it was "very hard to find grounds for agreement with the Soviets on anything beyond perhaps removing restrictions on crabmeat and this was really unilateral."[22] Kennedy wanted the next move to be made by Khrushchev. "Mayor Brandt said that he entirely agreed to this position and the West Berliners fully understood it."[23] Further, it proved Kennedy feared Berlin was a place where a confrontation was most likely to take place. Kennedy wanted any threat to world peace to begin with the Soviet Union. He could not have been pleased to hear from Thompson that it would not take too long.

Thompson sent a telegram to Kennedy on 16 March 1961 that confirmed the president's fears. In this telegram Thompson told Kennedy, "All my diplomatic colleagues who have discussed [the] matter appear to consider that in [the] absence [of] negotiations Khrushchev will sign [a] separate treaty with East Germany and precipitate [a] Berlin crisis this year."[24] Thompson went on to write that his own view was "that while [Khrushchev] would in these circumstances almost certainly conclude [a] separate treaty, he would likely attempt [to] avoid [an] immediate crisis on Berlin by some method such as instructing [the] East Germans not to interfere with Allied access for [a] given period [of] time." This was rather prophetic, as this would eventually be the status of West Berlin from 1971 to 1990. This strategy of leaving Berlin as "status quo" while attacking the larger issue of the German peace treaty points to the 17 February meeting between Kennedy and Foreign Minister Von Brentano. That "subtle pressure" pushed the administration to define foreign policy. Thompson argued that an "important factor in Khrushchev decision will be status overall Soviet relations with West at time decision made. Present outlook is not favorable."[25] Thompson said that there should be prepared remarks for the president on this issue, especially if there were a meeting between the two leaders any time soon. Khrushchev, he said, might push this issue, and "it could involve real possibility of world war, we would almost certainly be led back to intensified Cold War relationship."[26] These circumstances are a far cry from the pre-inaugural hope of a new relationship between the Soviets and the United

States. With the threat of a nuclear war mentioned in the earlier correspondence of 10 March and now the inevitability of a confrontation over this peace treaty, Kennedy, after less than two months in office, was confronted with staggering issues and devastating results should he fail.

"Berlin is of the greatest importance"

Henry Kissinger and Dean Acheson had their own ideas for solving the Berlin issue. Kissinger's role in the administration was minuscule; however, he was able on several occasions to get information to McGeorge Bundy that may have provided insight to the president. In this instance, Kissinger commented on maintaining rights in Berlin in a 4 April 1961 memo on national security. "Words may not be enough," he wrote. "Thus it may be worthwhile to consider whether it may not be wise to stake the President's prestige deliberately to the freedom of Berlin."[27] It seemed that Kissinger preferred a cautious approach to how the young administration attached itself to Berlin. Since Kennedy planned to visit France, Kissinger advised that "consideration be given to a brief stop in Berlin either just before or just after the visit to Paris." He saw this act, signifying a commitment to Berlin, as a boost for the morale of the population on Berlin and as having a profound impact on the public opinion in the Federal Republic.[28] Kissinger clearly saw action as the only way to signify a strong stance on Berlin. Kennedy, however, would not take the advice, and in his trip to Europe two months later did not make an appearance in Berlin. While it seems trite to state that Kennedy did not consider Kissinger's views, it seemed more likely that Bundy did not agree. After all, all the correspondence went through his office. The next day, Acheson was at the White House and had his own idea on how to approach the issues in Berlin.

In a very high level meeting on 5 April 1961 with British prime minister Macmillan, Kennedy, and other officials including Bundy, Acheson gave his opinion on how to approach the issue in Berlin. Having this meeting in the first place signified that Germany was a major issue between the Allies. Kennedy specifically asked Acheson to prepare a paper on this topic. While Acheson was still working on the conclusions, he felt that he could share what he had so far. He started by saying that "there was no satisfactory solution to the Berlin problem aside from a resolution of the German problem. It did not look as though the German problem were in train for immediate solution."[29] Acheson also concluded that "it looked as though the Soviets would press the Berlin issue this year." Finally he said that "he could see no proposals on the whole of Germany which would be better or put the West in a more favorable position."[30]

Acheson advised the group that they "must face the issue and prepare now for eventualities. Berlin is of the greatest importance. This is why the Soviets press the issue." Talk was not an option at this point. "There has got to be some sort of military response." He stated that defining "when we would come to a military response is a difficult question."[31] He argued that if anything interfered with the traffic into or out of Berlin, that would be the place to make a stand. "There are three ways of responding," Acheson told the group, "on the air, on the ground or by threat of a nuclear response. The last is not wise, but reckless and would not be believed. This brings us to a ground or air operation."[32] The minutes describe Acheson's view:

> Since the last airlift ... developments have caught up with the use of aircraft as a test of will. He did not think the West had the capability of forcing access versus determined Russian opposition. What is needed is a test of will. He hoped the test would make it clear to the Russians that Western interest in access was more important than Russian interest in stopping access. Berlin is vital to us but not to them.[33]

There are two things that are vital to understand how Kennedy was advised in this situation and how it became policy. First, when Acheson described this response as a "test of will" he demonstrated the symbolic value in Berlin. A "test of will," however, might involve nuclear weapons. Second, he made that clear to JFK when he stated that Berlin was "vital" to the United States and not the Russians. It also pointed to a philosophy on how to defeat the Soviet Union. Cold War tactics dictated that JFK take a stand in the face of aggression to show U.S. resolve. It symbolized Western presence. It also was an important gesture to maintain the Western alliance. Losing Berlin would hurt American prestige as well as its relationship with European nations. Should Kennedy have to recognize the GDR, he would lose a level of prestige with the FRG and Europe. Acheson had a very specific way to approach this issue.

Acheson argued in that meeting, "A small battalion or a brigade is not enough. A division with a division in support is required. Then we would have a very formidable weapon."[34] The use of the term "formidable weapon" pointed to Acheson's hawk-like tendencies. Acheson believed a mere visit to the city was not enough. Instead, there needed to be a military presence to stop the Russians. Acheson concluded to the group that these were his recommendations to the president and that the president had not decided on what course of action he would take. Here was a clear example of how advising a president took shape. With advice from Kissinger and Acheson and inside commentary from Thompson, the president was nearing a decision. He would apply some of this advice first in a meeting with Adenauer at the White House.

On 13 April 1961, Kennedy met with Adenauer and had some questions as to what the response of other nations would be in the event of a crisis in Berlin. It may also have been a way to mollify the strong militarism of the Joint Chiefs of Staff and the Central Intelligence Agency. While he had met with the British, he was uncertain what the French would do in this instance. "The United States," Kennedy said, "wanted to strengthen the military probes in the event that a formal blockade of Berlin might be undertaken by either the Soviets or the East Zone." Here was a clear sign that Kennedy hinted at Acheson's recommendation. While it was not entirely hawkish, it demonstrated that Kennedy was looking at military options. This also goes to the heart of the strain on the Atlantic alliance and a military presence in foreign policy decision-making.

The French and the FRG were afraid that the United States would back down from a confrontation in Germany — leaving Europe in the cold. JFK "indicated that he could hardly say that any final conclusions in this matter had been reached with the British and he felt that discussions would probably have to continue for some time."[35] In this statement to Adenauer, Kennedy showed resolve on the issues in Berlin. This was less than three months into office. Indeed, Kennedy wanted to look strong on Berlin, in order to gain prestige abroad. However, events that began four days after this meeting would plague JFK and his effort to establish prestige abroad as well as at home.

"in view of the absence of desirable alternatives"

On 18 April 1961 Cuban revolutionary forces aided by the CIA landed at the Bay of Pigs in an effort to overthrow the Castro regime. As the reports trickled in from that day, it was apparent that the invasion would not succeed without further assistance from the United States. Kennedy was confronted with the prospect of sending in air support to the Cuban rebels trapped by Castro's men. When asked by Admiral Arleigh Burke, chief of staff of the navy, if he could send in two fighters to aid the Cubans, Kennedy responded, "No, I don't want the U.S. to get involved in this." The admiral replied, "Hell, Mr. President, we are involved."[36] As a result, the advice to the Cuban revolutionaries was to utilize guerrilla warfare in an effort to survive. All attempts to salvage the mission were in vain, as the revolutionaries were caught and held by the Castro regime. Kennedy publicly admitted the U.S. involvement, and the situation caused problems for the young president. When Robert Kennedy was brought into the plan he stated that JFK said, "failure was almost impossible." RFK wrote later, "This as it later turned out, was completely incorrect."[37] The Bay of Pigs was something that Kennedy and his advisors needed to explain to the American people. As an integral part of defining U.S. policy in national security, Bundy had his version of the story.

On 4 May 1961 McGeorge Bundy wrote a memo to General Maxwell Taylor regarding the account of the Bay of Pigs. Taylor, at Kennedy's request, chaired a committee to investigate the Bay of Pigs. While Taylor led this endeavor, Robert Kennedy was intimately involved as well, questioning the decisions of military leaders. This event was a turning point in Kennedy's presidency. As a result, JFK would revolutionize the White House and employ a system of advisement contrary to the previous administration. "It seems to me," Bundy wrote, "that I can do a better job of presenting my views on this matter by sending you a memorandum covering my position on the points which are discussed in the Memorandum of Record."[38] In this five-page memo, Bundy gave his account of what transpired and how the Bay of Pigs unfolded in April 1961. "The President," he wrote, "on his entry into office was faced with a decision of disbanding or using the Cuban force in Guatemala. He was informed that the force must leave Guatemala within a limited time, and that it could not be held together in the United States for a long period." Bundy wrote that Kennedy did not agree with the plan, which included an amphibious landing and requested a different plan that was rejected by the Joint Chiefs of Staff.

"The military," Bundy wrote, "certainly wanted the operation to proceed; I do not think that this was because of a deep conviction that this was the best possible plan — it was rather that in view of the absence of desirable alternatives and the press of time, the Military believed that the prospects were sufficiently favorable and that it would be best to go ahead." Bundy stated that he "would not wish to go further into detailed analysis of the motives or positions taken by the Joint Chiefs."[39] With silence on the topic there was blame. Bundy changed the record and included his remarks that the Joint Chiefs were to blame for the debacle. He was writing for the president. Kennedy could not comment like this for the record, as it would seem as though he were trying to lay blame. Bundy implied blame on the Joint Chiefs. Once again, here was an example where Bundy was close to the center of the decision-making; therefore, he was also close to being responsible for failure.

Bundy was protecting his boss, while at the same time clarifying his version of what happened. He stated that he saw success of the operation depending on a Cuban uprising. He wrote to Taylor, "I do not think that the President was led to feel that the landing operation depended for its first success on immediate uprisings in Cuba." While he stressed this point, Bundy did acknowledge that there were reports that led people to believe there was great discontent toward the Castro regime. Bundy discussed the prospects of different approaches that included guerrilla warfare and possible escape routes. He recalled, "The President steadily insisted that the force have alternative means of survival, and that he was steadily assured that such an alternative was present."[40] Once again, this is evidence that Bundy had a hand in developing policy, especially regarding the issue in Cuba. Like Berlin, this was a situation that could lead to larger issues, because of Cuba's relationship with the Soviet Union.

Bundy was more than an advisor in this memo; he became a man defending his role in the affair, as well as an advocate for the decision-making by Kennedy not to provide air support for the invading force. The T-33 aircraft pinned down the Cuban revolutionaries. Bundy commented on the decision to refrain from offering air support. "This is a matter which arises from a conversation with the President and the Secretary of State, and I do believe," Bundy wrote, "I am the right man to comment on it.... The impression was conveyed to the President that there would be no strikes on D-Day that could plausibly come from an airstrip in Cuba."[41] For Bundy to say that he was the right person to comment on such an important aspect of this invasion made it clear that he not only had the authority to make decisions with the executive, but that he was the expert on such matters. Indeed, he was at the center of this operation. Bundy later made sure his version of events were a part of the record and condemn the judgment of the Joint Chiefs and the Central Intelligence Agency, as they were the proponents of this venture.

In this memo, Bundy argued that people who advised the president were still part of the earlier administration and "became advocates, rather than impartial evaluators of the problem. Moreover," he wrote, "I believe that many people were reticent in their representations to the President." In a clear and blatant effort Bundy laid a level of blame that the president could not. "Mistakes were made," he wrote, "in this operation by a lot of people whom the President had every right to trust."[42] Bundy had a very large role in the Bay of Pigs. This memo helps others see his point of view. But the main object of this document was to help the president maintain prestige and fault the military and intelligence establishments. This was an important aspect to understand since the Bay of Pigs now hindered the relationship between Khrushchev and Kennedy.

Kennedy's First One Hundred Days

John Kennedy wanted to be at the center of foreign policy decision-making with his team on the outer edge, informing, advising, and presenting his actions. The outer edge, however, in some ways contributed to the actions of the center. The team did not have the success it would have liked in those first one hundred days in the Oval Office. Bundy's tenacious involvement, Thompson's inside chats, and Rusk's communication of policy were not enough to give Kennedy the edge he needed on Moscow. These three men, with Kennedy at the center, were over-cautious. This guarded approach may have backed Khrushchev into the corner, leaving him no choice but to act on certain issues. Khrushchev's pre-inaugural overture to the president may have been an effort to establish a coalition between the two leaders—especially since the Chinese and the Soviets were having problems. The lack of communication and response in those opening months created major problems in the Kennedy-Khrushchev period of the Cold War. In addition, the Bay of Pigs incident gave Khrushchev the necessary material he needed to persecute Kennedy as aggressive, inexperienced, and imperialistic.

It was clear that before the inauguration Khrushchev wanted a dialogue with Kennedy. The Soviet premier offered the safe return of the RB-47 pilots. Kennedy and his advisors chose not to respond until he was in office. Did Kennedy's advisors fail him in this instance? Khrushchev gave the 6 January hard-line speech supporting "wars of liberation" appeasing his hardliners and, in some ways, the Chinese government. That speech prompted a strong reply from Kennedy in his inaugural and state addresses. The administration went from warm overtures to familiar Cold War rhetoric. It was possible that Kennedy's advisors were not able to evolve into détente because they were groomed on Cold War ideology and a world war. Indeed, the military structure, led by Lyman Lemnitzer, the chairman of the Joint Chiefs of Staff, embraced Cold War thinking. The bellicose tone they set with the Bay of Pigs hurt Kennedy's chance to establish a rapport with Khrushchev. In fact, Khrushchev commented that he wanted to establish a relationship that mirrored that of FDR and Stalin. Only a few months into JFK's presidency it seemed that was not the case.

The Kennedy team addressed two main issues in those first one hundred days—Germany and Cuba. Thompson argued that Khrushchev would push the German issue that year. At the first high-level meeting of 11 February 1961, the group wanted Khrushchev to make the first move, which implied that the United States had formulated a reactive policy on the Soviet Union. The main problem with this policy was that from the very beginning there seemed to be no "real" reaction from the White House to Khrushchev. The team was so busy trying to carefully craft a response to Khrushchev and issues that they missed an opportunity to define the Kennedy doctrine.

McGeorge Bundy went to great lengths to establish an office that would both assist and advise the president. From suggesting a lift on crabmeat restrictions to initiating the NSAM, it was clear that Bundy was at the center of decision-making. The greatest example of this involvement is evident in his 11 March 1961 memo regarding actions with Cuba. He basically outlined the Bay of Pigs invasion. His office was the hub of information for the president and others in the administration. Thompson, on the other hand, was the insider that utilized this core of presidential decision-making by feeding it information.

Thompson was in many ways the eyes and ears of the administration. The German question permeated his advice to the president. With Rusk, he played a role in releasing the fliers. More importantly, his many conversations with Khrushchev influenced the president. A great example of this was the 10 March 1961 telegram in which he told the president that Khrushchev planned to sign a peace treaty that year. As a result, Kennedy commented to people involved in the West German government, as well as the British, that he was planning to make a decision on Germany and Berlin. With that action came advice from Dean Acheson, which also played a role in his decision-making. These recommendations from Acheson, combined with Thompson's discussions, gave

Kennedy the information he needed at the center. It seems, however, that events in Cuba would hinder these decisions.

Bundy's 4 May 1961 memo to General Taylor is another example of how he influenced the Kennedy White House. Bundy said he was the "right man" to comment on the issue. Moreover, his condemnation of the Joint Chiefs and other policy makers in this memo attests to his position of authority with Kennedy. Bundy's claim that those advisors gave the president faulty intelligence was a very strong indictment. His impassioned five-page memo demonstrated that he was personally involved in the decision-making, placing him closer to the center than to the outer edge.

The Kennedy administration still had a great deal to prove. Their overcautious approach to the Kremlin resulted in Khrushchev's posturing over issues such as Germany. With a summit in Vienna coming up months after the Bay of Pigs invasion, it was more important than ever to advise the president. This team needed to have a strong showing in the realm of foreign affairs. In the first one hundred days of this administration, two issues Kennedy inherited hampered his ability to create a doctrine in foreign policy: the invasion of Cuba and issues in Berlin. His response in those early days changed those issues from being remnants of previous administrations to being unique problems within his own. Kennedy needed to demonstrate to the world, and more importantly himself, that he deserved to call the shots in foreign policy. The Harvard student of foreign affairs was now the architect of U.S. foreign policy, and he would have only one chance to succeed in this endeavor.

Part Two

*Mission to Vienna:
The Preparation of the
Commander in Chief and
the Impact of a Summit*

3

The Art of Diplomacy

"A more harmonious relationship between our two countries"

On 21 February 1961, Kennedy and his advisors met to send a message to Nikita Khrushchev. The letter, dated 22 February 1961, proposed that the two leaders meet. Kennedy wrote that he "would ... like to set before you certain general considerations which I believe might be of help in introducing a greater element of clarity in the relations between our two countries." Kennedy said, "I am sure that you are conscious as I am of the heavy responsibility which rests upon our two Governments in world affairs."[1] In this passage from the 22 February letter Kennedy utilized three themes that would permeate their exchange. The theme of "clarity" to prevent a catastrophe was common rhetoric from both the United States and the Soviet Union. In an effort to avoid war based on miscalculation, Kennedy wanted to avoid confusion. Debating and examining the need for "clarity" helps uncover what may cure the present situation in the world. Kennedy, in 1961, knew that there were limitations to where the Soviet Union and the United States could agree.

Much like FDR, Kennedy was a realist. The "disagreements" between the United States and the Soviet Union were something Kennedy tried to address in his response to Khrushchev. "I do believe," Kennedy wrote, "that the manner in which we approach them and, in particular, the manner in which our disagreements are handled, can be of great importance." Kennedy wrote that he hoped to use other diplomatic channels in creating a relationship between the two countries. "I hope it will be possible," Kennedy wrote, "before too long, for us to meet personally for an informal exchange of views in regard to some of these matters." JFK wrote that he trusted Thompson to convey to Khrushchev his position on various international issues and concluded by stating that he could foster "a more harmonious relationship between our two countries."[2] Kennedy wanted to bring out Khrushchev and see where he stood on issues. In addition, he wanted to meet with him in person to gauge how the leader reacted under pressure.

Thompson returned to Moscow with the letter and asked Andrei Gromyko, the Soviet foreign minister, to meet with Khrushchev, saying he would go anywhere. Khrushchev was in Novosibirsk meeting with Siberian farm workers, and Gromyko asked Thompson to fly there.[3] Khrushchev received the letter from Thompson and said "it could serve as a good beginning."[4] In a 10 March 1961 telegram to the president, Thompson told his story: "Khrushchev said it would be necessary [to] study [the] President's letter but he inclined [to] agree with proposal and thought [it] would be useful [to] become acquainted with [the] President."[5] Thompson went on to say, "Later at [a] luncheon Khrushchev said he hoped it would become possible to issue [an] invitation for [the] President [to] visit [the] Soviet Union." Thompson said that Khrushchev "would receive him with all their traditional hospitality; they would like welcome him and his family and show him their country but time not now ripe for this."[6] Kennedy took advantage of Thompson's close relationship with Khrushchev and sent the message through the ambassador because he was certain that Khrushchev would see the letter. For nine weeks, however, there was no response from the chairman regarding the summit.

Michael Beschloss argues, "Kennedy's proposal of a summit had been based on the hopeful atmosphere of February." After the Bay of Pigs it was a much different international atmosphere: "After his embarrassment over Cuba and the souring of relations with Moscow, [Kennedy] was glad to be spared the ordeal of seeing Khrushchev."[7] However, after nine weeks, Khrushchev decided that it was indeed time to meet with the new president; he may have wished to take advantage of this situation. Khrushchev expressed to his son that he did not understand Kennedy: "Can he really be that indecisive?"[8] William Taubman argues that Khrushchev reached two conclusions at this point: "First, that there was absolutely no difference between Republican and Democratic presidents ... and second, that now was the time to meet with a weakened Kennedy."[9] Khrushchev got a message to the president and, surprisingly, Kennedy accepted.

On 4 May 1961, Thompson transmitted a telegram to the State Department that said Khrushchev wanted to meet regarding the letter he received in Novosibirsk. Thompson wrote, "Events that took place lately yet again confirm necessity of contacts between [United States] and [Soviet Union] including contacts at highest level." Thompson went on to write, "Soviet Union owes debt in sense they have not yet replied by letter to confidential letter of President Kennedy in which was formulated proposal on meeting. Before sending reply they naturally would like to know how matters will take shape now."[10] After the Bay of Pigs, Khrushchev wanted to test the waters. In addition, Kennedy had backed himself into a corner. If he refused to meet with Khrushchev he would look weak at home and abroad. There was only one option at this point for JFK.

In another telegram of the same date, Thompson expressed that he hoped the president would meet with Khrushchev. Thompson also expressed in that telegram, "Despite recent sharp exchanges and Soviet actions [I] do not believe there has been any major change in Soviet policy or Khrushchev's intentions." Thompson said further, "While it has always been clear that Soviets seek communization of world Khrushchev continues advocate peaceful means."[11] While this insight was invaluable it is clear that Thompson misread his Soviet emissary. Khrushchev's attitude was much different after the Bay of Pigs. Nevertheless, the president and his advisors needed to work with the factors they now made for themselves. Rusk replied to this telegram on 6 May 1961 from Washington by stating, "The President remains desirous of meeting Khrushchev." He went on to be more specific and inform the Soviet ambassador that Kennedy needed to solidify his schedule.[12] This was the message Khrushchev needed to make the next move. Kennedy met with Soviet officials and solidified the meeting.

On 16 May 1961 Kennedy met with Ambassador Menshikov and Georgi Konierko at the White House. They gave the president a letter from Khrushchev dated 12 May 1961. "I welcome the spirit of cooperation in which this message was composed," Khrushchev wrote, "and I think I will not be wrong if I say that it cannot be a bad beginning for our personal contacts and mutual exchange of opinions."[13] However, Khrushchev made it clear that the Bay of Pigs hindered his ability to reply to the president's request for a meeting. "Unfortunately," Khrushchev wrote, "the international atmosphere has recently become somewhat heated in connection with the well-known events relating to Cuba, and a certain open falling out has taken place in the relations between our countries."[14] This is an important aspect to acknowledge. Khrushchev used the Bay of Pigs to stall talks with Kennedy. However, it was clear that Khrushchev also saw the attacks as an opportunity to exploit what he saw as indecision on the part of JFK. Indeed, this was representative of how Khrushchev approached Kennedy. In about a year from this date Khrushchev would make a decision to put missiles in Cuba, hoping to move JFK on Berlin.

At the start of the Kennedy administration the Soviet Union was welcoming and amiable. After the Bay of Pigs, they changed their rhetoric. This letter is evidence that the Soviet Union saw the period with FDR as a great time in U.S.–Soviet relations. "I think," Khrushchev wrote, "that the bilateral exchange of opinions between the leaders of the U.S.A. and the USSR, so fruitfully carried out during the time of Franklin Roosevelt, can also now contribute to the achievement of this aim to a significant degree."[15] FDR had an uncanny ability to connect with almost anyone and did so when he and Stalin met at Tehran. Moreover, lend-lease was extended to the Soviet Union during the war, which helped ease tension. Khrushchev had the advantage in many ways at this juncture. Kennedy needed to make a decision that would give him the upper hand. With that in mind every piece of information he could gather on Khrushchev was crucial. At first Kennedy had not planned to meet with Khrushchev and in many ways was glad not to have that prospect on the horizon. After the Bay of Pigs, however, JFK went into a malaise and often in the middle of conversation would say, "How could I have been so stupid?"¹⁶ JFK needed a victory. Therefore, he accepted the invitation in an effort to gain an advantage. However, the events which followed most certainly brought him closer to war.

"Look here Georgi."

Robert Kennedy's role in the creation of foreign policy was limited in the first one hundred days of the administration. Robert Kennedy provided many details regarding what transpired behind the scenes in the Kennedy White House. Eventually, the attorney general played an important role in decision-making. While there were several incidents that helped to establish this role, the first begins with the creation of a back channel to the Soviet Union through a Khrushchev emissary.

One way that Kennedy was able to gauge what the Kremlin was thinking was through a back channel. This was an important factor later for JFK, but the foundation for such communication began with RFK. Robert Kennedy and Georgi Bolshakov maintained a constant relationship during the Kennedy administration. Bolshakov was an information secretary for the Soviet embassy. He approached Frank Holeman of the *New York Daily News*. "I'd like to meet the Attorney General," he said, "Could you help me arrange it?"[17] Holeman told Robert Kennedy and he in turn consulted the president. John Kennedy wanted his brother to meet with Bolshakov and find out what he wanted.[18] The Kennedys were famously suspicious of many governmental personnel. This avenue may have been the channel that they hoped for in contacting the Kremlin about sensitive issues and moving toward détente.

Bolshakov was very well connected. Aleksei Adzhubei, Khrushchev's son-in-law, was his close emissary in Moscow. He served in the 1950s as an aide to the Soviet Defense Minister Marshal Georgi Zhukov, World War II hero.[19] On 9 May 1961, he was escorted to the Department of Justice. Robert Kennedy was waiting for him on the steps of the building. The two men walked down Constitution Avenue and discussed this new connection. "Look here Georgi," Kennedy said. "I know pretty well about your standing and about your connections with the boys in Khrushchev's entourage.... I think they wouldn't mind getting truthful first hand information from you, and I presume they'll find a way of passing in on to Khrushchev."[20] From that point on a relationship developed that would assist in the immediate issue of a summit between the two leaders and also craft a solution to the issues in Berlin at the end of the year. Schlesinger writes that in 1964 RFK said that he "met with [Bolshakov] about all kinds of things.... Most of the major matters dealing with the Soviet Union and the United States were discussed."[21] RFK, however, said that he never wrote anything down. "I just delivered the messages verbally to my brother and he'd act on them and I think sometimes he'd tell the State Department and sometimes perhaps he didn't."[22] The largest question from this evidence is what role did this information play in presidential decision-making? If JFK utilized this verbal information it is difficult to judge its impact.

Bolshakov played a role in the Vienna summit. It was, however, a role that many in the administration did not approve. Michael Beschloss writes, "Rusk and Bundy were … unenthusiastic about the channel. Neither knew that the President's brother was seeing Bolshakov so frequently…. Thompson's misgivings about the Bolshakov channel went beyond the professional aversion to informal diplomacy. He thought it an 'error in judgment.'"[23] Regardless of how the advisors felt about the channel, it did allow the president to attain information. It also epitomized how the Kennedy brothers controlled information. The largest issue, as brought up by many historians, is that Robert Kennedy was a major part of the administration. Bolshakov could be written off by the Kremlin should he say or do something that hurt the relationship.[24] Robert Kennedy could possibly be implicated in anything that went wrong with the exchange. Evan Thomas writes, "The Kennedys were, in the family manner, bypassing normal channels…. Thompson was a savvy and balanced expert on Soviet affairs. But the Kennedys did not yet know Thompson well enough to trust him, and they scorned State Department bureaucracy."[25]

The Bolshakov connection assists in understanding the Kennedy brothers' style. After the Bay of Pigs, JFK was very suspicious of any advice. This channel provided two things that Kennedy could gauge. First, his brother was the messenger. These two brothers may have been different in many ways, but they shared that "indestructible bond" Schlesinger writes about. Second, this was a source that potentially directly linked the chairman to the president. This was essential for Kennedy to maintain the clarity he longed for in his relationship with Khrushchev. It should be known, however, that the initial meetings with Robert Kennedy and Bolshakov were muddled and did not amount to much. While the idea of the channel was to give Kennedy another outlet, it seemed that it was too early to test the water. Evan Thomas writes, "Bolshakov indicated, or so RFK thought, that Khrushchev might be willing to negotiate a test ban treaty. Kennedy, with his untrained ear for diplo-speak, may have misheard Bolshakov, or the ebullient Russian agent, excited to be talking to the brother of the American President, may have exaggerated his master's willingness to compromise."[26] This issue would come back to Kennedy during the second day at Vienna. While this channel would prove effective down the road, it was too early for it to have an impact on the summit. Both people were still trying to understand each other. With that being said, this channel was another example of how Kennedy attained information. Therefore, it became a part of how he was advised on certain issues. Robert Kennedy played a role that is difficult to measure due to unreleased papers and private off-the-record conversations with the president. Acknowledging this relationship between the

Soviet agent and the attorney general, however, gives some bearing on how RFK contributed to United States foreign policy in 1961. He would have a larger impact when crisis threatened his brother's presidency.

"I conclude that this is not really how you like to begin the day."

McGeorge Bundy went to great lengths to assist the president in organizing the White House after the Bay of Pigs invasion. After a news article that stated there was disorganization in the White House, Bundy made it a point to discuss a few things with Kennedy. He outlined his ideas to JFK on how to run the White House more effectively in a 16 May 1961 memorandum. "I'm giving this to Walt Rostow," he wrote, "to give you on the way back from Canada because it can wait till then and because I hope you will be in a good mood."[27] Bundy planned to point out some flaws in JFK's leadership and hoped to build him up before he put him down. "Except for a brief period of disorder right after Cuba, the White House under your direction since January has been the center of energy—and controlled energy—which has revived the executive branch," Bundy wrote. "Don't take my word for it—take the word of all the old-timers who now fear that because of Cuba we may turn back to cautious inactivity."[28] Bundy eased into his critical analysis of the president. It is a clear example of Bundy's influence as well as his policy of action. However, he was also trying to strengthen the White House and clearly saw flaws that he wanted fixed.

Bundy acknowledged, "Cuba was a bad mistake. But it was not a disgrace and there were reasons for it.... Cuba is a nit-pick—it must not throw us off balance."[29] Did Bundy see Kennedy in a depression after the failure of the Bay of Pigs? Was this his way to bring things back on track? "But we do have a problem of management; centrally it is a problem of your use of time and your use of staff." Bundy stated, "You have revived the government, which is an enormous gain, but in the process you have overstrained your calendar, limited your chances for thought, and used your staff incompletely." Bundy also said that Kenneth O'Donnell, Ted Sorensen, George Ball, Robert Kennedy, and Dean Rusk were in agreement. This was a great example of Bundy's influence. He was trying to get the president to agree to new methods of management in the White House. By this time, they had agreed to the summit with Khrushchev, and this was a way to get the White House back on track for the upcoming months, which would be very difficult.

Bundy had some ideas to assist JFK's effectiveness. "You are altogether too valuable to go on this way; with a very modest change in your methods you can double your effectiveness and cut the strain on yourself in half,"[30] Bundy wrote. He was very gently telling Kennedy that he needed to focus. Kennedy needed to have a strong foundation and he would be more effective. Therefore, instead of blaming the failure of the Bay of the Pigs on the man, he was diverting it to an ineffective system that helped make that decision. What follows was a very blunt and to the point explanation of where Bundy saw the administration heading. Bundy gave Kennedy three ideas to get the White House moving again. First, he said, "you should set aside a real and regular time each day for national security discussion and action.... It is at least a matter of taking time for reports on current action, review the problems awaiting solution, and planning of assignments that have long term meaning."[31] In addition to this Bundy said that "planning a trip to Canada or a trip to Paris can be about three times as effective if you take part in it ahead (underlined) of time, not just the morning before you leave. Or again, you can not get what you need on a problem like test resumption if you don't take plenty of time to hear the arguments— and send back for more." There was a hint of frustration in this memo to JFK. Was this his way of assuring that the same things did not happen in Vienna that occurred with the Bay of Pigs?

Bundy went on to write that Truman and Eisenhower got their foreign policy briefings first thing in the morning. Bundy stated to Kennedy in that same memo that he "succeeded in catching [JFK] on three mornings, for a total of about 8 minutes, and I conclude that this is not really how you like to begin the day." Bundy had some suggestions:

> Maybe another time of day would be better for daily business. After lunch? Tea? You name it. But you have to mean it, and it really has to be every day, with an equal alternate time when your schedule requires it. Right now it is so hard to get to you with anything not urgent and immediate that about half of the papers and reports you personally ask for are never shown to you because by the time you are available you clearly lost interest in them.[32]

With Vienna on the horizon, Bundy needed to get his boss to focus on the tasks at hand, which included learning how to manage his time. In addition, the national security advisor looked to streamline his time with JFK. With a hint of frustration, Bundy commented that JFK needed to stay focused on certain issues and maintain a daily meeting.

Finally, Bundy focused on the staff work. He said that Kennedy should feel confident that "(a) there is no part of government in the national security area that is not watched over closely by someone from your own staff, and (b) there is no major problem of policy that is not out where you can see it and give a proper stimulus to those who should be attacking it."[33] This memo is clear evidence that Bundy had a major role in getting information to Kennedy. Moreover, he determined how the president would digest this information. While this was Bundy's plan, there are two examples of how he put this into effect with the president.

Bundy wrote a memo on 26 May 1961 that had reading materials on Vienna for the president. "Here are some beginnings of some of the interesting dope on Vienna,"[34] he wrote. Bundy organized this memo into six different topics for Kennedy to digest. The first one was a compilation of various conversations between Khrushchev and other people such as Richard Nixon and Dwight Eisenhower who, Bundy said, "seem most interesting to me." The second one gave Kennedy background on Berlin. Bundy emphasized the section from 1959, "in which there was more meat than in any other recent year." Third was a book on the background of heads of the government conference in 1960. Bundy highlighted the parts that mentioned the Khrushchev ultimatum in 1958 and the Camp David communiqué. Fourth, Bundy gave Kennedy a book on the foreign ministers at Geneva. "Together," he wrote, "these documents give the essence of the Berlin story as it has been in the past."[35] Bundy also attached Thompson's dispatches, and finally he gave Kennedy a CIA short analysis of Khrushchev's character and style. McGeorge Bundy told the president what was important. Taking the evidence from the previous memo into account, the president did not have enough time to read these papers for himself. Therefore, Bundy gave him the "highlights" he believed were important.

In another memo to the president on 27 May 1961 titled "This supplementary briefing book," Bundy provided a number of special papers that he suggested "may be of some interest."[36] There were eleven topics that Bundy covered such as an article on the general posture of the Soviet Union, memoranda from Walt Rostow that aimed at the "theme of the meeting," two papers from Rusk and McCloy that employed a "purple" phone that connected the White House and the Kremlin, a briefing paper from Khrushchev's visit in 1959 which emphasized the rigidity of the chairman, three papers on NATO and finally, to get Kennedy's attention, some family gossip about Mrs. Khrushchev and her daughters. Bundy also mentioned that there were some other papers on nuclear arms that were too sensitive to transmit to Hyannis Port. Clearly from the May 16, 26, and 27 memos, Bundy had a hand in how the information got to Kennedy as well as what he read. Indeed, in the absence of a chief of staff, Bundy took over that role very effectively. With all this evidence in mind one can conclude that McGeorge Bundy was as responsible for any failure in diplomacy as the president himself. Conversely, he should celebrate any success. Bundy, however, was not the only one who told Kennedy what to expect at Vienna.

"Laugh about it, don't get into a fight."

Preparing the president for his trip to Vienna took time. Thompson, once again, gave his opinion, saying in a 27 May telegram to JFK that Khrushchev might lead the discussions at Vienna and might exploit the administration's weaknesses: "In any discussion [of] self-determination he will probably bring up our failure carry out elections Viet Nam. In any discussion our concern over expansion Soviet influence Latin America via Cuba he will bring up question our bases and activities on Soviet periphery."[37] Thompson also said that Laos was an area of agreement, but Khrushchev would challenge the president on other issues such as the Congo. In addition, Khruschev was likely to see where the U.S. stood on China. "At appropriate time and possibly during President's talk [it] would be advisable [in] my opinion [to] attempt [to] put on Khrushchev responsibility for seeing that Laos in fact remains neutral and that this will be gauge of over-all Soviet intentions." Thompson went on to say, "Unless and until there is radical deterioration of our relations believe this could have real value as domination Laos itself not major Soviet interest particularly in view Chinese angle."[38] Thompson saw Laos as a possible point of strength for the United States. This advice is evidence that he wanted to meet Khrushchev with strength. It may also prove that Thompson believed that this was something that JFK lacked. Indeed, Thompson did not want Kennedy to challenge Khrushchev.

On 2 June 1961 Rusk received a telegram from George Kennan in Belgrade regarding the meeting between Khrushchev and Kennedy. Kennan wrote, "I do not share [the] frequently stated view that Khrushchev needs to be personally assured at this time of our determination to resist any overt encroachment that would bring into play our obligation under UN or existing alliances." He went on to write that Khrushchev was "well acquainted with our situation in these respects and knows that we will not hesitate to react with determination if challenged in this manner." Kennan assured the president that he did not have to use the same rhetoric that comes from the White House. Kennan wrote that Khrushchev

> does not I am sure, propose to offer us such challenges, if he can help it, particularly such as would threaten to embroil us directly with Soviet forces. Whatever pressures he may be planning to exert on U.S. in Berlin in coming period, they are not likely to be ones which, in his opinion, would present us with an overt and clear challenge of this nature.[39]

Kennan wrote that the president's approach should focus on three themes.

First, the situations throughout the world would take time to fix, since these issues were "of such difficulty that much time and patient preparation of public opinion would be involved before any practical negotiating approach could be made to their solutions."[40] Second, the U.S. would like to "cultivate" a lasting atmosphere to tackle these issues. Finally, however, he wrote, "it is idle to attempt this in face of the impressions recently created by violent Russian statements." Kennan finished the memo by saying that he thought "Khrushchev has, for various reasons, a greater interest in relaxation of tensions between Russia and the West than have his Chinese allies."[41] Kennan's analysis came right before the president spoke with Khrushchev in Vienna. How did this piece of advice assist the president? Kennan clearly did not see Khrushchev posturing over Berlin. Moreover, he characterized Khrushchev as wanting to strengthen the relationship between the West and the Soviet Union. Like Thompson in the previous memo, however, it seemed that Kennan did not want him to challenge the Soviet leader.

Before Kennedy arrived in Vienna, he stopped in France to meet with French president Charles de Gaulle. Berlin was a major piece of the French and American relationship, and when asked about it de Gaulle commented, "Khrushchev has been saying and repeating that his prestige is engaged in the Berlin question and that he will have a solution in six months. This seems to indicate that Mr. Khrushchev does not want war.... If he had wanted war about Berlin, he would have acted already."[42] De Gaulle seemed adamant that Khrushchev would not challenge Kennedy. While there were other aspects of this meeting, the notion that Khrushchev did not want to pressure the West seemed a common idea. In addition to de Gaulle, Averell Harriman, a diplomat who represented Roosevelt and Truman, asked to speak with Kennedy at a dinner in Paris. "I hear there is something you want to say to me," Kennedy said to the diplomat. "Go to Vienna," Harriman said, "Don't be too serious, have some fun, get to know him a little, don't let him rattle you.... His style will be to attack and then see if he can get away with it. Laugh about it, don't get into a fight. Rise above it. Have some fun."[43] It seems clear that most people were encouraging Kennedy to take it easy at the conference. The problem with that is he could not afford to take it easy and "have some fun."

Thomas Paterson writes that there are many factors that hindered Kennedy's ability to address foreign policy. JFK could not change to any significant degree due to his "own deep-seated foreign policy views, his personality, prior American commitments, domestic politics, and the intractability of many foreign issues."[44] Paterson's research demonstrates that the Kennedy administration stemmed from early Cold War ideology. While Paterson delves into several aspects of how Kennedy did not achieve his goals, there are two significant to this study: his generational influence and personality.

Paterson argues that JFK and his advisors were "captives of an influential past."[45] Cold War ideology influenced Kennedy's decision-making. The Kennedyites meant what they said, while most people termed it as nothing more than Cold War rhetoric. In addition to this, JFK's personality drove his foreign policy. This element seemed to permeate most foreign policy during the Cold War. According to Paterson, Kennedy's "combativeness [was] induced by political ambition and athletic competition, or precarious health ... Kennedy personalized issues, converting them into a test of wills."[46] Kennedy and his associates often spoke in "tough" or "soft" terms. Kennedy always preferred the former. With this in mind, Kennedy was always in competition with Khrushchev which immediately put him at a disadvantage. The Vienna summit went from an "informal exchange of views" to a "test of wills."

After the Bay of Pigs, Kennedy needed to appear strong. Moreover, JFK wanted to show Khrushchev that he had resolve on issues that concerned the

Soviet Union—especially Berlin. Kennedy could approach this situation with Harriman's advice in mind, but his own competitive nature hindered his ability to do so. While some of his apprehension was from his previous foreign policy mistake in Cuba, another aspect of it was ego. Did this advice have any impact on how Kennedy approached the first day of the summit? The varied pieces of advice came in close proximity to each other. One can only assume that JFK digested this information and it left an impact. Beyond Kennan, Thompson, de Gaulle and Harriman, the United States government gave Kennedy plenty to read before he set foot into Vienna.

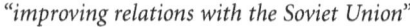

"improving relations with the Soviet Union"

The State Department prepared several papers for Kennedy that dealt with different aspects of how to approach Khrushchev. On 23 May 1961 Kennedy received one titled "Scope Paper." This paper had five points. The first point dealt with a list of United States objectives. The first objective stated that the United States wanted to "improve the prospects of finding an acceptable and workable basis for improving relations with the Soviet Union." This was the ultimate objective of the summit in many ways, but it was not the only one. The three that followed dealt with communicating U.S. resolve against the Soviet threat, demonstrating that the president had a grasp on the world situation. The final objective was "to gain a clearer understanding of Khrushchev as a man and of Soviet policy and intentions."[47] Particularly interesting was the point regarding Kennedy's grasp of world affairs. This seemed to be a reaction to the failure of the Bay of Pigs. Once again, this is evidence of how that failure dictated Kennedy's approach to Khrushchev and the administration's tone in foreign policy.

The second point of the paper dealt with Khrushchev and what to expect from him. First, it was obvious to the writer of this memo that Khrushchev would push the Soviet system and attest that it would eventually become dominant in the world. However, the paper stated, "Khrushchev probably is confident that the communist chances in the long run are good. However, he has a healthy respect and probably a reasonably accurate understanding of the military power and productive capacity of the Western nations, particularly the United States."[48] The report concluded, "He, therefore, has little taste for risky adventures." Khrushchev would, however, "undoubtedly press hard his position on Berlin and a peace treaty with East Germany and will try to get some form of commitment to negotiate the Berlin question."[49] This paper gave the president a background of United States objectives as well as a brief comment on where Khrushchev would stand on certain issues. A section on tactics in dealing with Khrushchev followed.

"In an exchange of this type," the report went on, "particularly with so outspoken a leader as Khrushchev, it is not practicable to expect that the course of the talks can be charted in advance." Despite the administration's efforts to define the issues, this paper offered an approach in dealing with Khrushchev. The paper argued that the Soviet Union must know that first, "it can not seek to encroach on the free world. In this event, force will surely be met with counter-force, the costly and dangerous arms race will be continued and probably accelerated and the risk of nuclear war will probably become acute."[50] This prediction of a heightened state seems to differ from Harriman's suggestion to have fun. The second alternative stated that the Soviets "can seek an accommodation of legitimate Soviet national interests with ours, reduce the intensity level of our confrontation, open up the prospect of arms limitation with its attendant benefits and broaden the area of mutually profitable cooperative endeavor."[51] These approaches demonstrate the volatility in the Soviet-American relationship in 1961. On the one hand, Kennedy should show great resolve and even hint at nuclear war. On the other hand, Kennedy should state that the Soviet Union and the United States could work together.

On 23 May 1961 Kennedy received even more advice. The next paper from the government was titled "Talking Points." In this paper, the State Department tried to prepare Kennedy for possible conversation points. The first topic of conversation was the test ban. This was an area in which Kennedy's advisors felt they could find success. Further, RFK's Soviet ally, Bolshakov, hinted to the attorney general that Khrushchev would welcome a test ban treaty; this would be proved wrong. The memo discussed the great importance attached to this topic and noted that there was a great commitment on the part of the U.S. to make this happen. The paper also had advice if there was no progress in the talks. "If Khrushchev's position is rigid and if—but only if—we have made a decision to resume testing in the absence of progress at the talks," the paper stated, "the president should convey to Khrushchev, in whatever terms seem appropriate, the understanding that we regard resumption of testing as our only alternative if no agreement can now be reached."[52] It seemed clear that the State Department wanted strength in the absence of compromise.

The next topic that the paper covered was the "world situation." The State Department told Kennedy, "We reject the Soviet view of the world and particularly the shift of power to the bloc, and stress that for the USSR to act on it will mean an intensification of the arms race, a blow to the chances of disarmament and greater risk of the war all should seek to avoid." This was an obvious position of the United States; nevertheless the State Department was sure to include it in its advice to the president. The fact that this advice was present may signify the confidence that the State Department had in their commander in chief. It may also be an indicator of the thinking of the time. Indeed, these were fundamental concepts of foreign policy. After a discussion of resisting attempts to spread communism worldwide, the State Department wrote, "We detail our concept of a more stable order. Mention could be made of the broad scope for cooperative action — in outer space, in help to under-developed countries, in the fields of science and technology." It finished by stating, "If the talks have made the moment propitious, cooperative endeavor and expanded exchanges might be discussed in greater detail."[53] The paper moved on to disarmament and discussed the mutual need for such an endeavor, but the real issue that would play such a key role in the summit was Germany and Berlin.

While disarmament was the first topic of importance, Germany and Berlin was secondary and just as volatile. The State Department argued, "Aspects of the situation in Berlin and Germany are unsatisfactory to the Western powers as well as to the Soviet Union but nothing is intolerable to either; the security interests of the Soviet Union are not threatened."[54] It went on to further point out,

> The wisest course is to leave the situation alone until arms reduction makes solutions easier.... In Berlin the U.S. has undertaken firm commitments and obligations together with its allies. It must and will honor its commitments regardless of the cost.... As Khrushchev will doubtless press the matter, we should be prepared to say that we will undertake negotiation of the problems of Berlin and Germany at a suitable time, but only as part of a broader discussion of problems of concern to both of us.[55]

This was the essence of the tension between the United States and the Soviet Union. The issue here was more than access rights and the flow of refugees to the West; there was a symbolic value attached to defending Berlin from the GDR. Kennedy needed to maintain the current situation if he wanted the French and the FRG to remain in the West. This was not the last piece of information from the State Department the president would utilize to prepare for the summit.

On 25 May 1961 Kennedy received the next paper that gave him information on the Soviet Union. This, titled "Background Paper," was perhaps the longest. However, the backbone of the paper begins with the section titled "Trends and Pressures in Soviet Policy." "Soviet diplomacy over the past year," it said, "has shown marked inconsistencies. These inconsistencies have been partly the result of immediate circumstances, but in almost every instance they also reflect certain deeper, inherent features of present-day Soviet foreign policy."[56] This inconsistency was something this administration could use to its advantage. The paper gets to the heart of Soviet foreign policy post Stalin in saying

> The implications of the nuclear age, the political isolation in which Stalin's rigid policies placed the USSR and the communist movement, and internal requirements of the Soviet regime, compelled Stalin's successors to develop a new look in foreign policy — a strategy based on minimizing the risks of nuclear war, consolidation of Soviet holdings in Eastern Europe, a paternalistic alliance (where possible) with the forces of

nationalism in the underdeveloped world, a generally gradualist approach to the goal of bringing communist parties to power, and more open and normal state relations between the West and the USSR.[57]

The nuclear age had made the USSR and the U.S. both victims of its power. Conversely, it seemed that nuclear arms, though powerful enough to destroy the world, may have saved the world by restraining otherwise ambitious ideologies. This approach, the paper argued, would eventually lead to better relations between the two countries, "On the other hand, the USSR's acquisition of a growing strategic strike force and increasing economic power have lent a new, assertive impulse to Soviet policies in recent years."[58] Here is a great example of how advice, however well prepared, can contradict itself and confuse. On one hand the advice seems sound and ready for peace, while on the other hand the trend moves forward to conflict.

The background paper went on to say under the section titled "Approach," "Despite the agreement to keep the Vienna meeting informal, Khrushchev will regard these talks as far more important than a mere probing of President Kennedy's views." This was contradictory to what Kennedy believed was the case. Kennedy wanted to keep these talks as informal as possible. This paper argued that Khrushchev wanted more. If that was the case then Kennedy should have prepared more for the engagement. The paper argued, "During the talks, Khrushchev might, for effect, strike a note of anger and bluster — particularly in response to strong language on sensitive issues. But it seems likely that he will generally assume an attitude of reasonable firmness, coupled with a pitch for improved U.S.–Soviet relations."[59] Kennedy needed this meeting more than Khrushchev. After many defeats in those first one hundred days, Kennedy needed to appear strong in the eyes of the world, to overcome his youth, and to the Soviet leader, to signal that he would not back down on Berlin.

These papers offer many integral pieces of insight for Kennedy. However, he needed practical experience to really gain some perspective on how to deal with someone like Khrushchev. This experience needed to happen in person. Kennedy's advisors gave him as much information as possible in approach and comprehension; indeed, these papers are evidence that the State department gave Kennedy the knowledge to perform competently. The insight and background were all significant and timely when the two leaders met in June 1961. It seems clear, however, that Kennedy needed more than the papers and advice from so many experts. In fact, Kennedy himself would say that it was a "very sober two days."[60]

4

"A very sober two days"

"You can't blame me for being interested in getting a look at him."

Video footage from this meeting between Khrushchev and Kennedy offers some insight. The JFK Library has several pieces to illustrate the atmosphere, tone, and look of the summit. Particularly interesting is the Russian film. This video opens in the streets of Vienna where vendors sold pictures of Kennedy and Khrushchev to willing buyers. It cuts to a scene where Khrushchev approached the city on a train while people flocked to the station to watch him arrive. Holding his white fedora, dressed in a dark suit, Khrushchev greeted the excited crowds. People were holding pictures of Lenin in the crowds and they cheered Khrushchev.

Once in the city, this little stubby bald man moved clumsily down the stairs of the train station, took flowers, and greeted even more people. He went into his open-top limo with full escorts riding motorcycles. After the motorcade moved away the next scene opens with Khrushchev on a balcony waving to the crowd. These images from the Russian film show strength, power, sentimentality, and command.[1]

It is important to look at how Kennedy finally approached Khrushchev when they met in Vienna. An examination of both the meeting and Kennedy's reaction demonstrates the impact his advisors had on foreign policy as well as how good Kennedy was at being his own secretary of state. When Khrushchev and Kennedy met, the press gathered around and took many pictures of the occasion. Once again, the Russian video aids in seeing the exchange. The photographers shouted, "Another one." Kennedy, fresh from a dose of a controversial medicine from Dr. Jacobson for his back, replied to his interpreter, Alexander Akolovsky, "Tell the Chairman that it's alright with me if it's alright with him."[2] From one angle JFK looked very puffy in the face, an after-effect from his shots. When asked to shake hands again, Khrushchev shrugged his shoulders in agreement. He forcefully shook Kennedy's hand and with a forced smile looked JFK square in the eyes. Enough pleasantries; the game had begun.[3] Kennedy put his hands in his pocket and looked Khrushchev up and down. He told Kenneth O'Donnell later, "After all the studying and talking I've done on him the last few weeks, you can't blame me for being interested in getting a look at him."[4]

Many people have analyzed the events that transpired after their handshake. Alexander Akolovsky, through interpreting the conversations, had one version of what took place between Kennedy and Khrushchev. Dean Rusk, in his cables to Washington, also had a version of what transpired on each of the days these two leaders met. At 12:45 P.M. on 3 June 1961, the two leaders sat down and talked face to face. According to the video, they sat in separate chairs half facing each other and the cameras. Their hands were on their legs close to the knees. The body language signified that the two leaders were open to ideas. As they exchanged some first thoughts, they motioned to each other, but both leaders seemed stiff — even nervous. This was clearly a time when they were learning about each other.

In this first meeting, it was clear that they were testing the waters. Khrushchev was there to show Soviet resolve, stamina, and will. Those people that met him at the train station gave him, if anything, reason to be strong against the West. The president, on the other hand, had been told by some of his advisors to "have fun." Khrushchev was like the prize fighter moving toward the ring. The president, Akolovsky wrote, "said that he had talked to the Soviet Foreign Minister and the Soviet Ambassador and that he was extremely interested in discussing at least to a certain extent matters affecting the relations between the two countries."[5] In addition to this, Kennedy said that he hoped these days would be useful. The chairman agreed and commented that he remembered Kennedy from his meeting with him during his tour of the United States when the president was a senator. The two leaders began their discussion over a large coffee table with an exchange involving the differences between communism and capitalism. Kennedy believed that

> the Soviet Union was seeking to eliminate free systems in areas that are associated with [the United States]. So while objecting to efforts directed at eliminating Communism in areas under the Communist system, Mr. Khrushchev appears to believe that it is appropriate to exert efforts to eliminate free systems. This is a matter of very serious concern to [the United States].[6]

Obviously Khrushchev did not agree with this interpretation of communism's ends. His reply was, "The Soviet Union proceeds from one assumption alone, namely, that any change in the social system should depend on the will of the peoples themselves. The Soviet Union is for change." This back and forth on ideology was not the best way to begin the summit. Thompson himself had said that Kennedy should "avoid ideology, because Khrushchev will talk circles around you."[7] Kennedy sat with Rusk, Thompson, Soviet expert Charles Bohlen, and the Assistant Secretary of State for European Affairs Foy Kohler behind him. Richard Reeves wrote, "The first thing the Soviet chairman noticed was that Kennedy rarely looked at his aides, much less talked to them. He was different from Eisenhower, who rarely spoke without turning to his team, especially his Secretary of State, John Foster Dulles."[8] Kennedy wanted to make it known he made his own decisions in foreign policy. He wanted Khrushchev and his staff to get this point at Vienna.

Kennedy continued the dialogue and moved further down the path where Thompson warned he should not venture. Akolovsky wrote, "The President said that he believed that the most important problem for the two sides was to have some understanding of their respective views on the differences that exist." The United States, the president stated, was for free choice.[9] Since Woodrow Wilson, self-determination was a fundamental part of U.S. doctrine. It was prudent for the president to start with this elemental idea when endeavoring to grasp Soviet perceptions. Ironically, the Soviet Union had the same impression of the United States. They saw U.S. action as highly imperialistic, which contradicted self-determination. The two leaders continued on the concept of ideology and the conversation hit a wall. The main reason why these two leaders were staring at each other over coffee was to avoid war. However, the more they discussed their ideological differences the more war seemed likely.

Kennedy brought the conversation back to where they had intended it to be when they agreed to the meeting. He told Khrushchev that their "basic objective should be preservation of peace and if we fail in that effort both our countries will lose." The modern weapons, Kennedy went on, could destroy the world. Both countries lost a great deal in the Second World War. "However," Kennedy went on, "if our two countries should miscalculate they would lose for a long time to come."[10] Khrushchev responded to this by saying that "he had often seen similar statements in the U.S. press. Miscalculation, he said, was a very vague term. However, it looked to him as if the United States wanted the USSR to sit like a school boy with his hands on his desk." Khrushchev went further and stated, "The Soviet Union supports its ideas and holds them in high esteem. It cannot guarantee that these ideas will stop at its borders."[11] Khrushchev skillfully brought the topic back to ideology — a fight that Kennedy was visibly losing. This stymied any chance of this summit's moving forward on issues. Moreover, it hindered Kennedy from getting the great start he was hoping. Khrushchev went on to state that "he wondered what the meaning of the term 'miscalculation' was." Further, he said that "the Soviet Union would defend its vital interests and the United States might regard some of such acts as 'miscalculation.' However, the USSR believes in defending its interests." Kennedy wanted to be clear on his point regarding miscalculation. He said, "It was impossible to predict the next move of any country. As Mr. Khrushchev knows, history shows that it is extremely difficult to make a judgment as to what other countries would do next."[12] The first meeting ends with Khrushchev stating that the reason they are meeting was to strengthen the relationship between the two countries. Indeed, this was not the best way to begin such talks.

This first encounter between Kennedy and Khrushchev had many faults.

Kennedy wanted his advisors to see strength in his leadership by making independent choices in dealing with Khrushchev. In addition, Kennedy wanted to demonstrate to Khrushchev that he was able to make decisions without his advisors. This was a perfect situation for him to demonstrate his intellect and wit in foreign affairs. His choice, however, was flawed. Richard Reeves writes, "Kennedy was having trouble getting into the conversation, much less persuading or impressing." Khrushchev was very passionate about ideology. His responses to JFK were characterized as "harsh" and "angry."[13] Reeves stated, "The American President's arguments did seem old and defensive. He was taken by surprise, caught in a web of Communist cant.... The Marxist coal miner was tying him in knots."[14] Kennedy asked Thompson after the meeting, "Is it always like this?" Thompson responded by saying that it was "par for the course."[15] But according to Reeves, there was some concern from the men who sat behind Kennedy. They could not believe that Kennedy sat there and took those shots without any response.

After their first meeting Khrushchev went back to the Soviet Embassy. When asked what he thought about Kennedy, Khrushchev responded, "What can I tell you? This man is very inexperienced, even immature."[16] While Khrushchev may have been telling people what they wanted to hear, it seemed clear that he felt he had an upper hand over Kennedy. At lunch, Kennedy asked what the two medals were that Khrushchev wore on his jacket. Khrushchev stated that they were the "Lenin Peace Prizes." "I hope you get to keep them," Kennedy responded.[17] Their conversation was largely informal over lunch. Overall, Khrushchev bombarded Kennedy with Communist ideology. In some ways, Kennedy tried to use his charm, much like FDR, to break the wall surrounding Khrushchev. Khrushchev came back with Cold War rhetoric. Kennedy's strategy, though flawed in many ways, was to create a rapport with Khrushchev. He was trying to make a connection. FDR brilliantly made some connection with Stalin at Tehran. He knew that he needed to give the Russians something if he were to realize his vision of the post–World War II world. This realistic approach to foreign policy was how JFK hoped to tame the Cold War. Kennedy was hoping that he could have the same impact on American-Soviet relations, but was not ready to concede anything to the Soviets. Perhaps the largest difference between these two instances was that Stalin had respect for FDR. If FDR had opposed Stalin, it would have ended differently at Tehran. Khrushchev saw JFK in a different light. There was great pressure for this venting of ideas. Therefore, the conversation continued after lunch in the garden.

"He treated me like a little boy."

At 3:00 pm the two leaders met in the garden. Robert Dallek writes, "During the stroll in the garden after lunch, Kennedy tried to establish greater rapport with Khrushchev. But the Soviet premier was unrelenting."[18] Kennedy suggested that the two leaders discuss the Laos situation. In addition to that, he had hoped that they could discuss Germany and the nuclear test ban. Ideology permeated the first session, and it seemed that Kennedy wanted to move on and get to the heart of the differences between the USSR and the U.S. As Kenneth O'Donnell watched from an embassy window he commented that Khrushchev was "carrying on a heated argument, circling around Kennedy and snapping at him like a terrier and shaking his finger."[19] Kennedy suggested they move inside where he discussed Khrushchev's notion that capitalism was to be succeeded by communism. Kennedy commented by saying, "This was a disturbing situation because the French Revolution, as the Chairman well knew, had caused great disturbances and upheavals throughout Europe." Kennedy went on to comment, "Even earlier the struggle between Catholics and Protestants had caused the Hundred Year War. Thus it is obvious that when systems are in transition we should be careful, particularly today when modern weapons are at hand."[20] This unpredictability inherent within transition was the heart of what he was trying to explain to Khrushchev. "Modern weapons" was something that Kennedy wanted to bring to the table.

Kennedy wanted to drive home to the chairman that miscalculation could destroy the world. JFK had recently read *The Guns of August*, by Barbara Tuchman, and believed that the First World War was largely a result of leaders mistakenly believing they understood each others' moves. JFK commented to Khrushchev that "in Washington, he has to attempt to make judgments of events, judgments which may be accurate or not; he made a misjudgment with regard to the Cuban situation." Kennedy's acknowledgement of the Bay of Pigs exemplified his wish to meet Khrushchev at a new, different level of diplomacy than previous presidents. This frank admission illustrates Kennedy's attempt to establish a rapport with Khrushchev. He went on to say that "he has to attempt to make judgments as to what the USSR will do next, just as he is sure that Mr. Khrushchev has to make judgments as to the moves of the U.S." Kennedy emphasized that the purpose of this meeting was to introduce "greater precision" in decision-making in an effort to survive this very dangerous period in both countries' history.[21] The conversation, unfortunately, moved in different directions.

Khrushchev moved to Cuba and said, "Castro is not a Communist but U.S. policy can make him one. U.S. policy is grist on the mill of Communists, because U.S. actions prove that Communists are right." Khrushchev went on to comment that "he himself had not been born a Communist and that it was capitalists who had made him a Communist." When confronted with nuclear weapons in Turkey and Italy, Kennedy replied to Khrushchev that those small countries were not a threat to the USSR. Khrushchev responded by saying, "The USSR is stronger than Turkey..., just as the U.S. is stronger than Cuba." He went on to remark, "This situation may cause miscalculation, to use the

4. "A very sober two days" 59

President's term. Both sides should agree to rule out miscalculation. This is why, Mr. Khrushchev said, he was happy that the President had said that Cuba was a mistake."[22] Kennedy said that the United States had three interests. Rusk stated in a 4 June 1961 telegram to Washington that Kennedy explained the United States was committed to "(1) insuring right free choice to all people through free elections. (2) Strategic interest.... (3) Next decade proceed so not to disturb greatly the balance of power."[23] There was also talk about how the Chinese situation might disturb the balance of power. The conversation moved to issues such as Laos and Africa, but there was no common ground attained. Nor was there mention of Germany until the end of the conversation at 6:45 P.M.—over three hours later.

Kennedy suggested that in view of the late hour, they could save the topic of nuclear tests and Germany for the next day. Khrushchev said he would like to discuss both nuclear tests and Germany the next day. However, he stated, "The main problem in this latter matter is that of a peace treaty. The Soviet Union hopes that the U.S. will understand this question so that both countries can sign a peace treaty together." Khrushchev argued, "This would improve relations. But if the United States refuses to sign a peace treaty, the Soviet Union will do so and nothing will stop it."[24] On that note Kennedy went to his quarters, where he got into a steaming tub in an effort to soothe his aching back. Some of Kennedy's advisors commented to him that he seemed pretty calm while Khrushchev was giving him such a hard time. The exasperated Kennedy responded, "What did you expect me to do? Take off one of my shoes and hit him over the head with it?"[25] Pacing the residence Kennedy later remarked with rage, "He treated me like a little boy, like a little boy."[26] This is another difference between Kennedy and FDR. Roosevelt always had self-confidence. He was able to convey to others that he knew what he what he was doing and it was right. Kennedy, on the other hand, was very insecure in his ability to conduct foreign policy. Perhaps it was his early failure in Cuba, but it was clear that this element of his personality hampered him from making sound decisions. Indeed, JFK had to establish himself not only in the eyes of Khrushchev and his own advisors, but also himself.

Khrushchev felt he could take advantage of the young president and in many ways did. Since Kennedy was already insecure about his position abroad as well as how his advisors saw him, Khrushchev's approach worked in breaking down the president psychologically. His comments at the end of the day are evidence of his frustration but also of his feeling of insecurity. The lack of confidence in his ability to relate to the Marxist was exactly what Khrushchev wanted. His physical condition may have had an impact as well. Robert Dallek argues, "As the day wore on and an injection Jacobson had given him just before he met Khrushchev in the early afternoon wore off, Kennedy may have lost the emotional and physical edge initially provided by the shot."[27] This raises some question as to Kennedy's approach. He may have felt over-confident in the early part of the meeting, which is why he trumped his advisors and focused on ideology. Additionally, it may also explain why he had a difficult time keeping up with Khrushchev later in the day. Nevertheless, Dallek goes on to argue that while Khrushchev was the aggressor Kennedy was not blameless. Despite the fact that JFK placated Khrushchev on some issues such as Cuba, "he was intent on the competition for international prestige as the Soviets. It was common knowledge," Dallek writes, "that the president regularly monitored the United States Information Agency (USIA) polls on international opinion toward the U.S. and the USSR."[28] Overall, Kennedy needed a stronger showing the next day. The pressure overwhelmed this man from Boston.

"Let's get down to business."

Kennedy's advisors had various reactions after that first day. Most of them believed that their boss should have done a lot better. As a result, they approached the second day a little differently. Thompson was upset that Kennedy did not stay away from ideology as he had suggested. He thought that the president still did not realize that Khrushchev could not yield even if he wanted to.[29] Bohlen remarked that JFK got a "little bit out of his depth" and should not have let Khrushchev draw him into that debate on ideology. Rusk advised Kennedy to take the approach, "You aren't going to make a Communist out of me and I don't expect to make a capitalist out of you, so let's get down to business."[30] The second day of the summit took place in the Soviet Embassy. Kennedy took his secretary of state's advice and tried to focus on the main issues of their meeting. The second day was as grueling as the first, but there was some progress made on three issues: Laos, nuclear testing, and finally Berlin.

The two leaders sat down and turned to the topic of Laos. The day before, "both sides had agreed that Laos was of no strategic importance and was not vital to either side.... The President said that his interest was to secure a cease-fire and to stop the fighting."[31] Kennedy said, "Laos is not so important as to get us as involved as we are." Khrushchev responded by saying that he "liked the concluding part of the President's remarks to the effect that the two countries should not get involved." Khrushchev then said that "it would be bad if the United States were to attempt to claim special rights on the grounds that it had vested interests. If the President would pardon the blunt expression, such policy stems from megalomania, from delusions of grandeur."[32] Khrushchev, once again, took the offensive. Perhaps after the first day he felt that he could really test the boundaries of how far he could push the president. It seemed that he really finished the attack when he said, "The United States is so rich and powerful that it believes it has special rights and can afford not to recognize the rights of others."³³ In this instance, it was clear that Khrushchev was picking at the president. This approach signified the lack of respect that the chairman had for the president. It also demonstrated to those involved in this summit that Kennedy was letting a lot of these comments go without a response. Perhaps he did so because there was some truth in Khrushchev's statements.

Kennedy responded to these remarks by stating that when he took office on 20 January 1961 these things were already in progress. He believed that "the United States and the USSR should adopt the policy of creating a neutral and independent Laos." This policy should be the ultimate goal of these two leaders. Khrushchev responded by saying, "The President's argument would be that all these commitments had been made by the previous administration. However, the Soviet Government has rescinded all the unreasonable decisions made by the previous governments under Malenkov and Bulganin."³⁴ Here was a clear example that beyond the ideology, Khrushchev did not understand the U.S. system of government any better than Americans understood that of the USSR. Kennedy could not ignore the policy of the previous administration. While this was a fundamental and even obvious difference, it did help to explain why these two countries could not bridge the divide during this period in Cold War history. In other words, this is one of many elements that contributed to the creation of an atmosphere where two of the world's largest countries almost went to war. Nuclear testing was something on which, according to Bolshakov, Khrushchev was willing to find common ground with the president. That, unfortunately for the battered Kennedy, was not the case.

Kennedy believed through Georgi Bolshakov that Khrushchev was willing to work with the United States on the issue of a nuclear test ban. In May, Robert Kennedy was told by his Soviet emissary that Khrushchev was ready to accept twenty inspections a year in order to reach an agreement.³⁵ Khrushchev, however, told the president that he would agree that "three inspections a year would be sufficient. A larger number would be tantamount to intelligence, something the Soviet Union cannot accept." Here is another example, perhaps, of how when Khrushchev finally met Kennedy, he felt he could push him on topics that he originally thought he would have to relent on. On the other hand, Bolshakov could have been wrong. Regardless, Khrushchev was not anywhere near where Kennedy believed. Khrushchev did not trust the United Nations and was hesitant to involve it in this issue. In addition, it seemed that Khrushchev did not have faith in this action. He commented, "The danger of war would remain, because the production of nuclear energy, rockets, and bombs would continue full blast." Kennedy agreed and stated, "A nuclear test ban would not of itself lessen the number of nuclear weapons possessed by the USSR and the U.S. Nor would it reduce the production of such weapons. However, a test ban would make development of nuclear weapons by other countries less likely."³⁶ Indeed, his last point has become an awful reality for the 21st century.

The two leaders went back and forth on the stipulations within the treaty.

One point that Khrushchev made was to link disarmament with the test ban. Another suggestion he made involved creating a troika in the UN, something that he had been arguing for some time, because he did not trust the structure of the Security Council. In the final comments Khrushchev again alluded to the act of espionage. Kennedy remarked, "The problem of espionage mentioned ... paled if compared with the problems which would result from the development of nuclear capabilities by other countries. This is bound to affect the national security of our two countries, and increase the danger of major conflicts." Kennedy was prophetic in his statement. However, it was clear that once the bomb was "out of the bottle," so to speak, it would be very difficult to put it back in. Much like Laos, they could not come to an agreement on a test ban treaty and moved on the next topic: Berlin.

"So we have to act."

The German issue elicited the greatest emotional response from Khrushchev. This topic was close to his heart and that of the Soviet people. In most of the exchanges on this issue, Khrushchev referred to the Second World War and the loss of Russian lives. He claimed that he feared a powerful Germany and that the lack of a peace treaty and certain restraint on the German people would result in the rise of Hitlerism once again. Khrushchev proposed that the United States and the Soviet Union sign a peace treaty and create a unified Germany. If Kennedy felt battered at this point, a red storm was on the horizon. Khrushchev had every intention to sign a peace treaty with Germany — ending Soviet guarantee of U.S. rights in Berlin. Khrushchev was frank with the president and said, "If the U.S. rejects this proposal ... the USSR will sign a peace treaty unilaterally and all rights of access to Berlin will expire because the state of war will cease to exist."[37] Kennedy appreciated the candor, but had his own response.

Kennedy's advisors knew that this would be an issue. It is fitting that Berlin was the last issue they would deal with, because it tainted their relationship for the remainder of the year. Kennedy said, "Here, we are not talking about Laos. This matter is of greatest concern to the U.S. We are in Berlin not because of someone's sufferance. We fought our way there, although our casualties may have been not as high as the USSR's." Kennedy went on to say,

> This is an area where every President of the U.S. since World War II had been committed by treaty and other contractual rights and where every President has reaffirmed his faithfulness to his obligations. If we were expelled from that area and if we accepted the loss of our rights no one would have any confidence in U.S. commitments and pledges. U.S. national security is involved in this matter because if we were to accept the Soviet proposal U.S. commitments would be regarded as a mere scrap of paper.[38]

4. "A very sober two days" 63

If Kennedy made mistakes earlier, he was very clear in making this point. The U.S. would show great resolve in that region. The fate of Western Europe was tied to the national security of the United States. "So when we are talking about West Berlin," Kennedy said, "we are also talking about West Europe." According to Michael Beschloss, the Eisenhower administration planned to make some concessions over the situation in Berlin. Kennedy renounced all of those concessions. Beschloss argues, "Now, in Khrushchev's view, [Kennedy] was arrogantly brandishing the superior might of the United States. Despite his earlier rhetoric about parity, Kennedy seemed to be saying that since America was more powerful, it could afford to ignore Soviet concerns about Berlin."[39] This was the point where Khrushchev's anger came to the surface.

Khrushchev responded to Kennedy by saying, "The U.S. is unwilling to normalize the situation in the most dangerous spot in the world. The USSR wants to perform an operation on this sore spot — to eliminate this thorn, this ulcer — without prejudicing the interests of any side, but rather to the satisfaction of all peoples of the world." Khrushchev was always trying to seem as though he was doing something for the interest of the world, but in reality, this was rhetoric he used to justify his own means. According to Khrushchev, all the Soviet Union wanted was "a peace treaty. He could not understand why the U.S. wants Berlin. Does the U.S. want to unleash a war from there?" Kennedy did not want war, but it was clear that he could not relent on Berlin by any means. This was the position that the United States was committed to defending at all costs. The conversation went in circles, and there was no agreement on how the two countries would approach the situation. They broke for lunch and Kennedy went back to his room. That was supposed to have been the last meeting of the leaders. Kennedy told aides that before he left he wanted to speak with Khrushchev one more time. "I can't leave here without giving it one more try.... I am not going to leave until I know more."[40] After pleasantries over lunch the two leaders sat down with only their interpreters for one last meeting.

Kennedy started by saying that "he recognized the importance of Berlin and that he hoped that in the interests of the relations between our two countries, which he wanted to improve, Mr. Khrushchev would not present him with a situation so deeply involving our national interest."[41] The essence of Kennedy's position was that he wanted to find a common ground, but that he was unwilling to change U.S. policy regarding access rights to Berlin. Khrushchev responded by saying that

> the U.S. wants to humiliate the USSR and this cannot be accepted. He said that he would not shirk his responsibility and would take any action that he is duty bound to take as Prime Minister.... He must warn the President that if he envisages any action that might bring about unhappy consequences, force would be met by force. The U.S. should prepare itself for that and the Soviet Union will do the same.

This clear challenge from Khrushchev was something that Kennedy had hoped he could avoid. Here they were in private, and now two countries with the ability to destroy themselves and the world in the process were poised to start a third world war. Khrushchev continued and said that, "he wanted peace and that if the U.S. wanted war, that was its problem." Kennedy responded, "that it was the Chairman, not he, who wanted to force a change." Khrushchev reiterated that "the decision to sign a peace treaty is firm and irrevocable and the Soviet Union will sign it in December if the U.S. refuses an interim agreement."[42] Kennedy responded by saying, "If that is true, it's going to be a cold winter."[43]

Rusk commented that he thought Khrushchev "was trying to act like a bully to this young President of the United States."[44] Kennedy went back to his suite after the final meeting and met with James Reston of the *New York Times*. He spoke frankly with the reporter and said that the summit was the "roughest thing in my life." He remarked that he had a "terrible problem. If [Khrushchev] thinks I'm inexperienced and have no guts, until we remove those ideas we won't get any where with him. So we have to act." Kennedy figured Khrushchev was hostile because of the Bay of Pigs, "So he just beat the hell out of me."[45] Overall, the issue of Berlin took up a great deal of the administration's time. Air Force One lifted off from Vienna — its next stop was London, then the United States.

Conclusions on Vienna

Did Kennedy's advisors contribute to his failure at Vienna? Conversely, did Kennedy's reluctance to listen to his advisors cause him to fail? It seems clear that Kennedy had the resources available to make sound decisions. He was briefed on various aspects of Soviet background. In addition, he had a great deal of information on Khrushchev himself. Kennedy had a major advantage through his youth and vigor to offset the elderly, yet still very vigorous, Khrushchev. Two things, however, contributed to his failure at Vienna. The first was the Bay of Pigs. Before Kennedy arrived at Vienna he was already at a disadvantage. Khrushchev saw weakness in JFK's decision-making skills. As a result, Khrushchev may have seen this summit as a means to gain an advantage over the United States. Secondly, once the two leaders sat down on that first day he should have listened to his advisors and not pressed ideology on the chairman. By the time Kennedy tried to steer the conversation elsewhere on the next day, it was too late. Khrushchev had decided that he would push this inexperienced young president.

Kennedy should have suspected that this summit was going to be hard. After nine weeks Khrushchev suddenly responded to Kennedy's letter of 22 February 1961. Why did Khrushchev wait until then to respond to JFK's request?

The international climate suited the Soviets and this was the opportunity to take advantage. After what was arguably Kennedy's greatest defeat politically, he chose to meet with Khrushchev. This is another example on how the Bay of Pigs impacted the relationship between the United States and the Soviet Union. The meeting was something that Kennedy did not expect; therefore, he was not prepared. Bundy's 16 May 1961 memo is evidence that the Kennedy was not managing time very well. Bundy specifically points to instances where JFK could have taken more time to prepare for certain trips or meetings. Nevertheless, it can be argued that the famous Kennedy competitiveness prevailed over reason. Kennedy needed a triumph after his worst defeat; hence, he chose to meet with Khrushchev. As a result, he needed to prepare for a meeting that would define his presidency for much of 1961.

The information Kennedy utilized to prepare for this meeting varied. Robert Kennedy's contact, Georgi Bolshakov, is an example of how JFK was thinking outside the box, regardless of what his advisors warned. This instance is also evidence that Kennedy did not feel the need to constantly adhere to the counsel of his advisors. Moreover, it seemed clear that after the Bay of Pigs, JFK wanted Bobby closer and part of his foreign policy team. The Bolshakov connection was only the beginning. RFK was only beginning to play a role in this endeavor. With that being said, JFK's advisors still had plenty of advice to offer the young president.

McGeorge Bundy's 16 May 1961 memo was the first piece of evidence that points to his attempt at reining in Kennedy. Two other good sources are the 26 and 27 May 1961 memos. These two memos point to the control Bundy had in Kennedy's decision-making. Bundy editorialized about what he thought was the most important aspects of the information. In addition, he presented the material to JFK in such a fashion that the president would be more likely to pay attention. For example, he included a paper on NATO and then followed up with some Khrushchev family gossip. As harmless as this was, it is evidence of a style that Bundy utilized in order to get JFK's attention. With that in mind, it seems clear that his views were very influential to the Kennedy White House. Beyond Bundy, however, several people lent their ideas and style to this preparation.

Thompson, as usual, gave his point of view on what Khrushchev would stress. His advice was typical in that he stressed Southeast Asia as a talking point. Thompson believed in finding strength and sticking to that point. In addition, he famously told Kennedy to avoid ideology. It was clear that Thompson wanted to play it safe with the chairman. He wanted Kennedy to come off as experienced as well as sympathetic to the Soviet needs. Thompson lacked faith in Kennedy's ability to go head-to-head with Khrushchev on certain issues such as ideology. His "stick to the script" advice is clear evidence of this. Kennan's advice holds a similar tone in that he felt Khrushchev would not challenge the United States or the president in an effort to avoid war. Kennan states that he felt Khrushchev was willing to "relax tensions" between the Soviet Union and the west. The 2 June 1961 memo may have contributed to Kennedy's failure. Kennan and Thompson almost describe Khrushchev as someone who wants to meet JFK and "have fun." If Kennedy assumed that Khrushchev was not hostile, he may have approached the meeting differently. Kennedy, after all, just wanted to meet the man and flesh out some ideas. He did not expect Khrushchev to attack like a bulldog. Khrushchev, it was obvious, wanted to challenge what he saw as an inexperienced, young, and arrogant president.

In addition to Thompson and Kennan, Kennedy also got advice from Averell Harriman and de Gaulle in France on his way to Vienna. De Gaulle felt that Khrushchev would have acted in Germany if he wanted war over Berlin. Harriman told Kennedy to "have some fun." While Harriman did say that Khrushchev would be on the attack, it did not sufficiently prepare the president for the chairman. Harriman was correct in telling Kennedy not to fight, but it was another example where Kennedy was told to relax when in reality the atmosphere he walked into was tense. Both the Kennan telegram and Harriman's advice came on the eve of the summit. These people may have left a lasting impression on JFK. Beyond his advisors Kennedy also consulted papers from the State Department.

It is important to examine the State Department papers as to what the president was given in preparation for the summit. However, there is no way one can be certain that he read each piece. Bundy himself, in frustration, commented that Kennedy often ignored certain advice in these documents. It seemed that above all, these papers wanted Kennedy to convey United States dominance and resolve. Additionally, they warned of a hard-line Khrushchev as well as difficulty in pinpointing issues to discuss at the summit. In some cases there was a heightened alertness to the nuclear situation. The three papers outlined in this study are evidence that the State Department gave thought-out and thorough advice. They covered topics ranging from Khrushchev's character to how the "world situation" impacted both countries. Did Kennedy heed this advice or did he ignore the papers and concentrate on what his advisors told him? The one thing these papers could not offer was practical experience. Kennedy was able to ascertain something about Khrushchev from those who met with him before, such as Thompson and Harriman. Is it possible that Kennedy saw those sources as more reliable than the State Department?

Kennedy's summit with Khrushchev made an already strained world situation worse. The result of this exchange was that Kennedy needed to demonstrate greater strength and resolve. Some of that could have been avoided. Kennedy overextended himself at Vienna. Pressure gave way to a sick president. While there is no concrete evidence that his back condition played a role in these talks, it is obvious from the record that he was less than outstanding. The transcripts show Khrushchev dominating the conversations. Additionally, there is proof, through other accounts, that his pain may have played a role in the past. Kennedy's Addison's disease may have played a role at Vienna. Therefore, it could be argued that his condition perpetuated a coming crisis that may have involved a nuclear exchange. Khrushchev pushed Kennedy on that first day to the point where his confidence was damaged for the second day. When Kennedy tried to regroup and stick to the issues on the second day it was too late. Khrushchev was, in so many ways, the victor — and they both knew it.

Overall, Kennedy was given sound advice. He ignored some and relied on back-channel advice regarding nuclear testing as well as character analysis from diplomats. Kennedy wanted to show the Soviets that he was in control of his foreign policy. In addition, he wanted his staff to see him succeed in this venture. Kennedy, however, was so busy letting his insecurities get the best of him that he nearly ruined any chance at leaving the legacy he wanted in foreign affairs. The pressure to produce that legacy contributed to his failure. As a result, Kennedy and Khrushchev squared off at the most dangerous place in the world in 1961: Berlin. That confrontation, however, produced a solution that both Kennedy and Khrushchev could live with.

Part Three

*"Once more unto the breach":
Constructing the Wall Between
America and the Soviets*

5

The Vienna Effect

"If He has a place for me, I believe that I am ready."

After Vienna, Kennedy made a stop in England to consult Prime Minister Harold Macmillan. On that Monday morning Macmillan offered Kennedy a "peaceful drink" and "chat" instead of a formal meeting. Kennedy told Macmillan that Khrushchev was more of a "barbarian" than he thought.[1] After his meeting with the prime minister and a few other formal events in London, the president boarded Air Force One, ordered soup and asked for Hugh Sidey of *Time* magazine to accompany him. He told Sidey that he thought the meeting with Khrushchev had been "invaluable." That night, before he went to bed, Kennedy wrote an Abraham Lincoln quotation on a piece of paper: "I know there is a God, and I see a storm coming. If He has a place for me, I believe that I am ready."[2] The Vienna summit brought the Berlin storm to Kennedy's doorstep.

Kennedy's advisors received a Soviet aide-mémoire as they left Vienna. This document stated that the Soviet Union would seek a peace treaty in Germany. Once they signed this treaty with the German government, the United States would lose all access rights to Berlin guaranteed by the Soviets. This document gave credence to Khrushchev's threat as well as presenting to the Kennedy administration its largest issue to address in foreign affairs. McGeorge Bundy gathered as much information as possible and brought it to the president. JFK's task was to determine how he would answer this new Soviet ultimatum in Berlin and how his actions would impact American prestige.

Bundy sent a memo to Kennedy on 10 June 1961. In this memo, he addressed a reply to the Soviet aide-mémoire, as well as outlining the perspectives of Henry Kissinger and reporters Joe Alsop and Walter Lippman on the approach Kennedy should take on this issue. The draft reply by the State Department was a document that Bundy accepted; however, he wanted to find a better way to communicate the United States position on Berlin. With that in mind, he gave Kennedy various insights to the problem. Bundy wrote, "Kissinger's fundamental conclusion is that we should 'take the offensive' on German unification."[3] Alsop argued "for a strong and essentially unyielding position, carried all the way to war if necessary." Bundy said that these two men had a firm stance on Berlin. He wrote that they and "most of your advisers, would hold that any neutralization of West Berlin would be a form of surrender, followed by great damage to the whole position of the West." It seemed that Bundy was leaning toward Lippman on this issue.

Lippman argued "for a negotiated solution, and has interesting ideas on what it should be. In essence, he would like to have us propose measures looking toward the genuine neutralization of West Berlin, in return for guarantees spelled out in detail by all parties."[4] Bundy tried to move Kennedy away from Kissinger and Alsop. He wrote,

> Lippmann's answer is that a real normalization of Berlin would be a gain to us and no real loss to Adenauer or anyone else. He holds that if you take the lead in this direction, the net result would be a gain, not a loss, in U.S. prestige. I find his proposition well worth considering, but I must say that I cannot see any good in accepting a Soviet presence in West Berlin, which Lippmann is prepared to do.[5]

This is evidence that Bundy was more of a centrist with regard to Berlin. While he realized that some action was necessary, he also thought that any aggressive action meant war. Therefore, in this memo he tried to bring Kennedy into the center.

In that 10 June memo, Bundy was strategic in what he highlighted for Kennedy. He said that there were some things on which Alsop and Lippman agreed. "First," Bundy wrote, "they share my view that in extraordinary measure this problem of Berlin is one which you will have to master and manage, under your own personal leadership and authority." He wanted Kennedy to understand that while it was important to consider all points, JFK needed to make his own conclusions on how to handle the crisis. This was a theme that came up in many of his memos to JFK, and is evidence that Bundy constantly tried to rein in his boss. Bundy wrote, "This is true because whatever course you determine upon will require a much higher level of understanding and support from the American people than we can now be sure of. It is true also because only your lead can provide the necessary degree of common direction to the West." Bundy argued that the American people and U.S. allies went hand in hand. If Kennedy persuaded these groups to support his action, then he would have the political upper hand both domestically and globally.

U.S. allies were always a difficult issue to tackle politically. Bundy wrote, "Four-power parleys will almost surely produce uncertain postures." He went on to say, "If you wish to be wholly unbending, you will have to confront the British with your own decision that this is how it must be. If you want to explore a new arrangement, you will have to find ways of making Adenauer accept your decision."[6] This was an example that the complex relationship with Europe made a difference in presidential decision-making. After addressing the issue of dealing with allies, Bundy brings up the other major problem with American foreign policy in 1961: the Bay of Pigs. Bundy wrote that Alsop and Lippman both agreed that the "Cuban error" needed to be avoided. He argued that Kennedy "must not plan a firm line which runs out of gas with a local defeat. If we do not mean to press the issue right up to war, even Joe [Alsop] would prefer that we now negotiate an accommodation."[7] Once again, the Bay of Pigs was a major factor in decision-making for JFK. Indeed, it would prove a formative event for the rest of the administration.

In the end Bundy had his own way to approach the situation. He knew that there needed to be action, and it was clear that he did not like the draft reply to the Soviet ultimatum. He said,

> I myself think there may be ways of having the best of both Alsop and Lippmann, by making serious military preparations now, while at the same time we strengthen the attractiveness and acceptability of our political posture, both before the world and also before the Russians.

With this advice, Bundy pushed the president to take military action, but also to explore other alternatives to give a varied approach to the problem. "This," he wrote, "might or might not take us to the particular position which Lippmann advocates, but it would probably have a more open and forward-looking flavor to it than the draft reply which is enclosed." Bundy knew from the Bay of Pigs that if Kennedy did not have his mind in the right place, then all talk would be moot and there was a greater chance that the "Cuban error" might occur once more. Bundy said, "These are merely marginal notes. The first order of business, I think, is for you to make sure in your own mind that ways and means of work are established which will put you in immediate, personal, and continuous command of this enormous question."[8]

There are some things, however, that Bundy clearly did not want Kennedy to consider. Bundy did not address the Kissinger approach. He mentioned the Kissinger paper to Kennedy, but did not reference it in his advice to JFK. Bundy placated Kissinger on numerous occasions, but it seems clear that he disregarded his advice when it came to important matters of state. In addition, Bundy steered Kennedy clear of the draft reply to the Soviets. That indicates that he wanted to see action in response to this threat. This was the first attempt of the Kennedy administration to solve the Berlin crisis in 1961. On 16 June 1961 the Coordinating Group on Berlin Contingency Planning met to discuss other alternatives on how to approach Berlin. Dean Acheson presented a paper to the administration that foretold a chilling outcome.

"Passivity did not increase deterrent credibility."

On 16 June 1961 the Coordinating Group on Berlin Contingency Planning met. Acheson and Kissinger were among the many participants in this meeting. The president wanted to see where Acheson stood on the response to the

Soviet ultimatum on Berlin. Acheson said that "his purpose was not to interfere with any present operation but rather to stimulate further thought and activity." Acheson went on to say that "Berlin contingency planning was not simply an exercise divorced from reality because we had no choice but to assume that Khrushchev meant what he said. Decisions had to be made, and we had to act resolutely or not act at all."[9] The strongest part of Acheson's contribution to the group was his insistence that any response to the Soviets must be made "resolutely or not at all." From Acheson's point of view, he wanted it made clear that Khrushchev meant business. This goes to the heart of what he felt the Berlin crisis was moving toward: confrontation.

Berlin was fundamental to United States prestige abroad. Acheson's approach is something that should be studied with great care. Kennedy charged this man with crafting a response to the crisis. Additionally, there were other times where JFK consulted him in similar and even more dangerous circumstances such as the Cuban Missile Crisis. Therefore, whether he followed them or not, JFK most likely paid attention to Acheson's conclusions. At this meeting Acheson went on to say that "he thought Berlin was very, very important indeed, certainly involving deeply the prestige of the United States and perhaps its very survival." The notion of pinning the United States' "survival" to Berlin demonstrated that Acheson was resolute on the importance of Berlin to foreign policy. The transcript goes to say that Acheson "did not believe a political solution was possible. The question was essentially one of U.S. will, and we had to make up our minds and begin to act regardless of the opinions of our allies."[10] Ironically, Acheson's unilateral approach to the situation is something that could have hurt the prestige of the United States. This arrogance in foreign policy decision-making is something that should have been avoided.

Frank Costigliola argues, "European resentment of those who assumed themselves to be the best and the brightest helps explain why Washington's official relations with Western Europe cooled during the Kennedy years in spite of JFK's personal popularity among Western European peoples." Costigliola utilizes evidence from members of the administration such as Theodore Sorensen, who stated that when the situation was vitally important to the United States JFK did not feel "that approval of the Alliance was a condition that pressed on him."[11] While Costigliola's study focused on the Cuban Missile Crisis, a case can be made that the behavior was consistent throughout the Kennedy administration and started with the Berlin issue. Acheson and many others argued that the allies needed to be "told," not asked, about the solution.

The use of nuclear weapons was a fundamental part of the Acheson argument. Not only did the president have to be "resolute" in his decision-making to avoid the "Cuban error"; he also had to want to use nuclear weapons. According to the same transcript from the 16 June meeting, Acheson continued by saying he began with the premise that our action depended on our determination to use nuclear weapons if we had to. Otherwise, we should not start. It was absolutely essential to increase the belief that we would use nuclear weapons to oppose Russian advances.[12]

This was a belief that Acheson wanted Kennedy to realize. Based on this evidence, Acheson saw the Bay of Pigs as an example of indecisiveness under pressure; therefore, he wanted Kennedy to be ready to act when the time came to use nuclear weapons. Acheson went on to say, "Passivity did not increase deterrent credibility. By itself, the threat to use nuclear weapons did not increase the belief that we would use them." He concluded, "Nuclear weapons should not be looked upon as the last and largest weapon to be used, but as the first step in a new policy in protecting the United States from the failure of a policy of deterrence."[13] Acheson, like many Cold Warriors, did not see nuclear weapons as a doomsday scenario. Instead, these weapons should be used like any other. The problem, of course, was that they were not like any other weapon. Kennedy was keen on this point and sought to avoid a nuclear response to Soviet aggression.

The threat of nuclear conflict was not enough, according to Acheson. The president needed to be willing to use the weapons if necessary. Kennedy wanted to avoid the use of nuclear weapons at all costs. Acheson felt that Kennedy did not have the nerve to use these weapons. Secondly, Acheson was a part of the only administration that used atomic weaponry; therefore, his perspective was unique. After all, the result was a period where the United States established greater prestige in the world due to economic and military dominance. Acheson knew no other way to bring stability and peace. He was making these assertions with old Cold War tactics. These tactics no longer applied in 1961. While the results were good for the might of the United States, they have also contributed to the problems faced in the 20th and 21st centuries.

Acheson went on to argue that the administration needed to focus on sending a message that Kennedy would use nuclear weapons. He said that "the military experts had to work out the use of force over a period of time beginning around the first of July and timed as an increasingly somber course.... The U.S. had to make preparations and act as if it were prepared to use force up to, and including, nuclear force, if necessary. The only alternatives would be to have more luck than could be expected by any stretch of the imagination, or to withdraw from Berlin."[14] Acheson's insistence to push this course demonstrates that from his chair Khrushchev would push this crisis to a dangerous level and the Kennedy administration needed to show the world it was willing to go to war. Moreover, his assessment consistently predicted that the conflict meant either nuclear standoff or giving up U.S. rights in Berlin.

Acheson also commented that if "he were right in his conclusion that Berlin was vital to the power position of the U.S., withdrawal would destroy our power position. We had to act so as neither to invite a series of defeats nor precipitate ourselves into the ultimate catastrophe." As mentioned in the Bundy memo to the president, Cuba was a major piece in foreign policy. Kennedy's noncommittal approach to the incident raised eyebrows across the world. Khrushchev was one of the many that believed JFK would not use force in defending Berlin. Indeed, this was the time for the Soviets to act. Acheson believed that other countries would feel the same way and that this was the best time to show U.S. resolve in a place that had been the symbol of East versus West since the end of the Second World War. In addition, Acheson was personally invested in the situation. He had presided over the last Berlin crisis and did not want his efforts to end in vain.

Acheson, speaking to the committee, went through how the events would unfold: "There would then be a symbolic probe, followed by certain political actions, and then a battalion would go up the Autobahn, be stopped, and we would have demonstrated that a blockage existed." Acheson presumed "that present Berlin contingency planning meant that nuclear weapons would be used, but his criticism was that everything would come too late to affect Soviet decisions before they were made."[15] Acheson's constant reminder to the administration that the Soviets needed to know the United States would use nuclear force is evidence that this man did not believe JFK would in fact commit. "Nothing," Acheson said, "was planned to increase the belief that we would use nuclear weapons. This would really amount to preemptive war with nothing being done first to increase credibility. It would involve the use of nuclear weapons without getting the benefit of their deterrent effect." On one hand nuclear weapons were peace negotiators vaguely threatening nuclear war. On the other hand, nuclear weapons were the last resort that would bring this conflict to a level that threatened the world. Acheson's overall conclusion was, "It would be better to build up our preparations toward the use of force in order to put ourselves in the best possible position to act, as well as to make deterrents more credible."[16] This advance was both sound and safe. Acheson wanted to position the United States to respond to an attack. This realism in foreign policy was probably why Kennedy looked to him for advice.

Acheson told Kennedy to not only give the notion he was ready to use nuclear force, but also be prepared to go all the way: "If we were not prepared to go all the way, we should not start. Once having started, backing down would be devastating." Acheson stressed this concept to the president as well as being clear on the U.S. position with its allies. "The reactions of our allies," Acheson argued, "were the crux and the hardest part of the whole matter. If our allies had serious inhibitions against action, we had better find it out. We should proceed not by asking them if they would be afraid if we said 'boo!' We should, instead, say 'boo!' and see how far they jump." United States foreign policy was always entwined with Europe as well as trying to protect national security. This proposal by Acheson furthers Costigliola's argument that the United States would not consult its allies on matters that threatened United States prestige.

This recipe was not always the best course of action, and created a tension among the Allies that would endure longer than the crisis in Berlin.

Dean Acheson gave JFK an exigent approach to the Berlin crisis in June. After Kennedy's performance in Vienna it was clear that Acheson advised that the United States needed to show the world, and especially the Soviets, that it was willing to use nuclear force. This approach to the Soviets would not only further the deterioration of Soviet-American relations, but also scare the rest of the world. This insistence on asserting U.S. resolve and strength without consultation with U.S. allies was detrimental.

"There is, also, a substantial possibility that war might result."

Acheson followed up his report to the NSC with a paper for Kennedy. In this paper he clarified his position on taking an offensive with strong posturing on nuclear war. "Until this conflict of wills is resolved," Acheson wrote, "an attempt to solve the Berlin issue by negotiation is worse than a waste of time and energy. It is dangerous."[17] Acheson saw this as a conflict of wills because he approached this issue with the old ideology that Thomas Paterson argues hampered JFK and his advisors. If Acheson had been able to step back and understand the complexity in Germany he would have seen that Khrushchev was under pressure from the Chinese and the GDR. This situation was more than a contest of wills, and his inability to see this put his advice to JFK into question. Acheson went on to comment that knowing Khrushchev's "state of mind" regarding these matters was integral to the ability of the United States to make the right decisions. It was clear that at that point in the crisis the administration had to guess where Khrushchev's "state of mind" was with regard to Berlin. In his paper Acheson reiterates for the record his position on using nuclear war as both a deterrent and possibility to maintain United States prestige.

Acheson wrote, "The capability of U.S. nuclear power to devastate the Soviet Union has not declined over the past two years.... The decline in the effectiveness of the deterrent, therefore, must lie in a change in Soviet appraisal of U.S. willingness to go to nuclear war over the issue which Khrushchev reiterates his determination to present." Therefore, the main problem was that the Soviet Union's appraisal of the United States was that Kennedy would not go to all-out war over this issue. How did the Bay of Pigs and the Vienna summit play a role in this decision-making? Kennedy was not only battling advisors but also his past performance. Acheson wrote that per his current appraisal, the Soviets did not believe that the U.S. would go to war over Berlin, and so "the problem is how to restore the credibility of the deterrent — that is, how to cause Khrushchev to revise his apparent appraisal of U.S. willingness to resort to nuclear war, rather than to submit to Soviet demands."[18] Was Kennedy willing to use nuclear weapons? Acheson was not only willing, but he expected there to be an exchange between these countries. With this frank and immediate advice to Kennedy, the paper went on to state what would happen if the United States did in fact go to nuclear war.

Acheson summed the situation by saying, "There is a substantial chance, not subject to evaluation, that the preparations for war and negotiation outlined here would convince Khrushchev that what he wants is not possible without war, and cause him to change his purpose." However, a more cryptic result was that there was "a substantial possibility that war might result."[19] Acheson then wrote,

> It is, therefore, essential to make an early decision on accepting the hazard and preparing for it. The "substantial possibility" of the success of the course of action here depends on the existence of a core of hard decision, understood in all its grimness and cost. Furthermore, the condition of the country in the event of war will also depend on an early and deliberate decision. A hasty and improvised decision in the eleventh hour of approaching panic and hysteria could add vastly to the cost of war.[20]

Acheson was clear and to the point: he wanted Kennedy to make a decision and stick with it regardless of the outcome. The "eleventh hour" comment can be linked to Kennedy's indecisiveness earlier in 1961 when he refused to provide air support to the Cuban exiles in the Bay of Pigs invasion. In addition, it also seemed clear that Acheson wanted the American people apprised of the situation in advance, which would not only signal to the American people the nature of the situation, but also signal to the world that the United States meant business.

As a result of the NSC meeting and the recommendations Acheson gave the president, Bundy issued National Security Action Memo number 58 on 30 June 1961, which stated that the NSC must "evaluate various proposals for U.S. approaches to the Berlin problem."[21] According to this directive, the secretary of defense should "prepare recommendations concerning the timing and nature of the preparations to be taken to create a capability for: (a) a garrison and civilian ... airlift by October 15; (b) naval harassment and blockade of Bloc shipping by November 15." In addition to those directives, McNamara needed to be prepared for

> large scale non-nuclear ground action within four months of such time after October 15 as it may be ordered — with tactical air support, as necessary — assuming appropriate use of forces in Europe and assuming reinforcement from the U.S. as necessary to permit the use of two, four, six, and twelve divisions in Europe for the purposes stated in section C of chapter IV of Mr. Acheson's preliminary report to the President, including preparations which will ensure that nuclear weapons now in Europe are not used in the course of such action without direct Presidential authorization.[22]

This directive is evidence that Kennedy did agree with some of Acheson's recommendations, and therefore made decisions based on that advice. Kennedy may not have liked Acheson's assessment, but it was clear that pressure from within his cabinet was mounting for him to take action. Kennedy needed to show the men around him that he was able to make decisions. Additionally, it was an example of how likely this administration thought it was that this conflict might grow into an all-out war with the Soviets. Also, this memo wanted the Strategic Air Command in a state of "maximum readiness." Bundy's memo was clear:

> These preparations should include only steps which are directly related to the four military purposes set forth above, and should not include measures primarily designed for psychological effect which could be considered provocative or measures which run counter to the U.S. policy toward NATO.[23]

This insistence to stay on task with the four main goals was evidence that Kennedy was reluctant to use nuclear weapons as a deterrent as Acheson advised without consultation from the allies. It also supports the idea that Kennedy did not want to hint at the use of nuclear weapons yet in this diplomatic game with Khrushchev. There were some in the administration that did not want to stand on the advice that Acheson so powerfully provided the administration, and one of those people was a historian from Harvard.

"All wars start from stupidity."

On 7 July 1961 Arthur Schlesinger wrote Kennedy, providing him an assessment of the Acheson paper. Schlesinger started by summing up Acheson's position for the president and then focused on "major issues" with the Acheson premise. He wrote that according to the paper, "Khrushchev's principal purpose in forcing the Berlin question is to humiliate the U.S. on a basic issue by making us back down on a sacred commitment and thus shatter our world power and influence."[24] Schlesinger went on to write, "From this premise flows the conclusion that we are in a fateful test of wills, that our major task is to demonstrate our unalterable determination, and that Khrushchev will be deterred only by a demonstrated U.S. readiness to go to nuclear war." He wrote that under this premise "negotiation would be harmful" until the crisis was fully developed.

He explained from his point of view the problems with Acheson's assessment, arguing that Acheson's paper avoided some major concerns. For example, he wrote, "What political moves do we make until the crisis develops?" This question is important for Schlesinger, because from his point of view, Acheson's recommendations were contingent on an escalation of the crisis. "If we sit silent, or confine ourselves to rebutting Soviet contentions, we permit Khrushchev to establish the framework of discussions. As we do this, we in effect invite him to demand from us a definition of the guarantees we would find acceptable." The result of these events, Schlesinger argued, "casts the U.S. as rigid and unreasonable and puts us on the political defensive."[25] Schlesinger went on to point out the political objectives in this exchange with the Soviets. The paper, he argued, "defines an immediate casus belli; but it does not state any political objective other than the present access procedures for which we are prepared to incinerate the world."[26] By this statement, Schlesinger made apparent that the world hung in balance over "access rights." Such circumstances seemed difficult for this man to comprehend.

A nuclear exchange was something that Schlesinger did not take very lightly. "It is essential to elaborate the cause for which we are prepared to go to nuclear war," he wrote. "Where do we want to come out if we win the test of wills?" These were important moral questions to consider. Indeed, Schlesinger looked at the events differently. The historian's trained eye saw through bellicose rhetoric and asked why the United States was embroiled in such a standoff. Besides upholding the prestige of the United States, Schlesinger wanted to know what were the main objectives in threatening to "incinerate" the world? Was one German unification? Did the United States really want to start a nuclear exchange over access rights? Kennedy said to Kenneth O'Donnell, "All wars start from stupidity.... God knows I'm not an isolationist, but it seems particularly stupid to risk killing a million Americans over an argument about access rights on an Autobahn."[27] If Kennedy really felt that way then how much did someone like Acheson impact his decision-making? Moreover, did Schlesinger give Kennedy the reasons to not escalate this crisis into all out war?

Schlesinger went on to state that Acheson's paper "covers only one eventuality — that is the communist interruption of military access to West Berlin. Actually there is a whole spectrum of harassments, of which a full-scale blockade may well be one of the least likely."[28] While there was no mention of a wall between the sectors, it seems clear that Schlesinger was looking at this crisis with a different perspective. Acheson, on the other hand, was fighting this crisis with his own experience when he was on the White House staff. Schlesinger went on to say, "The paper hinges on our willingness to face nuclear war. But this option is undefined. Before you are asked to make the decision to go to nuclear war, you are entitled to know what concretely nuclear war is likely to mean."[29] Again, Schlesinger's need for a definition of nuclear war is another example of how his questions gave Kennedy a new angle to consider. Schlesinger's criticism of Acheson's vague premise to be ready for a nuclear conflict was valid. The largest difference between the two papers was that Acheson tried to get JFK to make a stand and be firm, while Schlesinger tried to get Kennedy to see what his objectives were in the conflict. Schlesinger also pointed out that the Acheson paper did not look at the possibility that the Allies might not go along with this course of action.

On 17 July 1961, Kennedy, Rusk, McNamara, RFK, and Bundy were among the principal people who met regarding the Berlin Crisis. The meeting addressed several questions regarding Berlin such as military options, discussing policy with U.S. allies, and a position toward the GDR. Bundy wrote the memo for the record. Rusk wanted to be "low key" while at the same time insisting, "necessary military strength should be built up and the Department would concur in a budgetary increase of $4.3 billion and a call of National Guard and Reserve units if needed." McNamara stated, "A declaration of national emergency was not needed before September 1st or October 1st, although there would be a probable need for a call of air units before the end of the year."[30] There was a great deal of discussion regarding the number of troops and military planning. In the final analysis they all agreed that the president should "review these questions of military policy with the Joint Chiefs of Staff before [a] final decision was made." This meeting had advice from all aspects of the Kennedy circle. JFK put this team together to handle these situations, and he was sure to take every point of view before he committed the United States to a war. Rusk went on to discuss how the administration should handle the issues with its allies.

While getting the military in the proper mode was a major obstacle in times of crisis, getting the United States allies to agree with JFK's course of action was another issue altogether. Rusk said, "The second large item for discussion on Wednesday would be the planning of the negotiating position of the U.S., preparatory to discussion with our Allies." He went on to ask, "What negotiating position should we have, and how should its development be timed?"[31] These are questions that the Acheson paper did not address, and maybe the Schlesinger paper had an impact on the meeting. Rusk indicated "his view that the opening posture of the West should be an emphasis upon self-determination, and that probably we would wish to spin out the discussion in order to make it difficult for Mr. Khrushchev to proceed with concrete steps at an early stage."[32] On the same day, Rusk issued a memo to the president that emphasized the "low key" approach. JFK was very much his own secretary of state, but it seemed that Rusk was suddenly offering more advice then he had done in the past. His point on emphasizing "self-determination" was nothing new. It always had been the policy of the United States to promote self determination. He did, however, have another piece that he brought to the group.

Rusk, like Schlesinger, wanted to be clear on the objectives of the administration's actions in this crisis. Rusk brought out "the question of our eventual position toward the [GDR]." While it was clear that the administration would have to talk to a representative from that country, Rusk wanted to be sure that the administration did not come on too strong, making these discussions look like a defeat. Rusk said, "Our rights in Berlin certainly cannot be discussed, but there can at an appropriate stage be a discussion of the way in which our rights are to be maintained without impairment."[33] This meeting was a great example of the secretary of state giving his opinion on points that JFK should consider. Moreover, these recommendations demonstrated that Rusk was thinking about countries other than the Soviet Union. With that in mind, the military issues still needed to be addressed. McNamara made clear that a military operations plan would not be ready until 19 July, and General Maxwell Taylor asked about propaganda proposals. While the meeting was good in analyzing the complexity of the situation, it seemed that the United States was running out of time and the possibility of military conflict was very real.

"I'd think about it very hard and tell no one what I'd decided."

As discussed earlier in this book, McGeorge Bundy had a major influence on Kennedy's decision-making. While Bundy's earlier memo from 16 May 1961 effectively communicated to the president how he could better utilize his leadership skills, a 19 July 1961 memorandum from Bundy to the president demonstrated, once again, that Bundy had a hand in keeping Kennedy on task. The subject of the memo was "afternoon meetings," and it addressed how Kennedy should approach the NSC meetings regarding Berlin. The steering committee met at 3:00 p.m. and the NSC meeting was at 4:00 p.m. Bundy stated in the last line of this memo, "This is probably the most important NSC meeting that we have had."[34]

With several specific ideas in mind, Bundy outlined for Kennedy what he should concentrate on in the first meeting so it would in effect bring the issues up in the second meeting. Bundy stated that Kennedy should briefly review the military options regarding Berlin. Within this review, JFK should understand "the State Department's estimate that there will not be a strong allied response to requests for parallel action on their part. It thus becomes a major diplomatic question whether we want to ask strongly for something we may not get." In addition to that, Bundy told the president to consider Maxwell Taylor's "Third Course" which was outlined in a 19 July 1961 memo to the president. This memo stated, "This 'Third Course' would call for a substantial increase to the defense budget but would use the money for a permanent increase in the military establishment justified by the over-all world situation."[35] Bundy went on to tell the president, "Whichever military level you decide on, there is need for additional decisions about a national emergency and about standby controls and taxing authority."[36] Most of the people in this group believed that the U.S. did not have to declare a national emergency. According to Bundy, however, there were people such as Acheson who did not agree with that course of action. That would make sense considering that Acheson's whole premise was to signal to the Soviets that the United States was ready and willing to take this crisis to the next level. "It will be important," Bundy wrote, "to decide how to handle this matter in the 4 o'clock meeting so as to have as much harmony and unanimity in the government as possible, once the decision is taken."[37] Once again Bundy slowly pushed Kennedy to make a decision and stick with it. Moreover, he was preparing JFK for the obstacles that lay ahead and how to avoid them.

There was a third item that did not get much attention in the previous meetings. Acheson's insistence on taking the offensive permeated previous exchanges, but here Bundy mentions the prospect of economic sanctions. This idea of economic sanctions called for "a general economic embargo against the Sino-Soviet bloc if access to Berlin is blocked." Bundy said that this alternative was "worth reading, and it makes clear that we could do a lot of harm to the Sino-Soviet economy, at a considerable cost to ourselves."[38] However, Bundy made sure of JFK's focus by stating, "the most important subject for discussion in the first meeting, and the one which you may wish to put first, is the political scenario." This political scenario was discussed in a paper prepared by Dean Rusk. Bundy went through the highlights of the paper for JFK.

Bundy says that the first part of the paper was a summary of the issues and then it became "foggy" toward the end. He told Kennedy that he should ask Rusk to clarify on two items:

> The first is whether we should now make clear that neither the peace treaty nor the substitution of East Germans for Russians along the Autobahn is a fighting matter. The second is whether we should extend serious feelers to the Soviets with respect to the elements of an eventual settlement of the crisis.[39]

Bundy stated that he would try to draft up something for the 4:00 p.m. meeting based on the 3:00 p.m. meeting, but Kennedy should try to prioritize items according to their urgency. He even went as far to give him suggestions and the reasoning why. Bundy stated that first Kennedy should focus on the "level of military build-up," followed by other "immediate measures — national emergency? taxes? stand-by controls?" Then Kennedy should ask about the tone and content of his speech and a discussion on the economic sanctions policy. Finally, JFK should discuss the "immediate political steps" which included "a. Early talks with the Soviets? (Acheson against and Rusk undecided); b. An immediate decision on attitude toward the peace treaty and East German troops on the Autobahn. (The British are pressing hard for this.)" Not only was Bundy giving Kennedy advice on where to concentrate his energy; he was also dictating how Kennedy should run his meetings. This memo preceded a meeting where JFK determined his actions outlined in National Security Action Memorandum number 62.

During this summer in 1961 Kennedy asked Acheson, with only Bundy present, at what point nuclear weapons would be used. Acheson quietly said, "If I were you, I'd think about it very hard and tell no one what I'd decided."[40] On 19 July 1961, the NSC meeting was the final piece which determined JFK's course of action in response to the Soviet ultimatum regarding Berlin. The steering group met at 3:00 p.m. in the president's study on the second floor of the executive mansion. Dean Rusk opened the meeting with a discussion on the "political scenario" from his talking paper. "He emphasized in particular that we must not give our allies a veto, although in practical terms both Germany and France have such a veto de facto. He also emphasized that we must have public opinion on our side and that the force of such international opinion on the Soviet leaders is very great."[41] Rusk went on to state that he supported a military program with three characteristics: "1. A present build-up; 2. A capability to stop [GDR] troops by the end of 1961; 3. An ability to fight conventional war for several weeks against Soviet forces, at the same point in time."[42] It seems evident from this memo that the administration was getting ready for a conflict with the Soviets. However, it should be noted that the characteristics in Rusk's assessment of the military program called for a "conventional war."

McNamara added that "there would be no need for a declaration of national emergency before September 1 at the earliest. He believed that Congressional authorization could be obtained for a limited call-up of reserves without such a declaration." One of the main issues was how the president would attain the money to finance this new deployment of forces. A national emergency would give him some power to avoid Congress, and at the same time signify to the Soviets that JFK was willing to commit forces and money to Berlin. Kennedy, however, wanted to avoid this. The Cabinet members suggested raising taxes so the American people would feel that they were a part of the crisis.[43] Kennedy "raised the question whether the proposed military build-up would increase the credibility of the U.S. nuclear deterrent, and the Secretary of Defense replied that in his judgment this would be the effect, but the argument was not fully developed."[44] For JFK to ask such a question signified that he had considered the Acheson scenario. He believed that a nuclear deterrent might make a difference in this political scenario that they were discussing.

The meeting then turned to considering the Allies as well as the military build-up in Europe. Kennedy asked more questions regarding issues that had been discussed in previous meetings. The group "agreed that one major purpose of the measures now proposed is to effect preparation for a major build-up of forces in Europe, on short notice." Kennedy then asked "whether these preparations should go forward even if there were a negative response abroad to our proposals for concurrent allied military preparations." Kennedy was testing to see how the allies would respond to U.S. action in Europe. Their participation was crucial; otherwise, the United States would look like a bully in Europe's back yard. McNamara "answered that he would be in favor of the present build-up and of the further deployment of major U.S. forces to Europe as long as the Germans were willing to play their role, and he believed they would."[45] With this last piece, the steering committee ended business and the president with his cabinet members met with the overall contingent group on Berlin.

The 4:00 p.m. meeting started much like the steering committee, with Rusk reading his paper and McNamara outlining the military options. The president "emphasized his own view that the outlined U.S. preparations would not be adequate without an effective allied response, especially from the Germans and the French." What followed was what Bundy called an "important exchange" between Acheson and McNamara. According to the meeting minutes,

> Mr. Acheson initially appeared to wish for a present definite decision to declare a national emergency and begin the call-up of reserves not later than September. Secretary McNamara argued that it would be better not to make a definite commitment now, but to have the understanding that a declaration of emergency would be declared and larger ground reserves called up when the situation required.[46]

McNamara's reluctance to issue a national emergency was most likely caused by JFK's hesitancy to escalate the situation according to Acheson's plan. Kennedy, however, could not bring this up in this meeting, because there were already people who believed that he lacked the nerve to go to war. McNamara rejected this notion because he wanted to avoid a "rigid time-table in advance." Moreover, he did not want a large deployment of troops with no concrete mission.

Bundy wrote, "Mr. Acheson initially appeared to believe that the proposed course of action was not sufficiently energetic or definite, but the President kept the discussion going until it became clear that Secretary McNamara's flexible time-table would in fact permit a sufficiently rapid deployment in the event of deepening crisis, to satisfy Mr. Acheson."[47] "The essential point," Bundy wrote,

> was that the present preparations would rapidly create a force in being, in the continental U.S., of six Army and two Marine divisions. In the event of a rapidly developing crisis, appropriate numbers of these divisions could be deployed to Europe and reserve divisions called up to take their place, so that up to six divisions and supporting units could be promptly deployed as needed. The exact way in which this deployment and call-up would be interconnected in time was not spelled out in detail, but the up-shot of the discussion was a general agreement that the plans as presented by Secretary McNamara were satisfactory. Mr. Acheson specifically indicated his own approval.[48]

Clearly the president did not make decisions alone. Both Bundy and McNamara had a say in when JFK would deploy the military. Additionally, the men involved in this decision-making had an impact on executive authority. The process dictated his actions. Moreover, the resolution was very logical and had certain steps in the event the crisis worsened. These considerations satisfied men like Acheson that the administration was taking this threat seriously. It seemed clear, however, that Acheson expected Kennedy to take a stronger stance. While the rest of the meeting was devoted to informing the Allies of United States action it was clear that Kennedy had his decision and was ready to initiate his response to the Soviet Union regarding their ultimatum.

6

"Perhaps a wall"

"A High Noon Stance"

After the 19 July 1961 NSC meeting Kennedy was ready to state the administration's response to the Soviet Union. National Security Action Memorandum Number 62 was specific about how Kennedy planned to initiate his actions. On 20 July 1961 Kennedy sent similar letters to Adenauer, Macmillan and de Gaulle outlining his 25 July speech. This was very characteristic of the Kennedy administration. As previously mentioned, JFK did not consult the Allies—he informed them of the United States' decision. Walt W. Rostow had some words for Kennedy in a 22 July 1961 memo entitled "A High Noon Stance on Berlin." In this memo, Rostow discussed the Allies and how they factored into the planning of such an operation in Berlin. "On the one hand," he wrote, "the unity of the Allies is a factor on which Moscow has its attention carefully focused. They will take any sign of disunity and disarray as a cause for pressing their position with increased confidence."[1] Rostow went on to state that the "maximum degree of Allied unity is desirable; a minimum degree is essential." Additionally he said that the U.S. might have to stand alone "relatively isolated" as the crisis approached. However, he was clear in telling the president that "we should not let their stance necessarily determine our own."[2] Rostow told Kennedy that the administration should be prepared for what he called a "High Noon Stance," with a reference to Gary Cooper going at the bandits alone in parentheses.

Rostow gave Kennedy two reasons why the United States should prepare for this "High Noon stance." "First," he wrote, "it is on the United States—its will and its power—that the Russians will ultimately focus. We may have to pay something in the end for a degree of wilting on the part of our Allies." Rostow also said, "Although allied unity and American toughness will have to be carefully weighed, at each stage, the question of unity should not be automatically overriding."[3] Rostow's use of the terms "wilting" and "toughness" points to the issues Thomas Paterson argues, as mentioned earlier. As long as members of the administration viewed their response to the Soviets in these terms then there would be an issue relating to the pressure Khrushchev was dealing with. However, Rostow wanted to prepare Kennedy for the stark reality that he might have to give up some level of prestige or political capital to avoid war. "Second," Rostow wrote, "we must remember that the position of our Allies differs from ours in some important respects. We have the finger on the atomic trigger — not they." In perhaps the best piece of advice he could give JFK at this point, Rostow wrote, "It is one matter to face the possibility of atomic war, if your political leaders have their finger on the trigger: it is a quite different matter if someone else's leaders are in that position."[4]

While Rostow acknowledged that he might be wrong with his assessment, he emphasized, "We must be prepared in our minds for the possibility of a relatively lonely stage; and we should accept it without throwing our sheriff's badge in the dust when the crisis subsides."[5] Rostow acknowledged the Allied perspective to Kennedy while at the same time emphasizing that it was important that Kennedy not throw away United States commitments to its Allies regardless of their actions in this crisis. While Kennedy did *inform* England, France and West Germany, he did not *consult* them on his decision. It was evident in the NSC meetings that Kennedy was worried about how the Soviets would respond first and the Allies second. Some could argue that it would have been better for Kennedy to gather a coalition before acting. While that would have granted him international strength, it may also have suggested that he was unable to react independently; thus strengthening perceptions abroad that he was weak and indecisive. Dean Acheson wanted Kennedy to show resolve and military might regardless of the what the Allies thought. Kennedy was determined to maintain peace and believed that Acheson's advice had some merit, but he would not follow it. JFK told Acheson that he would not take such a strong stance. JFK did however take Acheson's advice regarding the Allies. Despite the fact that Kennedy took some of his advice, Acheson reportedly told a small group, "Gentleman, you might as well face it. This nation is without leadership."[6] Looking for a peaceful solution, Kennedy was determined to succeed in his endeavor without nuclear conflict. Acheson's comment illuminates Kennedy's struggle with some Cold Warriors. Indeed, the young idealistic senator-turned-president had the stark realities of the Cold War shoved in his face.

On 24 July 1961, NSAM Number 62 was issued by Bundy. This document outlined the president's action regarding the Soviet ultimatum. In this memo, JFK made it clear for the record that he did inform the Allies and was going to address the people on 25 July. In addition it stated, "The President has authorized a prompt strengthening of the United States' military position, in the light of the general international situation." Also, he asked for 3.2 billion dollars from congress to assist in this "strengthening" of U.S. forces. With regard to the allies the memo stated, "The President directed that negotiations be undertaken immediately with our allies looking toward their parallel participation in such a higher level of military readiness. In these discussions there will be no initial indication of any U.S. willingness to increase military assistance to our allies for these purposes."[7] Finally, the memo addressed the economic situation as well as how information would be delivered to the American people. This directive went out to the members of the White House staff and lent some finality to the pending question of a response to the Soviet ultimatum on Berlin. JFK would now address the people to outline his position and send a signal to Khrushchev.

According to Robert Dallek, JFK was administered additional steroids to assist in the tension surrounding his largest political maneuver since the Bay of Pigs.[8] He began by recapping for the people what had happened since his trip to Vienna to meet with Khrushchev. His speech emphasized Khrushchev's "grim warnings about the future of the world," and reminded the people, "In Berlin, as you recall, he intends to bring to an end, through a stroke of the pen, first our legal rights to be in West Berlin — and secondly our ability to make good on our commitment to the two million free people of that city. That we cannot permit." He largely blamed the crisis on Moscow; however, he offered the olive branch through negotiation, but also showed strength in a military build-up that would cost the American people, saying, "American families will bear the burden of these requests. Studies or careers will be interrupted; husbands and sons will be called away; incomes in some cases will be reduced." He continued with a strong sense of duty and history, "But these are burdens which must be borne if freedom is to be defended — Americans have willingly borne them before — and they will not flinch from the task now."[9] This was a speech that took a great deal of time and energy to produce. Much like the individuals already discussed, Ted Sorensen's efforts to paint a picture for the world with words contributed to Kennedy's Cold War policy. His strong, direct prose offered no confusion of the U.S. position. It was a message to the American people as well as a message to the world that JFK would not shy away from a challenge. It was a speech designed to bring the Allies into the fray as well as show Khrushchev that this man who was young enough to be his son was someone he had better watch. If anything this speech demonstrated his resolve, commitment to the Allies, and respect for the people of the United States. He was not afraid, as some presidents were, to invoke the notion that these actions might cause war. Also, he was not afraid to ask the people for sacrifice.

Khrushchev told John McCloy, Kennedy's chief negotiator to Moscow on disarmament, that the speech was a "preliminary declaration of war." McCloy said that Khrushchev was "really mad" and "used rough war-like language."[10] A week after this initial reaction to the speech he saw McCloy again and told him to deliver a message to JFK. "Please tell your president we accept his ultimatum and his terms and will respond in kind.... We will meet war with war." He went on to say that if there were war Kennedy would be the "last president of the United States."[11] This reaction from Khrushchev was expected, but it complicated JFK's negotiating power. Khrushchev needed to act in some way to counter Kennedy's build-up. One can argue, however, that had Kennedy took Acheson's advice, the two countries would have been even closer to war. Kennedy's administration needed to focus on what its next step would be in this global chess match with the Soviets.

On 26 July 1961 Kennedy met with the Berlin Contingency Planning Group. The beginning of the meeting dealt with where the administration was in negotiations. What were the major responses and how could they get the U.N. involved? A telling part of the meeting was when Rusk mentioned that Thompson meet with Khrushchev to "find out further what is on the Soviet leader's mind." Indeed, Kennedy and his advisors relied largely on Thompson's opinions to gauge the next step in diplomacy. Acheson, however, was pessimistic about negotiations. He said that the "first round of discussion would certainly fail and that in the second round we might wish to bring up an incomplete proposal which would give us room for a few final concessions at the end."[12] Acheson was most likely still vying for Kennedy to take his advice and use a grand show of force in that region — risking war, but maintaining U.S. prestige abroad.

In a 29 July 1961 telegram from Thompson and McCloy, JFK was told that Khrushchev was "really mad on Thursday after digesting President's speech." It went on to say, "War bound to be thermonuclear and though you and we may survive all your European allies will be completely destroyed." Their advice was that the "situation [was] probably not yet ripe for any negotiation ... by U.S. but too dangerous to permit it drift into a condition where cramped time could well lead to unfortunate action." McCloy went on to say that he and Thompson "sense [the] Soviets will be pressing allies with threats of destruction to weaken their determination to go along with us."[13] Most importantly, this account is evidence that Khrushchev was quick to mention "thermonuclear war" and its impact on United States allies. Clearly this was a bargaining position for Khrushchev. If he could convince Europe that Kennedy's actions would impact Europe, then the fragile support that Kennedy had would deteriorate. This was just another example of how frail the relationship was between the United States and its allies and why it was such a major factor in United States decision-making. With that being said, after the initial response, Khrushchev kept sending messages to Washington through Thompson.

According to a 31 July 1961 telegram from Thompson, Khrushchev was "personally so far out on limb on this issue now that he could abandon it only at price of concessions in other areas which we clearly could not make." Additionally, Thompson said, "Soviets will make strong effort however end occupation status as well as to stop refugee flow."[14] As mentioned earlier, the refugee flow to the Western zone in Berlin was staggering. With this embarrassing situation thrust onto the world stage, Khrushchev needed to act in some way. His advisors crafted a plan for a wall dividing the zones as early as March 1961, but Khrushchev felt that was too dangerous.[15] Kennedy and his team forced Khrushchev to make the next move. Hence, JFK would not initiate force.

According to William Taubman, Khrushchev believed that "the best way to restrain the American state ... was to scare the daylights out of it."[16] Therefore, there was some logic behind his outbursts to McCloy. Thompson followed up this telegram with another that outlined four approaches to the Berlin issue for the president to consider and gave his opinions on them. Additionally, the State Department had their own opinions on how to approach the Soviets. Finally, Dean Acheson offered his opinion once again to JFK on how to handle this current crisis. Bundy, however, would be the linchpin that assisted Kennedy in seeing all these points of view.

"important to have a clear view on some of these issues fairly soon"

In a 31 July 1961 telegram to the president, Thompson suggested his ideas for Kennedy. Option one focused on what he called an "all Berlin solution." This suggestion stated that all four powers would be in control of the city. Thompson was not a strong supporter of this solution. He stated, "From Soviet point of view successful amalgamation of socialist and capitalist systems within city would be powerful argument against their contention that this could not be done for all of Germany. Therefore I do not believe they would agree to or carry out such plan."[17] Thompson's second option was his favorite. He proposed a "peace package plan postponing for 7–10 years showdown on German reunification through free elections." In addition to the elections other measures included "Western commitment not support change in present frontiers, NATO–Warsaw non-aggression pact, prohibition of atomic arms to East and West Germany, etc." This may have appealed to Thompson because it would postpone this crisis until new leadership could address these circumstances. Additionally, Thompson made it clear that this option appealed to him because the Soviets might be tempted "by such solution [because] they could easily find means of evading elections when time came by accusing West of violations."[18] Finally, Thompson suggested for his third and fourth option respectively a similar peace treaty with West Germany or a peace treaty with some "interim arrangement on Berlin." Each option is evidence that JFK's advisor was trying to think differently. After Kennedy's speech and Khrushchev's tough talk, Thompson may have felt that this could result in a nuclear confrontation. With that in mind, he may have been trying to get Kennedy to approach this topic differently and find a more plausible solution than nuclear war.

The steering committee met on 2 August 1961 at 4:00 P.M. and discussed three items pertaining to the Berlin situation. According to a Bundy memo that outlined the meeting, Dean Rusk took the lead, suggesting that "Ambassador Thompson, perhaps with associates, might meet with Khrushchev later in August in an attempt to get him to talk and to clarify certain aspects of the

Soviet position."[19] It seems clear from the evidence that Rusk was trying to also get the ball rolling with respect to a solution to the current crisis as soon as possible. "The immediate and urgent problem was propaganda," Bundy wrote, "and there followed an extensive discussion of ways and means of making our case more strongly all around the world." Presenting the case to the American people was only part of the problem. The group decided to stay on target with the principles outlined in Kennedy's 25 July speech stating "keep the peace and keep Berlin free." In addition to these two mainstays of the administration's message, they thought to add self-determination as another goal. Finally, the group addressed military concerns. One of the main issues discussed was how Rusk should approach the European powers. He was going to Paris for a meeting with the major powers from 4 to 9 August 1961. Bundy wrote, "The first urgency on the military side is to get agreement among the major Governments on the basic policy of a strong military build-up."[20] Once again the problems with U.S. allies plagued this administration as they had in the past and would in the future. It was imperative that the United States was able to confront the Soviets in Berlin and have the support of the other major powers. Bundy's memo was evidence of the major concerns these men faced that August as well as a statement of how they would handle these problems. Bundy, however, had some specific ideas for the president that would help JFK make decisions on Berlin.

On 3 August 1961, the day after the meeting with the Steering Group on Berlin, Bundy wrote Kennedy a memo regarding two papers on Berlin: one paper was written by Dean Acheson and the other by the State Department. Bundy took the points of these many pages and distilled them down to a short memo for the president. In this memo Bundy stated, "The two papers are thoughtful and careful, and in their basic outlines much alike." He went on to summarize the major points for the president. Both papers divided the Berlin issue into three phases. Phase one went from the current time to the proposed elections in Germany on 17 September, phase two covered the period from the elections to a possible peace treaty, and phase three focused on after the peace treaty.

Phase one was the first issue that Bundy outlined for the president.

> There should be no actual negotiations of a formal sort. We need time to concert our military build-up, and public substantive negotiations before the German elections would create turmoil in West Germany.... At some time in this period the Western states should make a proposal for negotiations in a four-power Foreign Ministers meeting [which should] be preceded by a Western Summit for the purpose of concerting a Western negotiating position.[21]

Bundy spent a little time outlining the plan for phase one, but it seemed that he had more questions for the president to ponder.

Bundy focused a good amount of the memo on major questions with regard to phase one. This implies that he was not completely in favor of this venture. He presented the question to Kennedy, "Should there be a 'quiet approach' to the Soviets before the German elections?" Bundy mentioned that Acheson's paper argued that someone could drop a hint that the United States was strengthening its position. "This quiet approach," Bundy wrote, "would not be discussed with any of our Allies—otherwise it could not remain quiet." He mentioned that Rusk would want Thompson to explore further conversations with Khrushchev, but his "own hunch is that unless Thompson is in a position to send up some new signal of his own, all we shall get at present is a repetition of what everyone has been hearing since Vienna." Bundy went on to ask further questions on the summit as well as when things should be made public. He was certain, however, to address the issue of Kennedy's leadership.

Bundy wrote,

> On one further matter there is no disagreement but your own leadership and pressure are important—propaganda. It is agreed that we should use the next two months energetically to advance understanding of our position and of the low character of the Soviet effort.... The real problem is that the center of international sympathy should be directed toward people of West Berlin and not toward the official position of the U.S. Government, and this takes some doing.[22]

Bundy was looking for international support and he knew that the United States would not garner the support it needed without the assistance of other countries. However, the people of West Berlin might make a difference. He was suggesting to the president that the administration use the people in Berlin to assert American policy. "The Acheson report," he wrote, "states well and strongly the four central themes of freedom, peace, faithful trusteeship and self-determination. We are for all four, and the Soviets are currently in fact against them all on Berlin."[23] Propaganda was something Bundy stressed to Kennedy. Further, he demanded that the president lead in this category.

Bundy wanted the president to examine the papers himself before he spoke with Rusk. Bundy's assessment, however, was "that they are sensible within their limits. They do not, in my judgment, adequately examine wider alternatives like calling a peace conference, or proposing that the United Nations have a role in Berlin." While he thought phase two should be focused on negotiations, perhaps the best evidence of Bundy's role in this crisis is within his assessment of phase three. He believed that "the questions all turn around this general problem: what form of interference with access to Berlin triggers what form of response?" This was a loaded question for this administration. Did this mean that if the Soviets denied access rights there would be war? "These questions," he continued, "are very hard ones, and the consensus of the Steering Group yesterday was that they need not have first priority attention for the coming meeting. But as General Taylor points out, it is going to be important to have a clear view on some of these issues fairly soon."[24] It was imperative, according to Bundy, that JFK knew what he was going to do in reaction to defiance. Indecisiveness on JFK's part seemed to be a major concern of his advisors.

"Was there any warning in the last two or three days?"

During those tense days in August, Kennedy found himself meeting with many people. He was walking with Rostow outside the Oval Office, contemplating what would happen next. Multitudes of people in East Germany had been migrating to the West through Berlin. Kennedy said to Rostow, "Khrushchev is losing East Germany. He cannot let that happen. If East Germany goes, so will Poland and all of Eastern Europe. He will have to do something to stop the flow of refugees. Perhaps a wall. And we won't be able to prevent it."[25] Kennedy knew the storm surrounding Berlin would worsen before it got better. Moreover, he understood the pressures of being in a position where people wanted action. Kennedy's actions had put Khrushchev in a situation where he needed to react in some way.

The weekend when Khrushchev ordered the wall constructed, Kennedy was in Hyannis Port with his family. Bundy gave him "a checklist of the actions that you were obligated to take if and when you contemplate a decision on the use of nuclear weapons."[26] On 13 August 1961 Kennedy's boat, the *Marlin*, was called back from a lunch cruise with a "triple-priority" message waiting ashore. Wearing a polo shirt JFK greeted General Clifton, who gave him a yellow teletype that explained that a wall had been constructed separating East from West Berlin.[27] Kennedy called Rusk in Washington and asked, "What the hell is this? How long have you known? Was there any warning in the last two or three days?"[28] While this was an unforeseen circumstance, it was imperative that Kennedy seem as if there were nothing to panic about. Robert Dallek writes, "Kennedy responded to the border closing with studied caution." JFK went back to Washington on Monday, as scheduled, and let the State Department handle the initial response stating that this did not change the Allied resolve to maintain access rights to West Berlin.[29] Kennedy remarked to Kenneth O'Donnell, "It's not a very nice solution, but a wall is a hell of a lot better than a war."[30]

On 14 August 1961 the decision-making process on a response to this act began. Bundy wrote Kennedy a memo addressing Berlin negotiations and possible reprisals for the wall. Bundy suggested that negotiation was a good idea and said the staff was in accord: "I find unanimity in your immediate staff for the view that we should take a clear initiative for negotiation within the next week or ten days." However, the problem with the four powers persisted. Bundy wrote, "Since our allies are hesitant, the lead will have to come from you, at the highest level." Kennedy, Bundy was saying, must take a stance soon and make it clear to the allies that this was going to be the action, without any debate on the matter. Bundy went on to write, "The truth is that we're making very slow headway toward a clear position, as it is; a date for negotiation would put all our noses to the grindstone."³¹ There were some reprisals such as the ending of travel permits discussed by Bundy. However, Bundy wrote, "I doubt if we should take little actions in reprisal against this big one, especially when the punishment is unrelated to the crime." Bundy said that he agreed with Joe Alsop and George Kennan. First, "This is something they have always had the power to do; [secondly] it is something they were bound to do sooner or later, unless they could control the exits from West Berlin to the West; [finally] since it was bound to happen, it is as well to have it happen early, as *their* doing and *their* responsibility." Bundy's assessments were helpful to the president, but it seemed that JFK started to ask his own questions.

In a 14 August 1961 memo to Dean Rusk, Kennedy asked, "What steps will we take this week to exploit politically propaganda-wise the Soviet–East German cut-off of the border?" In addition to this JFK said, "This seems to me to show how hollow is the phrase 'free city' and how despised is the East German government, which the Soviet Union seeks to make respectable." Finally, Kennedy's assessment was that "the question we must decide is how far we should push this. It offers us a very good propaganda stick which if the situation were reversed would be well used in beating us. It seems to me this requires decisions at the highest level."³² Kennedy spent too much time asking questions and meeting with advisors and not enough time focusing on solutions. It seems from the record thus far that this is one of the first times he addressed his secretary of state and asked him to do his job. JFK was ready for new ideas. This situation was the catalyst that pushed Kennedy to explore advice on Cold War issues. Indeed, the remainder of his presidency would focus on gathering people whom he trusted for counsel. Once again, in all the meetings on Berlin, there was no mention of a wall or anything like it. Could Kennedy have been widening his circle of advice? Did this mean that he might have been about to take a different approach to foreign policy? At the start of the administration he was steadfast in appointing a soldier to the secretary of state position; now it seemed he was asking questions instead of ordering. With that in mind, was JFK asking these questions out of frustration or did he mean to get Rusk's input?

On 17 August 1961 the Steering Group on Berlin met, and Rusk proposed that the United States reinforce the West Berlin brigade over a letter of protest from the three Western heads of government. Kennedy decided that the reinforcement should be one battle group (1500–1800 men).³³ Kennedy asked if they should go to the UN, and Rusk said that there would not be enough support and that they should hold the UN "in reserve for a more important and suitable occasion." Rusk proposed the reinforcement and discouraged Kennedy from going to the UN — JFK agreed with both ideas. Additionally, this meeting had Robert Kennedy presenting the notion that more should be done with regard to propaganda. This was an issue that JFK wanted to exploit. His memo to Rusk is evidence of that point. It seems, however, that Robert Kennedy was the one to broach the subject with the group. This is evidence that Robert Kennedy made statements at the behest of his brother. This role is not unique, but does show a certain dynamic to the cabinet room. It's also evidence that RFK was playing a new role in the administration. The strong personal relationship between the brothers was something that influenced presidential decision-making. Since there are few papers on this relationship, one must read between the lines to see just how much a difference this alliance made in history. It is clear, however, that JFK was trying to approach these problems with fresh ideas and new people. RFK and Rusk were not as prominent in those first one hundred days as they were toward the end of 1961 and beyond. While it seemed that Rusk would have a major role to play in this crisis, Kennedy made it clear to him that things needed to be done soon, and he had a few ideas for the secretary of state.

On 21 August 1961, JFK wrote Rusk regarding Berlin political planning. Kennedy started the memo by saying that he wanted "to take a stronger lead on Berlin negotiations." Kennedy did not want to discuss this matter on the level with the four powers and believed that a U.S. position should be determined. "We should of course be as persuasive and diplomatic as possible," JFK wrote, "but it is time to act." Kennedy liked several of Rusk's ideas regarding negotiations, but Kennedy's impatience was very evident in this memo. Kennedy went on to suggest Chip Bohlen to negotiate for the United States and said that he did not want to try and "smoke" Khrushchev out with ambassadors. "Until we have something to suggest ourselves," he wrote, "we shall not get any more out of him than we have been getting since Vienna." Diplomacy was important and necessary, but time was now against this administration.

JFK suggested, "The Acheson paper is a good start, but it is not a finishing point. What you and I need is a small group of hard workers who can produce alternatives for our comment and criticism on an urgent basis." In addition to proposing the notion of the group, Kennedy also had a few ideas about who should be in it, the goals of the group and when they would meet to discuss their assessment. Kennedy finished the letter by saying, "Can I have your prompt reaction to this?"[34] This letter in tandem with Bundy's various memos demonstrates the influence that he had on JFK. In several of Bundy's memos there was an insistence for the president to make up his mind on various issues as well as get going on possible negotiations. Kennedy wanted action from his secretary of state and it seemed that this may have been prompted by Bundy. This letter from JFK to Rusk makes it seem that in the 14 August memo the president was asking questions out of frustration rather than for input. Kennedy's phone call to Rusk after he heard news of the wall is another example of Kennedy's frustration over Rusk's inability to give him the answers he needed to make decisions. Nevertheless, the president would have an opportunity to influence this crisis directly in his own words.

6. "Perhaps a wall"

"You wouldn't keep me waiting that long."

On 28 August 1961 Kennedy was informed that the Russians would resume nuclear testing. Despite the fact the Khrushchev had assured Kennedy at Vienna that he would cease testing and focus on a test-ban treaty, the chairman decided to follow up his wall with a bang. Both sides had observed a moratorium in testing since 1958.[35] For Khrushchev to come out and resume testing was a major slap in the face to Kennedy. Khrushchev had made this decision to resume testing on 10 July against some of the advice from his counsel.[36] With this element added to the situation, it seemed that the crisis was only getting worse. Kennedy needed answers and new ideas to make a difference in this high-stakes chess match with Khrushchev. Michael Beschloss writes, "the travails over Berlin and the resumption of nuclear testing illuminated Robert Kennedy's new place near the center of his brother's foreign policy government."[37] Lyndon Johnson reportedly told a friend, "Every time they have a conference, don't kid anybody about who is the top advisor.... It's not McNamara, the Chiefs of Staff, or anybody else like that. Bobby is first in, first out. And Bobby is the boy he listens to."[38] With this in mind, the crisis was about to turn to a relationship established by RFK before the Vienna conference.

Bolshakov left a message for Salinger, who was in Newport with Kennedy, on 29 September 1961 and told him that he had a message for Kennedy and must meet "immediately." Bolshakov wanted to charter a plane to Newport to meet with Salinger. The press secretary told Bolshakov to not do anything and contacted Kennedy and Rusk. It was decided that Salinger would travel to New York and meet Bolshakov the next day at three-thirty. Bolshakov replied, "If you knew the importance of what I have, you wouldn't keep me waiting that long."[39] Nevertheless Salinger met Bolshakov the next day in his room at the Carlyle Hotel in New York. The Russian showed up with newspapers under his arm which concealed a thick manila envelope. Inside was an English and Russian version of a letter from Khrushchev to Kennedy. Thus began an exchange between the two leaders where they could speak frankly and openly without the ridicule of the press and the world. Arthur Schlesinger writes of the exchange, "Behind the obligatory Cold War rhetoric, the two leaders were trying to forestall conflict and seek accommodation. All this built in the course of 1962 a measure of mutual understanding, even of mutual confidence."[40] There are several questions that should be addressed with regard to this act on Khrushchev's part. Why did Khrushchev initiate this exchange? What did he hope to gain? Additionally, what did Kennedy's advisors do to contribute to this communication?

Michael Beschloss argues that Khrushchev was going through some difficult times at home. "[He] was worried about his Twenty-second Party

Congress, scheduled for Moscow in October. He knew that the meeting could be rocky and unpredictable, with people saying many harsh things against the United States." Beschloss went on to argue, "A private correspondence would allow him to maintain quiet contact with the president and keep hostilities from escalating."[41] Khrushchev did not want his letters to be the topic of the Washington press corp. With that in mind, Beschloss writes that Khrushchev thought this method "would appeal to what he knew to be Kennedy's penchant for secrecy and convey the implied compliment that he was willing to use a channel with Kennedy that he had never used with his predecessor."[42] What did this letter say to the president in the middle of this crisis, and how did the Kennedy White House respond?

It is imperative to examine the approach Khrushchev took in conveying his thoughts to Kennedy. The tone and metaphors utilized by the chairman are important indicators of what he was thinking. For example, Khrushchev chose to tell Kennedy that he was writing from the Black Sea while relaxing. "This is indeed a wonderful place," he wrote. "As a former Naval officer you would surely appreciate the merits of these surroundings, the beauty of the sea and the grandeur of the Caucasian mountains." Khrushchev chose to approach the president in a personal way. Khrushchev knew that there was a lot at stake with Berlin as well as other issues. "Under this bright southern sun," Khrushchev wrote, "it is even somehow hard to believe that there still exist problems in the world which, due to lack of solutions, cast a sinister shadow on peaceful life, on the future of millions of people."[43] Khrushchev began the letter with a personal note as well as a regret. "I have given much thought of late to the development of international events since our meeting in Vienna, and I have decided to approach you with this letter." He went on to write, "The whole world hopefully expected that our meeting and a frank exchange of views would have a soothing effect, would turn relations between our countries into the correct channel and promote the adoption of decisions which could give the peoples confidence that at last peace on earth will be secured. To my regret—and, I believe, to yours—this did not happen."[44] Khrushchev's informal tone reappears several times in the letter. He wrote that he began with the "delights" of the Black Sea, but politics always crept back into the conversation: "They say that you sometimes cast politics out through the door but it climbs back through the window, particularly when the windows are open." The windows had been opened with the Berlin crisis.

Khrushchev spoke about several items, which included the need for the Soviet Union to stabilize Germany due to the lingering forces of Hitler who wanted to take over, a possible visit by Kennedy to the Soviet Union, and the dangerous situation that was unfolding. "I do not want here to engage in an argument as to who is right or wrong in this matter. Let us leave this aside for the time being." He wrote, "The main thing is that events are unfortunately continuing to develop in [an] unfavorable direction. Instead of confidence we are turning to an even greater aggravation." Khrushchev was attempting to connect with Kennedy on these issues. These elements demonstrate that Khrushchev wanted to use this channel for ideas to assist the relationship between the men and the nations. He went on to use various metaphors to discuss the problems between the Soviet Union and the United States. In an attempt to describe the situation, Khrushchev wrote, "There is an analogy here ... with Noah's Ark where both the 'clean' and the 'unclean' found sanctuary. But regardless of who lists himself with the 'clean' and who is considered to be 'unclean,' they are all equally interested in one thing and that is that the Ark should successfully continue its cruise." He went to say that they had "no other alternative: either we should live in peace and cooperation so that the Ark maintains its buoyancy, or else it sinks. Therefore we must display concern for all of mankind, not to mention our own advantages, and find every possibility leading to peaceful solutions of problems."[45] In the end, this letter was a major olive branch from a man who did not often attempt this avenue. Did Khrushchev feel that he could foster a relationship with Kennedy? Was the crisis so drastic that Khrushchev felt this letter was necessary to stop a full-blown nuclear war? Kennedy was grateful to those involved who brought him the letter. It was time, however, to see where this avenue would lead.

Kennedy called Rusk and Bundy after reading the letter, and they all agreed that JFK would respond. He instructed Salinger to inform Bolshakov that a letter would be forthcoming in the next week. Beschloss argues, "Kennedy felt that a correspondence would be in keeping with his often expressed desire for open communication, and it might postpone or muffle a showdown over Berlin."[46] It was imperative, however, that Kennedy be careful in what he wrote back to Khrushchev. Kennedy dictated a memo to himself to have Bundy and Sorenson review and analyze the letter.[47] Kennedy's response was important to his relationship with Khrushchev. He needed to be certain that the chairman was not tricking him on one hand, but also prepared if this was a genuine offer of a frank and informal exchange of views.

Kennedy replied to the chairman from his home in Hyannis Port in a 16 October 1961 letter. It is unclear whether any of his advisors had a hand in crafting this letter. With that being said, there are definite influences from his advisors and the past year that Kennedy had just endured. This letter is evidence that Kennedy was more confident in his ability to address issues. Further, it is also evidence that he was not afraid to engage in this dialogue and may even have seen it as necessary to avoid war. Finally, his response is a far cry from the beginning of his term when his team of the "best and the brightest" chose to wait until after the inauguration to respond to Khrushchev.

Like Khrushchev, Kennedy started on a personal note and talked about something very close to his family — Cape Cod. "My family has had a home here overlooking the Atlantic for many years," Kennedy wrote. "My father and brothers own homes near my own, and my children always have a large group of cousins for company. So this is an ideal place for me to spend my weekends during the summer and fall, to relax, to think, to devote my time to major tasks instead of constant appointments, telephone calls and details." Kennedy even tried to empathize with the chairman: "Thus, I know how you must feel about the spot on the Black Sea from which your letter was written, for I value my own opportunities to get a clearer and quieter perspective away from the din of Washington."[48] Here Kennedy was using the same approach as Khrushchev. Kennedy went on to say that he was grateful the chairman initiated this communication. "Certainly you are correct in emphasizing that this correspondence must be kept wholly private, not to be hinted at in public statements, much less disclosed to the press." Kennedy wrote that for his part "the contents and even the existence of our letters will be known only to the Secretary of State and a few others of my closest associates in the government." These are good examples of JFK setting the stage for his Russian counterpart. He wanted it known that Khrushchev was to keep this secret and that Kennedy was being genuine in his promise to do the same. With the pleasantries out of the way, the men were ready to discuss issues that threatened the world.

The letter goes on the talk about the importance of this exchange and how it would make a difference to the issues these countries confronted. "Whether we wish it or not, and for better or worse, we are the leaders of the world's two greatest rival powers," wrote Kennedy, "each with the ability to inflict great destruction on the other and to do great damage to the rest of the world in the process." Kennedy pointed to the importance of and difference in this new age. "We therefore have a special responsibility — greater than that held by any of our predecessors in the pre-nuclear age — to exercise our power with the fullest possible understanding of the other's vital interests and commitments." This was not a debate on ideology. Kennedy stayed away from such talk after the Vienna conference. This was Kennedy stressing to Khrushchev that the world was now a place where they needed to create new rules. This was a world that the founders of both countries could not have predicted.

Kennedy commented on Khrushchev's analogy to Noah's Ark by saying, "I like very much your analogy of Noah's Ark, with both the 'clean' and the 'unclean' determined that it stay afloat." He went to stress, "Whatever our differences, our collaboration to keep the peace is as urgent — if not more urgent — than our collaboration to win the last world war." There was a pervasive sense of urgency on both letters. Kennedy chose to meet Khrushchev with this tone in an effort to explain his point of view. In addition, Kennedy, it seemed, wanted to engage in this exchange whole-heartedly, hoping that it would create a thaw in the cold war. Kennedy said that his attitude in Berlin was one of "reason not belligerence." He went on to write, "It is not the remains of World War II but the threat of World War III that preoccupies us all." It is clear that Kennedy stayed on the message that the Berlin Steering Group meetings had discussed. He reinforced the United States' position in Berlin and stated that he wanted a "free" West Berlin. Kennedy, in fact, quoted Bundy and Rusk when he told Khrushchev that "We would be 'buying the same horse twice'—conceding objectives which you seek, merely to retain what we already possess."[49] The phrase was in a 2 October 1961 memo from Bundy to Kennedy regarding a meeting with Rusk.[50] It pointed to the talks between Gromyko and Rusk and how the Russians were focused on altering U.S. access rights. The fact that the Soviets were reaching out on Gromyko's level as well as Khrushchev's demonstrated that there must have been a feeling that the situation was getting out of hand and something must be done before a third world war.

This letter is also evidence that in matters of diplomacy Kennedy had come a long way from those days in Vienna. In addition to the fact that Kennedy did not engage in an ideological debate, he was also clear that if the two of them met again he would want things to be more productive. "As for another meeting between the two of us," Kennedy wrote, "I agree completely with your view that we had better postpone a decision on that until a preliminary understanding can be reached through quieter channels on positive decisions which might appropriately be formalized at such a meeting." The letter went on to discuss Laos and other matters, but Kennedy wanted to be sure that the current matter was resolved. He finished by saying, "I hope you will believe me, Mr. Chairman, when I say that it is my deepest hope that, through this exchange of letters and otherwise, we may improve relations between our nations, and make concrete progress in deeds as well as words toward the realization of a just and enduring peace." He finished by saying, "That is our greatest joint responsibility—and our greatest opportunity."[51]

This letter from Kennedy is evidence of maturity in foreign policy that was not present at the start of his administration. There is no evidence that anyone helped him write this letter, but it is clear that his many advisors influenced his rhetoric regarding Berlin and the position of the United States. With that being said, Kennedy brought to this venue his own charm and wit that had been absent at Vienna due to the overwhelming nature of the summit both mentally and physically. JFK was allowed to respond on his terms and in the manner he deemed appropriate. Khrushchev withdrew the ultimatum on Berlin on 17 October 1961, the day after the letter was sent from Kennedy to the chairman.[52] Despite that fact, the crisis in Berlin was about to escalate and this new relationship would play a role in stopping the conflict from getting out of hand.

On 25 October 1961, American and Soviet personnel engaged in a standoff at Checkpoint Charlie. Two members of the American military police drove through the checkpoint without showing their passports. Battle-ready soldiers in American Jeeps escorted them to the East German side. Three armored personnel carriers and ten American tanks equipped with a bulldozer to wage war on the Berlin wall were lining up on the boundary line.[53] By Friday 27 October, ten Soviet tanks lined up on their side of the line. This was the only time in the Cold War when Soviet and American tanks faced each other with the prospect of battle. Robert Kennedy initiated their back-channel communication with Khrushchev through Bolshakov to ask that the Soviet tanks back away from the line so the United States could do the same. There is some debate whether RFK promised anything in return for this action. Nevertheless, Khrushchev himself said that the United States "can't turn their tanks around and pull them back as long as our guns are pointing at them.... They are looking for a way out, I'm sure, so let's give them one."[54] The next morning Soviet tanks left the border. The United States did the same.

As the year ended the crisis in Berlin subsided and each side of the world prepared itself to fend off new issues. The problems in Berlin stemmed from a long, drawn-out year when Kennedy was trying to establish himself both at home and abroad. The exchange that began with these two letters proved useful in this circumstance. It was not so much the letters but the line of communication that made a difference in this crisis. Khrushchev and Kennedy now had a channel that would not be tainted by the press and other stresses in their countries. This exchange gave the two leaders a forum to flesh out issues before they brought them to the world. It is, however, another example on how the United States drafted policy without the assistance of its allies. Additionally, it is evidence that Kennedy was feeling more confident in his ability to influence matters of foreign policy both small and big. While it may have played a role in assisting in these matters, Khrushchev was getting pressure from other parts of the world to do something about the American problem. One person in particular resided about ninety miles off the coast of Florida.

Conclusions on the 1961 Berlin Crisis

The Kennedy White House learned how to handle a crisis that fall of 1961. After Vienna Kennedy had a new set of circumstances he had to consider when dealing with the Soviets. He did not trust Khrushchev and feared that nuclear conflict was certain. Those "sobering" days in Vienna assisted Kennedy in creating his own style of leadership. JFK's poor performance highlighted to himself that he needed to do something or else his presidency was in jeopardy. Therefore, Vienna prompted him to craft his own approach to foreign policy.

It was clear that Bundy consistently influenced Kennedy and how he approached problems at the executive level. Bundy's 10 June 1961 memo is evidence that he brought all the arguments to Kennedy's attention. Additionally, that memo highlighted the constant battle over how the United States would discuss these issues with its allies. Bundy contributed to the problems the United States had with its allies and played a major role in the Kennedy circle. His memos were written to influence Kennedy. While Bundy had a major influence in decision-making, it seems clear that Kennedy also wanted to hear from a former secretary of state.

Dean Acheson offered constant advice to Kennedy. Acheson gave his ideas and thoughts to the president because Kennedy asked and because he still had a lot of influence outside the administration in foreign policy. This is evidence that JFK wanted all the points on the table before he made a decision. Kennedy did not agree with Acheson, but he apparently respected his opinion as a former Cold Warrior. Henry Kissinger, on the other hand, was not as welcome in the decision-making. Acheson was at the center of all the major problems Kennedy faced in foreign affairs. The 16 June 1961 Berlin Contingency Planning Group meeting is evidence of his influence. Acheson's sense of urgency permeated the meeting. His influence did not end at the meeting table. His papers were also something that Kennedy referred to in memos and his advisors closely scrutinized.

Acheson's analysis had to play in Kennedy's thinking. His consistent reminder to Kennedy that nuclear weapons should be used a deterrent with the understanding that war might result had to resonate in Kennedy's thought process. JFK's decision-making demonstrated that he saw a nuclear exchange as inevitable — it was just the time and place. His job was to be certain that his administration did not bring the world to an end. NSAM Number 58 demonstrated that Kennedy saw some of Acheson's conclusions as valid and believed the administration should be prepared to meet force with force. Schlesinger's assessment of Acheson's paper and Kennedy's role in determining when nuclear war would take place is a perfect example of how Kennedy brought all available ideas to the table and then made a decision.

What impact did Schlesinger's letter have on Kennedy? At this stage of his development as a leader, he was sure to review all sides exhaustively until he felt comfortable with his decision. In some ways that hindered the response, but in many others it assisted in keeping the peace. Schlesinger attempted to provide clarity for Kennedy while Acheson focused on moving Kennedy to display a firm and resolute decision on the matter. Rusk, like Schlesinger, wanted the president to really know why they were going to war. In the 17 July meeting, Rusk focused on objectives rather than action. These two letters are evidence that there was some disagreement within the Kennedy White House.

Allied support was something that consistently plagued the administration. Rostow's assertion that the United States should prepare itself for a "High Noon Stance" was evidence that many saw the United States making unilateral decisions that would impact Europe more than the United States. Rostow told Kennedy to prepare for a confrontation "Gary Cooper" style. He foresaw the European allies as going against Kennedy. Additionally, he stressed to Kennedy that it was the United States that could bring the world to the brink. Rostow prepared the president for what he saw as the inevitable. Additionally, he wanted Kennedy to be sure he did not disregard these relationships after the dust settled. This advice pointed to the importance of maintaining a healthy alliance with Europe. It also foreshadowed major problems for the United States. Unilateral decisions by the United States threatened its relationships with its allies then and at the start of the 21st century.

Kennedy's 25 July speech was the turning point in the crisis that sent a message to Khrushchev that the Kennedy White House might not be as easy as he thought. The meetings preceding this speech focused on how the administration would handle both the Soviets and the world. This was important because after Vienna, Kennedy seemed unable to respond to threats. It should be noted here that the administration needed to show its teeth as a result of both the Bay of Pigs and Kennedy's poor performance in Vienna. The latter may have been the result of Kennedy's use of amphetamines to quell the pain in his back. If that was the case, then the United States reacted to a crisis as a result of a president's illness. Nevertheless, the bellicose speech had the reaction they were looking for, and Khrushchev made the next move with a wall dividing the East from the West in Berlin. This act resulted in Kennedy looking to his "best and brightest" to find a solution to Soviet posturing.

Bundy was the pivotal man in this decision-making process. He filtered all the information to the president, telling JFK what was important. Bundy told Kennedy on several occasions to keep his head in the game because every decision needed "leadership at the highest level." The urgency in Bundy's memos signaled that each decision was contingent on the next; therefore, Kennedy needed to be cautious in how he confronted each dilemma. For example, Bundy made clear to Kennedy what his major issues were regarding the Acheson premise. Additionally, he advised Kennedy to take a larger role in the construction of propaganda. As a result, both RFK and Rusk were made aware that this was an important piece of the war games they were playing and that it should not be forgotten.

After the construction of the Berlin Wall it seemed as if Kennedy was looking for any solution. He consulted Rusk and stated he was going to take a lead on the Berlin issue. Perhaps Kennedy was consulting the secretary of state out of frustration. Nevertheless, it is apparent the wall woke up something in Kennedy. He was suddenly asking questions that he had not in the past. After the Bay of Pigs, Kennedy was afraid to trust a lot of the people around him. As a result of this mistrust, he failed to take a strong stance in Vienna and managed to precipitate another crisis in Berlin. Kennedy may have seen that another debacle like the Bay of Pigs was on the horizon and he needed to take matters into his own hands. Therefore, he brought in other people to his circle that he was uncertain should play a role in foreign policy. These people would play significant roles in 1962 and 1963.

Robert Kennedy played an unprecedented role in foreign affairs toward the end of 1961 and the rest of the Kennedy presidency. His back-channel communication with Georgi Bolshakov, which was established before Vienna as a means to flesh out ideas, assisted in quelling the storm of Berlin. JFK's use of this channel, when it was presented to him, signifies that he was ready to take matters into his own hands. Finally, after a year of stumbling around his advisors, this was the moment he could decide what direction his foreign policy should move. The letters exchanged between the two leaders in September and October 1961 are evidence that these two men needed to talk without the press and advisors present. It took places like the Black Sea and Cape Cod for these men to see that they were people with extraordinary powers who needed to relate at some level. The overtures before the inauguration and the summit in Vienna were scrutinized by many people in and out of their administrations. While Kennedy did share his letter with "close advisors" and it did contain some obvious Cold War rhetoric, his personal approach may have made the difference in this crisis. This communication, through the next year, would prove useful in creating trust between the leaders. While it can never be certain what immediate impact these letters had on history, the fact that they continued this exchange demonstrated that both leaders were willing to talk, not fight.

The Berlin Crisis of 1961 was an integral part of Kennedy's education as president. This crisis prepared him for a larger issue one year later in Cuba. It was also one more instance that would lead Kennedy to craft a strategy of peace toward the end of his life. The system of advisement evolved into the famous EXCOMM, and Kennedy finally found his voice on foreign policy after the two countries squared off at Checkpoint Charlie. While this was a major step in Kennedy's growth, it was only a first step in a long crisis-driven presidency that would end in tragedy and unresolved agendas.

Part Four

*Brother's Keeper:
Robert F. Kennedy's Role in
Presidential Decision-Making*

7

Jack and Bobby

"I should have had Bobby in on this from the start."

Getting through both the Bay of Pigs and the Berlin crisis was not easy for a young president with little executive experience. John Kennedy was perplexed at how the people in government whom he was supposed to rely on were inept in their advice. Despite the fact that the Joint Chiefs of Staff and the CIA had been fighting communism throughout the fifties, they failed the president. This was something that John Kennedy wanted to change. The New Frontier was filled with hope and change. This new direction for the country meant that there would be new alternatives to fighting the Cold War. In addition to that, JFK also explored new methods in how he would prepare for crisis situations. Robert Kennedy was John Kennedy's unbiased and selfless advisor on the matters that could shape the presidency. RFK's influence went beyond his job description at attorney general and bordered on a combination of secretary of state and defense. Their bond was unlike any in history and it changed American government.

Arthur Schlesinger describes, in his book *Robert Kennedy and His Times*, the differences between the Kennedy brothers. "The two brothers," he wrote, "had moved in different directions in adolescence and manhood, John establishing his intellectuality, Robert his toughness, John his independence, Robert his commitment to the family."[1] The relationship between these two brothers was complex. Schlesinger writes, "Alike in so many ways, united by so many indestructible bonds, the two brothers were still different men. John Kennedy remained ... the Brahmin; Robert the Puritan."[2] It is now very clear that RFK played a role in shaping foreign policy. After the Bay of Pigs, Robert Kennedy was a part of the decision-making process regarding the Cold War. He later said that it was "just on Berlin or Laos or Vietnam or Cuba."[3] Those instances shaped the Kennedy presidency and many others afterward. They were defining moments in the Cold War and United States history. Analyzing the decisions of leaders who shaped these issues is important to attain a clear understanding of those problems. Robert Kennedy was one of those leaders.

7. Jack and Bobby

When JFK and RFK were contemplating cabinet positions, Robert Kennedy was very reluctant to take the attorney general position. When asked why he did not initially want the position, Robert Kennedy said, "[In] the first place, I though that nepotism was a problem. Secondly, I had been chasing bad men for three years [in the Senate], and I didn't want to spend the rest of my life doing that."[4] He went on to say that the "other reason I was opposed to it was just the fact that I had been working with my brother for a long time, and I thought I'd like to go off by myself."[5] However, as JFK met with each potential position in this new government, Bobby was right there to question them as well. Indeed, their father, who influenced both brothers, wanted Robert Kennedy close to his older brother. RFK said, "[My father] felt that, that if I as there, that I should be involved in all the major decisions that were made." He went on to say, "Secondly, he felt that ... Jack should have somebody that was close to him, and had been close a long period of time when he went into the job."[6] What made up his mind to take the job was when his brother told him that "it would make a difference to have somebody that he could talk to over some of these problems."[7] RFK worked with his brother to solve some of the most daunting issues that the country had faced up that point.

In addition to Robert Kennedy, the president trusted Robert McNamara a great deal and soon welcomed him into a close circle that involved Kenneth O'Donnell, McGeorge Bundy, and Ted Sorensen. Robert Kennedy described McNamara as "head and shoulders above everyone else."[8] These men played a role normally reserved for the secretary of state. As matter of fact, RFK said later, "Jack was his own secretary of state."[9] He also said, "At the end he was very frustrated with Rusk."[10] This was one of the main problems that laid the foundation for Kennedy to change the way that government operated. Indeed, with the problems that Kennedy faced, he needed to look elsewhere for solutions as these issues were like none other. The Bay of Pigs taught John Kennedy a great deal of things. Chiefly among those lessons was to keep Robert Kennedy close. Kennedy's kitchen cabinet started to take shape at the start of 1962.

Robert Kennedy's biographer Evan Thomas called RFK the "Attorney General and right hand man to the President."[11] Thomas described the younger Kennedy as a "chancellor to an empire.... Everything he did had to be measured not only against the particular—and burdensome—duties of chief law enforcement officer, but in the larger context of helping his brother rule, as they saw it, the 'free world.'"[12] Michael Forrestal, aid to McGeorge Bundy, had commented once, "If you wanted to get a dissenting idea into the White House ... the best channel—almost the only channel—was Bobby Kennedy."[13] While there are many differences between these two brothers, Robert and John formed a coalition after the Bay of Pigs debacle that was integral to foreign policy-making in the White House.

After the Bay of Pigs, Kennedy said to Kenneth O'Donnell, special aide to the president, as the bad news came in, that he "should have had Bobby in on this from the start."[14] Robert F. Kennedy shaped American foreign policy more than any other attorney general in United States history. Maxwell Taylor, who was very impressed with Robert Kennedy when they worked together to dissect the Bay of Pigs, stated that his relationship with John Kennedy was "a reversal of the normal fraternal relationship of a big brother looking after a younger one. In this case, Bobby, the younger brother, seemed to take a protective view of the President."[15] This relationship rooted in trust was the basis for many foreign policy decisions.

The Kennedys believed that Rusk mismanaged the State Department. Schlesinger writes, "The essential Kennedy problem with State was how to annex the department to the New Frontier."[16] Robert Kennedy later commented, "[The President and I] used to go back to his office — about how awful it was and about, that we should get rid of Rusk."[17] Rusk was good at putting a face on diplomacy while JFK handled the details that made things happen. These two brothers wanted to reinvent a part of the government to fit into their philosophy. With this is mind the two brothers went forward with new innovative methods to bring about peace. John and Robert Kennedy initiated great change in government. JFK did not have a chief of staff. Looking at the record, Robert Kennedy was the person who most closely filled that role. From 1962 to the end of the presidency this coalition was viewed with suspicion.

During the Berlin crisis Robert Kennedy had a say in some matters when it came to policymaking. For example, although JFK stressed the importance of fallout shelters, the attorney general opposed them. "I was in the minority of one," he recalled in a later interview. "I thought during that period of time that really you're never going to get it going very well and if we get too far out on a limb on it was just going to collapse eventually."[18] This is another example of how, after the Bay of Pigs, RFK always had a say in matters. By referring to himself as a "minority of one" it is evident that while he was not listened to then, he still had an opportunity to give his opinion.

John Kennedy found a confidant in his brother. This was not a political relationship, rather familial. JFK would confide his thoughts and feelings on a given topic. "I think there was an advantage of being ... in our relationship," RFK said, "because my motivation could never be questioned." He went on to say, "There wasn't anything to be gained by me ... [and] I surely think it had some advantage."[19] A good example of this was when the Soviets resumed testing nuclear weapons. RFK recounted that their meeting was the "most gloomy meeting at the White House ... since early in the Berlin crisis. I had talked to Jack previously and he was at a loss to explain Khrushchev's decision to resume testing. It was obviously done to try to intimidate the West and the neutrals."[20] Kennedy wanted his brother as close as possible. The Bay of Pigs had taught him a great deal about who he could trust in the government. Bobby Kennedy was not a yes man and always looked for a "snow job." That made him a unique individual to give the president advice. The Bay of Pigs led JFK to question his advisors. "It wasn't until after the Bay of Pigs," RFK said later, "that he found out that he couldn't rely on people, and the mere fact that somebody was head of the CIA or General Lemnitzer, had been in the army thirty, forty years, didn't mean that you could rely on them to ... be prepared, to give [the president] a correct factual presentation."[21] RFK went on to say, "It was a major change made in the government of the United States: it was based, really, on the Bay of Pigs."[22] Indeed, the change that Robert Kennedy refers to is a switch from the Eisenhower doctrine of "massive retaliation" to Kennedy's doctrine of "flexible response." Eisenhower believed that the United States should stockpile nuclear weapons in the hopes that the Soviet Union would be afraid to use them — thus preventing a nuclear war. In addition, the CIA was involved in counter-insurgency programs, especially in Latin America. Kennedy's "flexible response" came from Maxwell Taylor.

The Bay of Pigs brought Taylor to the White House in an effort to dissect the event to learn how it failed. Taylor worked very closely with RFK and others in questioning the men involved in the planning of the operation. JFK was taken with Taylor and wanted him involved more intimately with the government. In particular, JFK wanted Taylor to assist in bridging the divide between him and the Joint Chiefs of Staff. Moreover, it was also a switch in how a president used his advisors. Eisenhower had a hands-off approach to his advisors, while Kennedy particularly questioned his military advisors after the Bay of Pigs.

During the Berlin crisis, for example, there were military decisions that had to be made, and Robert Kennedy was right by his brother's side. Perhaps the best example of RFK's influence was when the administration was discussing a reaction to the Soviets if they fired on planes over West Berlin. He remembered in an interview that both General Lemnitzer and Taylor "felt very strongly" that the United States should fire back at the Soviets in the event that an anti-aircraft fired on a U.S. plane. McNamara was against firing on the Soviets and JFK wanted to have more control of the situation. "It is obvious that as we get closer to D-day the situation becomes more difficult. The people are less and less anxious to stand firm. It is my feeling that Russians feel this, feel strongly that if they break our will in Berlin that we will never be able to be good for anything else and they will have won the battle in 1961." RFK went on to say, "My feeling is they do not want war but will carry us to the brink.... After the meeting Jack asked me what I thought. I said I wanted to get off. He said, 'Get off what?' and I said, 'Get off the planet.'"[23] RFK's role at this meeting demonstrates both his brother's trust in him as advisor as well as the attorney general's unprecedented role in foreign affairs. This was the greatest crisis up to that point in the administration. JFK wanted his brother by his side — despite scrutiny from anyone in or out of the administration.

In addition to his role in the Berlin Crisis, RFK had insights into the crucial appointments within the administration. He recollected that JFK thought "the most highly of" McNamara. "The President and I discussed on a number of occasions [the possibility] after the [1964] election of moving Rusk out perhaps to the UN and appointing Bob McNamara Secretary of State." Dean Rusk had only committed to one term due to financial reasons. "Tommy [Llewellyn] Thompson he thought was outstanding.... He liked Ed Murrow, very much.... [But] he really felt at the end that the ten or twelve people in the White House who worked under his direction with Mac Bundy ... performed all the functions of the State Department."[24] It is no surprise the men who advised JFK in crisis were at the top of his list. Since the Kennedy administration was so crisis driven, those individuals rose to the top and became very influential in foreign policy decisions usually reserved to the State Department. Indeed, JFK wanted to be his own secretary of state and planned to reshape the department and his influence with his own advisors with RFK at his side.

Perhaps one of the best examples of RFK's influence in policy-making came in an April 1962 memo to JFK. In this memo, RFK was proposing specific language his brother should consider in a speech to the Foreign Service Association. "Innovations, imagination, yes even revolutionary concepts are essential.... It is your responsibility not just to carry out policies that have been established but to suggest and come forth with new ones." Arthur Schlesinger wrote, "Foreign policy, the Attorney General thought the President should point out, was no longer a matter of transactions among chancelleries." Schlesinger quotes Kennedy, who said, "More and more people themselves are determining their country's future and policies. Therefore, greater attention has to be given than has been true in the past to these new and sometimes revolutionary elements."[25] RFK went on to say that, "A major effort must be made to meet with representatives of all kinds of groups.... [In addition] They must know our history and our culture so that they can discuss these matters freely and with candor."[26]

Clearly John Kennedy took the advice very seriously and included some of Robert Kennedy's suggestions in his speech to the Foreign Service Association on 2 July 1962. "Instead of becoming merely experts in diplomatic history, or in current clippings from the New York Times, now you have to involve yourselves in every element of foreign life — labor, the class struggle, cultural affairs, and all the rest — attempting to predict in what direction the forces will move." This was the involvement that RFK discussed in the letter to the president. JFK went further by saying, "Now you have to know all about the United States, every facet of its life, all the great reforms of the thirties, the forties and the fifties, if you are going to represent the United States powerfully and with strength and with vigor."[27] Robert Kennedy was a force in the Kennedy White House. This fraternal relationship gave the attorney general a place in determining presidential policy.

Arthur Schlesinger argues, " John Kennedy used Robert in part as Franklin Roosevelt used Eleanor — as a lightning rod, as a scout on far frontiers, as a more militant and somewhat discountable alter ego."[28] In other words, JFK had a way to get his message across without having to say a word. Robert Kennedy could go out on a limb and push the president's agenda without its affecting JFK politically. Robert McNamara stated, "The President never hesitated to turn down Bobby's advice, but many, many times he took it when initially, he, the President, was in favor of an opposite course." McNamara went on to say, "They had an extraordinarily close relationship: affection, respect, admiration."[29]

"Cuba has made the President a different man regarding his advisors."

Robert Kennedy had some thoughts on the Bay of Pigs incident and outlined them in a 1 June 1961 memo. This memo, dictated six weeks later, was a good indicator of how he viewed the incident as well as the role he played. Of course, Robert Kennedy had no role in planning the invasion. That plan was initiated by the CIA under Eisenhower and was inherited by John Kennedy. There are many ways to explore this event, but Robert Kennedy meant to give some of his "thoughts on Cuba and the effect it has had on the administration and the President."[30]

Robert Kennedy was brought into the Bay of Pigs situation at the request of his brother. "Dick Bissell [the CIA's deputy director of plans]," he wrote, "at Jack's instructions came over to the department of justice and briefed me." RFK discussed in the memo how the military emphasized that there was no way this operation could fail. If the invasion had not worked, then the force would have become a guerrilla unit designed to be a "thorn in the side of Castro."[31] Of course, that was not the case, and Castro was able to destroy most of the landing forces. RFK stated, "I think that the President might very well not have approved of the operation if he had known that the chances of these men becoming guerrillas was practically nil." From this memo it is clear that Robert Kennedy had an insight into his brother's policy decisions. One can speculate that he came to these notions through discussions with his brother on the topic, which implies an intimate relationship between them.

When things looked as though they were not going to work, JFK immediately went to his brother for advice. "He called me down in Williamsburg where I was speaking and said we had run into trouble. He asked me to come to the White House." RFK went on to say that when he arrived the "situation already looked dark."[32] Indeed at the most crucial time of the event, Robert Kennedy's advice was an important factor. The invasion force was pinned down and JFK needed to decide whether or not to grant air support to the men. The CIA believed that if the United States ordered air strikes, then the chances of the invasion succeeding would increase. At first, according to the memo, "Jack was in favor of giving it." Dean Rusk was against it. Robert Kennedy said, "I took the position that we didn't really have enough information to know whether the air cover would make a difference or not. If the air cover should save the operation, perhaps we should take that step. On the other hand if it just meant the delay of a few hours before absolute and ultimate collapse, there wasn't any sense in it."[33] Ultimately, JFK did not order air cover and the invasion did in fact collapse.

Robert Kennedy argued that the failure of this invasion was due to "incompetency and lack of communication and nervousness." He also commented that this event had a "great physical effect on Jack. I noticed him particularly a week from the following Saturday when we had a talk for a half hour before the meeting began and even during the meeting he kept shaking his head, rubbing his hands over his eyes."[34] Retrospectively, JFK's health issues may have been worsened due to such a massive failure. This event shaped Kennedy's approach to foreign policy for the remainder of the administration. Robert Kennedy discussed the lessons learned in the same memo.

"What comes out of this whole Cuba matter," RFK wrote, "is that a good deal of thought has to go into whether you are going to accept the ideas, advice, and even the facts that are presented by your subordinates." He went to say, "The fact we have gone through this experience in Cuba has made the President a different man regarding his advisors, and the Joint Chiefs of Staff are well aware of this." Robert Kennedy had particular disdain for the military advisors on this matter. He wrote, "[The Joint Chiefs of Staff] study of the Cuba matter was disgraceful."[35] Indeed, Robert Kennedy was in a unique position to criticize the military-intelligence complex and would continue to do so for the remainder of the Kennedy years.

There were a lot of things that bothered both John and Robert Kennedy about the Bay of Pigs. This event, RFK argued, "Really revolutionized the, drastically altered the president's approach to government."[36] A good question to consider in this study is how deep was the impact of this event? Further, how did it bring the brothers even closer than they already were at the start of the administration? Maxwell Taylor had written in his book, *The Uncertain Trumpet*, a new way to fight the cold war. "The strategic doctrine which I propose to replace Massive Retaliation is called herein the strategy of Flexible Response."[37] John Kennedy was very fond of Taylor's idea and stated, "Nuclear war should not be the first step that you take."[38] JFK wanted to distance himself from Eisenhower's policy. "Now, he took responsibility," RFK said later, "which was the right thing to do, but it was based on people he had confidence in — not because he had known them himself, but just because they had been there."[39]

Robert Kennedy said that what really bothered both brothers was the lack of communication between the military and the people on the ground: "The lack of communications, the lack of intelligence information was what was particularly disturbing." RFK went on to say, "That's why we made a real effort afterwards to improve the communication in any kind of operation, and why at the time of the second Cuba a whole different system was established throughout the world dealing with communications."[40] What came out of this operation was that the Kennedys realized they needed to think about any operation and not take the advice of the military so readily. After the Bay of Pigs RFK said that they followed Francis Bacon's mantra, "A wise interrogation is half the knowledge."[41] While the president could not go behind all the reasoning of every decision, he needed someone he trusted to be in the room when decisions were being made or contemplated. From then on Bobby was involved in "all the international questions."[42] As a matter of fact Robert Kennedy said, "[The] Bay of Pigs might have been the best thing that happened to the administration."[43]

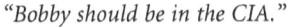

"Bobby should be in the CIA."

JFK saw the Bay of Pigs as a result of the unchecked CIA — one more thing to worry about as he tried to be his own secretary of state. "I made a mistake," the president said to Arthur Schlesinger while the Cubans were still fighting on the beachhead, "in putting Bobby in the Justice department. He is wasted there.... Bobby should be in the CIA."[44] According to Schlesinger, "Kennedy began redefining the [CIA's] mandate. In National Security Action Memos 55 and 57 he transferred paramilitary operations from CIA to Defense and sought to restrict the size of covert operations remaining to the CIA."[45] These two memoranda from the president attempted to redefine the Joint Chiefs of Staff mandate and define for the CIA proper methods in how to conduct paramilitary operations.

In the wake of the Bay of Pigs invasion JFK wanted to rein in the military-intelligence complex and be certain, for the record, that the Joint Chiefs did not overstep their boundaries. This is a significant shift from Eisenhower, who used the CIA as a means of covertly fighting the Cold War. Kennedy wrote in NSAM 55,

> The Joint Chiefs of Staff have a responsibility for the defense of the nation in the Cold War similar to that which they have in conventional hostilities. They should know the military and paramilitary forces and resources available to the Department of Defense, verify their readiness, report on their adequacy, and make appropriate recommendations for their expansion and improvement. I look to the Chiefs to contribute dynamic and imaginative leadership in contributing to the success of the military and paramilitary aspects of Cold War programs.[46]

In many ways this is a reaction to the failed intelligence from the Bay of Pigs situation, as well as a message to the Chiefs defining what their role as advisors should be. Especially interesting is the point that JFK regards the Joint Chiefs "to be more than military men and expect their help in fitting military requirements into the over-all context of any situation, recognizing that the most difficult problem in Government is to combine all assets in a unified, effective pattern."[47] The Joint Chiefs were supposed to advise not only on military matters, but also on the political and governmental pieces of the problem. In other words, they need to start thinking about better means of diplomacy and not so much about war, especially since war meant a nuclear exchange.

While in NSAM 55 JFK reined in the Joint Chiefs, in NSAM 57 he took away the ability of the CIA to wage their paramilitary actions without some oversight. These are prime examples of how Kennedy wanted to take control of the military complex. After World War II it had run unchecked. John Dulles, secretary of state, and Alan Dulles, director of CIA, were brothers, and often were able to conduct affairs without the bureaucracy that is innate to such situations. The Kennedys were another such team. The memo clearly states, "Any proposed paramilitary operation in the concept stage will be presented to the Strategic Resources Group for initial consideration and for approval as necessary by the President."[48] This group would be led by Maxwell Taylor with Robert Kennedy there to watch over the planning of paramilitary operations. Arthur Schlesinger writes, "To complete [this chain of reorganizing] the President quietly gave Robert Kennedy an informal watching brief over the intelligence community."[49] Perhaps the best example of Robert Kennedy's influence over this planning is from a 19 January 1962 memo from the CIA outlining how he led the group in discussing actions against Cuba.

"The Attorney General," it stated, "outlined to us 'How it all started,' findings as they developed, and the general framework within which the United States Government should now attack the Cuban problem."[50] RFK argued that after the failed invasion the United States should "lay low." In addition, the refugee flow was increasing, while the movement of the Cuban government to a police and communist state was "more rapid during this period than that made by any country in Eastern Europe in an equivalent period of time."[51] Because of this, the United States needed to act quickly. The memo goes on to state,

> The Attorney General had a discussion at the White House during the autumn of 1961 with the President, the Secretary of Defense, and General Lansdale. The Secretary of Defense assigned General Lansdale to survey the Cuban problem, and he (Lansdale) reported to the President, the Secretary of Defense, and the Attorney General.[52]

Clearly, Robert Kennedy was the president's envoy to the CIA when it came to dealing with Cuba. He outlined for those in attendance how it all started. Notice that General Lansdale reported to the president, the secretary of defense and the attorney general. In the past the attorney general had handled domestic matters. But it is clear that RFK played a much larger role in this administration. RFK was going to be a part of all decisions to do with Cuba, because it was the defining factor in the administration. Furthermore, he was going to spearhead any movements in that region for the president, as it would aid his brother. Once again, Robert Kennedy wanted to protect the Kennedy legacy.

The recommendations from General Lansdale stated that the Castro regime could be overthrown: the U.S. should attack the sugar crop and should create "internal problems" to keep Castro busy. The memo also said that Robert Kennedy made it clear this measure was very important to the president. Robert Kennedy stated to the group that the Cuba issue had "the top priority in the United States Government — all else is secondary — no time, money, effort, or manpower is to be spared." He went on to say, "There can be no misunderstanding on the involvement of the agencies concerned nor on their responsibility to carry out this job. The agency heads understand that you are to have full backing on what you need."[53] RFK also said the president said to him that "the final chapter on Cuba has not been written" and that this has to get done. He went on to stress the thirty-two tasks outlined in a report regarding Operation Mongoose, the invasion, of which General Lansdale was in charge. "It is not only General Lansdale's job to put the tasks," he said, "but yours to carry out with every resource at your command."[54] If the Cuba problem was top priority and Bobby had his hands on the wheel, doesn't that imply that he was pretty powerful? Moreover, the president had indicated to him that the final chapter "had not been written." This is another example of that kind of one-on-one discussion that they had had on the Soviets and Cuba. RFK took the power given to him by his brother and brought systemic change to American government, particularly dealing with foreign policy. His role in the counterinsurgency group as a watchdog for JFK enhanced the elder Kennedy's ability to find advisors he could trust.

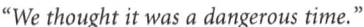

"We thought it was a dangerous time."

Robert Kennedy said that the first year of the administration was tough. "We had a helluva tough time, you see, after the Bay of Pigs, not just rising out of the Bay of Pigs but Berlin." He went on, "The president felt strongly, and I did, that we were very close to war at the time."[55] RFK went on to argue that Vienna may have played a role in this crisis. "I think," he said, "he went to Vienna, and in my judgment, Khrushchev thought he was dealing with rather a weak figure; he was dealing with a young figure who had perhaps no confidence."[56] He commented, "We thought it was a dangerous time."[57] In addition, he saw this as "test of strength for President Kennedy."[58] What this demonstrates was that Robert Kennedy had a unique insight into how these issues affected JFK. Robert Kennedy later said that 1961 "was often a very mean year because of Berlin, and what to do about Berlin."[59] He was a dedicated brother who came into the White House with very little motive to go further at the expense of his older brother.

"The problem," he said later in 1964, "was to get all of our allies in agreement, and that's what really brought home to us a lesson during that period of time." The specific lesson RFK was discussing was the fundamental difference between diplomacy in the United States compared to the Soviet Union. "What an advantage," he said, "the communists or a dictatorship had! You just decide what your policy is going to be and you don't have to publicize it."[60] This was a major obstacle for the Kennedy administration. Diplomacy had to act in tandem with the European alliance and the will of the American people. As discussed earlier, Kennedy had a very difficult time working with the European alliance. "The French," RFK said, "were the ones who gave the most difficulties." He went on to say, "The British were not much better, but the French would never give their concurrence ... always wanted to meet about it, didn't want to reach any conclusion as to taking any definitive steps, and that made it so difficult."[61] The alliance was something that heightened a tense situation. The Kennedy brothers would have to learn how to work with that relationship if they planned to bring the State Department into the New Frontier. Like other aspects of the Cold War, it was complex, but necessary in order to move toward détente. There were other issues, however, that perplexed the administration.

"The second great problem," RFK went on to say, "was ... in the planning during this period of time." Covert planning especially was an issue if you had to consult the Allies with every move in the region. "We always had the feeling that it would ... either get in the newspapers or it would get back to the communists so that they would know your every move."[62] The fundamental problems were a part of the diplomatic quagmire, but more importantly, Robert Kennedy's discussion of them in 1964 illustrates his intimate relationship in shaping foreign policy. His consistent reference to "we" implies that he was working closely with the president and the rest of the administration. Berlin was a multilayered issue, and he had an influence in many ways. Perhaps the greatest example of his involvement was with Georgi Bolshakov.

Kennedy's involvement with Bolshakov has been outlined in previous chapters. The Russian emissary to Khrushchev had delivered messages to the leader through a back-channel exchange. Robert Kennedy said that on the cusp of the Berlin crisis, they would meet "maybe once every two weeks, and so we used to go over all this, about whether the United States would stand up and went through Berlin."[63] Kennedy went on to say that when the Russians were concerned about Berlin, Bolshakov "would come to me, and talk about that."[64] When the Russians were poised at Checkpoint Charlie against American tanks, Bolshakov and the attorney general helped stave off, arguably, the seeds of another long, perhaps nuclear, war. "They were in their tanks," RFK recalled in 1964. "I ... got in touch with Bolshakov and said the president would like them to take their tanks out of there. We'd like to have them take their tanks out in twenty-four hours."⁶⁵ This is yet another example of how RFK had a major role to play in presidential decision-making and world affairs.

Berlin was a part of NATO, and any act of war was a war against that alliance. The ramifications of such an act had large potential to bring the world, if not into war, definitely into chaos. Robert Kennedy was the conduit for the president, leader of the free world, in a crisis situation that arguably kept the United States and its NATO allies out of war. According to RFK Bolshakov said he would speak with Khrushchev and "they took their tanks in twenty-four hours. So [Bolshakov] ... delivered effectively when it was a matter that was important."⁶⁶

"This is the most shameful object of mankind."

On 22 February 1962 Robert Kennedy went to Berlin. Arthur Schlesinger remembered that they arrived in Berlin "on a cold blowy, snowy day." He went on to say, "The streets were lined with cheering people, who had waited for hours in the bitter cold."⁶⁷ RFK went to Berlin as a representative of the United States, but also as the right-hand man to the president, the brother of the man who stared down Soviet aggression. The people lined the streets to see, arguably, the second most powerful man in the world. They arrived on Washington's birthday and Ted Kennedy met them there as well. When the American delegation dined with Mayor Brandt he made a toast to "the president, government and people of the United States." Robert Kennedy responded jokingly, "That's the three of us — the President, that's my brother; the government, that's me; and [looking at Ted] you're the people."⁶⁸ While Robert Kennedy was using humor, it is a good illustration at what the Kennedys were doing to the government. These brothers were taking institutions that had been there before they were in office and changing them to meet the needs of their own vision of where the United States should be going.

While in Berlin, Robert Kennedy said in an address at Free University, "We do not stand here in Berlin because we are against communism. We stand here because we have a positive and progressive vision of the possibilities of a free society."⁶⁹ He brought the New Frontier message to the crisis in Berlin. The *New York Times* reported that Robert Kennedy told "West Berliners that their freedom would be supported by the 'full strength of American Power.'" The article went on to say, "It was clear that the young Attorney General meant something special to West Berliners. His visit was a symbol of United States' commitment to West Berlin, an especially powerful symbol because he is the President's brother."⁷⁰ A sign in City Hall Square said, "Tell your brother what you see — Berlin wants democracy." This was how the Kennedys changed the world. They had people believing in their ability to get things moving toward change. According to the same article approximately 150,000 people came out in the "freezing cold." Their determination to see Robert Kennedy was a testament not only to their will to bring democracy to Berlin, but also the strength of the symbol, which RFK represented.

When he saw the wall, which was built months prior to his visit, he said, "This is the most shameful object of mankind." He went on to say, "To understand this, one has to see it."[71] At City Hall Plaza he emphasized America's determination to defend Berlin by saying, "An attack on West Berlin is an attack on Chicago, New York, Paris, London," and he meant it. Robert Kennedy could speak with conviction because he was in the cabinet room or the Oval Office when the administration discussed foreign policy. Moreover, he would be the person to advise JFK to stand firm on West Berlin. He spoke with conviction because he was an important element in the administration.

In his speech to the Ernst Reuter Society, RFK said, "On the dark side of the Iron Curtain despite rigid Communist controls, democratic ideas, democratic techniques, democratic fashions and democratic ideals are stirring." He went on, "Among its own intellectuals and it own youth communism finds itself on the defensive."[72] Robert Kennedy was a steadfast Cold Warrior, but he looked outside the status quo for a solution to problems that had plagued American foreign policy from the end of the Second World War. His ideas since the Bay of Pigs helped John Kennedy shape his foreign policy on important matters such as Berlin and Cuba. More importantly, JFK was weary of the men who had led him to disaster on Cuba and almost nuclear war in Berlin. He was looking for someone who would advise him without an agenda or an axe to grind. Robert Kennedy was that man.

8

RFK and the CIA

"social reform under pressure"

A byproduct of the Bay of Pigs investigation was a lasting relationship between the Kennedys and Maxwell Taylor. The Kennedy doctrine of flexible response was Taylor's brainchild. When Robert Kennedy talked in 1964 about the shift from massive retaliation to flexible response he said, "The most influential figure in it was Maxwell Taylor."[1] As a matter of fact, RFK went as far as to say, "Every decision the president made on foreign policy was made through Maxwell Taylor."[2]

It is clear that JFK did not trust the military complex after the Bay of Pigs. Being realistic, however, Kennedy knew that he needed the military. Maxwell Taylor was someone whom RFK had trusted. Robert Kennedy's faith in Taylor led John Kennedy to bring the retired general into the inner circle.

Robert Kennedy enjoyed working with Taylor on the investigating committee. He said in 1964 that he

> was really terribly impressed with him: his intellectual ability, his judgment, his ideas. He was ... the most effective person that I had met, and looking back over the past three years I would say that the two people that have made the greatest difference as far as the government is concerned are Bob McNamara and Maxwell Taylor.[3]

Kennedy went on to reemphasize that he was "terrifically taken with him, so the president brought him on as military advisor."[4] Arguably this was one of the most important decisions up to that point in the administration. Indeed it was a bold maneuver for the embattled commander in chief. By bringing in Taylor, Kennedy sent a message to Lemnitzer and Curtis LeMay. The Joint Chiefs of Staff had pushed their agenda on Kennedy. This move demonstrated that JFK would not give in to American militarism. Robert Kennedy found for JFK the link between the military and the president in Taylor. In addition, Taylor's philosophy outlined in *The Uncertain Trumpet* became the policy for the administration.

In such a crisis-driven period in American foreign policy, massive retaliation was a very dangerous notion. If President Kennedy followed through with this notion, then the United States could have found itself in a nuclear confrontation on several occasions. Perhaps it was the fact that Khrushchev did not respect this president as he did Eisenhower. It may also have been a combination of Kennedy's inexperience and bad counsel. Nevertheless, the United States found itself in difficult situations those three years that JFK was in office. After the Bay of Pigs, Kennedy employed the notion of flexible response. JFK wanted to stay away from nuclear options.

Maxwell Taylor had the respect of the Joint Chiefs of Staff. He had served with distinction in the Second World War, leading the famous Screaming Eagles in an attack on Normandy and through the Battle of the Bulge. JFK appointed him military advisor at the behest of RFK, and then eventually he would be appointed chairman of the Joint Chiefs of Staff. Before that role he served as chair of a special group that employed this notion of flexible response. This group was focusing on counter-insurgency measures as opposed to nuclear measures in regions where the United States needed to take a stand.

Robert Kennedy's role in the special group was important to the new Kennedy Doctrine of flexible response. While Taylor served as the chair of the Counterinsurgency (CI) Committee, RFK was there as well. His presence gave JFK the inside information he felt was necessary since the Bay of Pigs. Robert Kennedy said that this was not aimed at taking land, rather the "allegiance of man." He said, "That allegiance can be won only by positive programs: by land reform, by schools, by honest administration, by roads and clinics." RFK emphasized, "Counterinsurgency might best be described as social reform under pressure."[5] This special group was involved in Latin America and Southeast Asia, mostly. But this strategy also called for more men in Special Forces.

Robert Kennedy said in 1964, "After ... our investigation of the Bay of Pigs, I made a major effort to build up the Special Forces. We did that, but also the conventional forces, so that we would have troops over in Germany to respond.... We called up troops, enlarged the army. Then also, tremendous steps were taken to make our armed forces more efficient and better equipped."[6] These actions were the result of the Bay of Pigs almost leading the United States into another war.

Robert Kennedy went on to say, "If it hadn't been ... for Cuba, we would have sent probably large numbers of troops into Laos and Vietnam, which would have been very damaging."[7] Counter-insurgency was a better method to foster change in parts of the world where the United States needed a presence. This, combined with Taylor's notion of flexible response, became the policy of the administration and arguably kept them out of a larger conflict. Unfortunately, Lyndon Johnson would take a different approach to issues in Vietnam.

8. RFK and the CIA

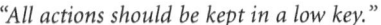

"All actions should be kept in a low key."

John Kennedy always had Castro on his mind. Ted Szulc, the *New York Times* Latin American correspondent, came to the White House at the behest of Richard Goodwin. JFK asked Szulc, "What would you think if I ordered Castro to be assassinated?" Szulc replied that it would only make the situation worse. According to Szulc's notes from the meeting, JFK said "he was testing [him], that he felt the same way." Kennedy went on to say he raised the question because he was under pressure to approve such a plan.[8] In fact on 16 November 1961, Kennedy addressed the University of Washington on its centennial anniversary. Kennedy said that since the university was founded during the Civil War, a lot had changed in America. The world in 1961 was complicated and dangerous. "We increase our arms at a heavy cost, primarily to make certain that we will not have to use them. We must face up to the chance of war, if we are to maintain the peace. We must work with certain countries lacking in freedom in order to strengthen the cause of freedom." Kennedy went on to say, "We cannot, as a free nation, compete with our adversaries in tactics of terror, assassination, false promises, counterfeit mobs and crises." This statement invoked both the struggle for the administration to attack new problems and Kennedy's condemnation of the use of "terror" and "assassination" in American foreign policy. He also said in that speech, "In short, we must face problems which do not lend themselves to easy or quick or permanent solutions."[9]

Cuba occupied both the White House and the CIA. The CIA had initiated assassination attempts on Castro since the Eisenhower administration, but had supposedly stopped under Kennedy. Indeed, when the attorney general found out that the CIA had hired the Mafia, he told CIA general counsel Lawrence Houston, "I trust that if you ever try to do business with organized crime again — with gangsters— you will let the Attorney General know." Houston said, "If you have seen Mr. Kennedy's eyes get steely and his voice get low and precise, you get a definite feeling of unhappiness."[10] The issue of Castro and Cuba was something that permeated JFK's presidency, and since the Bay of Pigs, Robert Kennedy involved himself in any planning. John Kennedy's discussion with Szulc and his speech were clear indicators that he wanted the nation to use new methods. Similarly, RFK's reaction to the Mafia's role in U.S. policy is evidence that the two brothers were trying to rein in the old intelligence establishment.

Robert Kennedy's hand-written notes from a White House meeting on 4 November 1961 give a little insight into his thoughts on the Cuba situation. Kennedy assigned various members of the administration to execute his plan. "My idea," he wrote, "is to stir things up on the island with espionage, sabotage, general disorder, run [and] operated by Cubans themselves with every group but Batistaites [and] Communists. Do not know if we will be successful in overthrowing Castro but we have nothing to lose in my estimate." Robert Kennedy was taking the lead on any plans to overthrow the regime. These plans did not involve assassination. They did, however, involve counterinsurgency. Robert McNamara, Dick Bissell, Alexis Johnson, Paul Nitze, and General Edward Lansdale were all present at this meeting. RFK went on to say, "[McNamara] said he would make [Lansdale] available for me — I assigned him to make a survey of situation in Cuba — the problems [and] our assets."[11] Lansdale came up with a scenario in which Cubans who were dissatisfied with Batista and Castro would take down the regime. This philosophy would give more power to the people and keep the United States out of the limelight. They called this Operation Mongoose.

Robert Kennedy's relationship with his brother gave him not only direct access to the Oval Office, but also powers to initiate actions in Cuba. Further, his relationship with Maxwell Taylor helped him when it came to military matters. The Kennedy brothers wanted to stay low in Cuba, but maximize any opportunity. Indeed, Maxwell Taylor reinforced that it was JFK's wish that "all actions should be kept in a low key."[12] The Kennedys would rather force a social revolution of the people. The action rang with the self-determination that Kennedy believed in. Additionally, a successful revolution from within Cuba would invalidate communism, which could have larger implications throughout the world. This notion was in tune with the counter-insurgency that RFK gave such credence. Indeed, Arthur Schlesinger said, "The CIA wished to organize Castro's overthrow itself from outside Cuba, as against those in the White House, the Attorney General's office and State who wished to support an anti–Castro movement inside Cuba."[13] Though slower, this revolution would have larger benefits than any military operation.

Maxwell Taylor and Robert Kennedy led a special group that focused on this operation in Cuba. On 11 January 1962, Taylor and Kennedy met with the CIA to discuss the progress of this operation. "Several members of the Group noted the difficulty of the task ahead," the memorandum said. CIA director John McCone called "attention to the fact that the prevailing spirit within Cuba appears to be one of apathy rather than resistance, and that a fanatical pro–Castro minority exists along with an efficient police mechanism." In addition the CIA was employing other means in an effort to foster rebellion from within Cuba:

> It was noted that the prevailing policy on sabotage is still in effect, i.e., that no actions which would be dangerous to the population will be undertaken, nor will major demolitions be done at this stage. It was agreed that whenever this policy appears to require change, the matter will be discussed with the Special Group.

In addition to efforts at "sabotage" the CIA also worked out a way to gather information in that region by setting up "an interrogation center for Cuban refugees in the Miami area" that was to be "adequately staffed to produce the optimum amount of intelligence on conditions inside Cuba."[14]

Robert Kennedy asked McCone in meeting on the same day for his "frank and personal opinion" on Operation Mongoose, General Lansdale's plan. McCone responded with four points:

> (a) an operation of this type, as presently planned, has never been attempted before, (b) it will be extremely difficult to accomplish, (c) the CIA and the U.S. Government are short on assets to carry out the proposed program, and (d) the Agency, however, is lending every effort and all-out support.[15]

The fact that Robert Kennedy was so intimately involved in the planning and execution of this plan demonstrates his influence on policy. Moreover, it is a clear indication that the men who employed these plans looked to him as a representative for JFK.

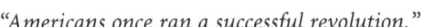

"Americans once ran a successful revolution."

Nikita Khrushchev's 6 January 1961 speech, which outlined for the world how he would wage "wars of liberation" to spread communism, had far reaching implications in the Kennedy White House. Robert Kennedy said in 1964, "The speech that impressed the president most by Khrushchev was his speech ... about wars of liberation." The speech talked about how communism would subvert democracy. Robert Kennedy said,

> Khrushchev talked about the wars of liberation that were going to be done through subversion, through overthrow of governments, through civil war, civil disobedience, and the president felt that our actions, steps should be tailored to meet those kinds of problems, and that too much in the past we had been ready to.... The big bomb with the buck, or whatever it was.[16]

These new methods to attack the Soviet Union were a priority for the young attorney general and his Special Group (Augmented). Moving away from massive retaliation, the Kennedys hoped to confront the Russian threat successfully. Taylor and his notions of flexible response and gearing up the United States' conventional forces led the way to attack this subversive strategy.

On 30 November 1961, General Lansdale outlined for the administration the goals of the "Cuba Project" in a document that was largely the result of the special group led by Taylor and Robert Kennedy. The first point outlined stated, "We will use our available assets to go ahead with the discussed project in order to help Cuba overthrow the communist regime." The main policy, as already mentioned, was for the United States government to covertly overthrow Castro from within. It went on to state that the operation would remain under the command of Lansdale and have periodic reviews. It concluded, "Knowledge of the existence of this operation should be restricted to the recipients of this memorandum."[17] This memo gave Lansdale power to conduct his counterinsurgency program in Cuba. Indeed, any "communist regime" had connotations of the Soviet Union playing a role in the Western hemisphere and threatened American hegemony in the region.

On 20 February 1962, Lansdale sent another memo to the president regarding the Cuba Project. In this memo he began by saying, "We still know too little about the real situation inside Cuba, although we are taking energetic steps to learn more." However, what the group did know was that "the Communist regime [was] an active Sino-Soviet spearhead in our Hemisphere and that Communist controls inside Cuba [were] severe." It went on to state,

> There is evidence that the repressive measures of the Communists, together with disappointments in Castro's economic dependency on the Communist formula, have resulted in an anti-regime atmosphere among the Cuban people which makes a resistance program a distinct and present possibility.[18]

Lansdale linked the Cuban government with the Sino-Soviet government and also brought in its intentions in the region. He went on to say, "The Cuban people feel helpless and are losing hope fast. They need symbols of inside resistance and of outside interest soon." Lansdale even went so far as to invoke the American Revolution.

"Americans once ran a successful revolution," he wrote. "It was run from within, and succeeded because there was timely and strong political, economic, and military help by nations outside who supported our cause. Using this same concept of revolution from within, we must now help the Cuban people to stamp out tyranny and gain their liberty."[19] Lansdale used phrases such as "tyranny" and "liberty" for the Cuban people. These had been and would be concepts that would justify American action in other parts of the world.

The Cuban Missile Crisis interrupted the plan outlined in the memo later that year. Nevertheless, it clearly demonstrated the willingness of the president and the military to intervene in Cuba. The project was broken up into six phases. The first phase states that in March 1962 the United States would "start moving in." Phase Two involved a "build up" from April to July 1962 wherein the U.S. would begin "activating the necessary operations inside Cuba for revolution and concurrently applying the vital political, economic, and military-type support from outside Cuba."[20] This was the revolution Lansdale hoped to create within Cuba. Phase Three and Four were entwined; the former would address the readiness of the operation and the latter would initiate guerrilla actions in Cuba from August to September 1962. Phase Five was an "open revolt" of the government occurring in the first two weeks of October 1962. Finally, phase Six involved establishing a new government friendly to the United States.

After Lansdale outlined the phases he went on to say, "The operational plan for clandestine U.S. support of a Cuban movement inside Cuba to overthrow the Communist regime is within policy limits already set by the President." While JFK had authorized the use of these "clandestine" operations, there was one piece he did not agree to: "A vital decision, still to be made, is on the use of open U.S. force to aid the Cuban people in winning their liberty." The military wanted to avoid another Bay of Pigs, where Kennedy refused to give air support to the Cubans landing on the island to take down Castro. Lansdale asked an important question: "If conditions and assets permitting a revolt are achieved in Cuba, and if U.S. help is required to sustain this condition, will the U.S. respond promptly with military force to aid the Cuban revolt?" Herein lay the major concern of both JFK and RFK. Lansdale said, "An early decision is required, prior to deep involvement of the Cubans in this program."[21]

This memo is evidence that the military truly believed that the Soviet Union had planned to infiltrate the United States. In turn, these men were planning to overthrow Castro from within. This covert plan was in accordance with RFK and Maxwell Taylor, two people whom JFK trusted and supported. Moreover, it is evidence that there were still issues with Kennedy's decision to deny air support during the Bay of Pigs. The military wanted to be certain that Kennedy would respond if this project needed higher levels of intervention.

---

*"No decision was expressed or implied
approving the use of such forces."*

On 12 March 1962, General Lansdale asked some questions about concerns he had regarding the United States' commitment to Mongoose. These questions were addressed to the Special Group Augmented, in which Robert Kennedy played a prominent role. He was the only non-military person in the group. "CIA desires to train small groups of Cuban nationals on the U.S. Air Force Bombing Range, Avon Park, Florida, immediately," Lansdale wrote; "Capture and interrogation of any of these covert agents could result in exposure (in international news media) of U.S. official involvement in efforts to unseat the present Communist Cuban regime." Of course any publicity was something that JFK did not want. With that in mind Lansdale concluded, "A policy determination is needed as to whether or not agents to be infiltrated into Cuba should be trained on U.S. Government installations." This discourse was necessary due to the National Security Actions Memos, which held back the CIA and the Joint Chiefs of Staff from doing any operation without presidential oversight. That was the role RFK played. In addition to this question, Lansdale went on to say, "CIA needs a policy determination on the supplying of arms and equipment to deserving Cuban guerrillas, as they are located, assessed, and request help."[22]

A 14 March 1962 memo provided some of the response from the president.

The response came from Maxwell Taylor. Attached to the memo was a handwritten note by U. Alexis Johnson dated 16 March 1962 which stated,

> The President expressed general approval on the understanding there will be further examination of use of Americans for airdrops etc. during first phase when risk estimates are completed.... The President also expressed skepticism that in so far as can now be foreseen circumstances will arise that would justify and make desirable the use of American forces for overt military action.... It was clearly understood no decision was expressed or implied approving the use of such forces although contingency planning would proceed.[23]

This memo clearly outlined for the military and the CIA that there would not be military action without presidential approval.

Taylor's 14 March 1962 memo went on to outline the "Guidelines for Operation Mongoose," saying there would be specific "assumptions":

> a. In undertaking to cause the overthrow of the target government, the U.S. will make maximum use of indigenous resources, internal and external, but recognizes that final success will require decisive U.S. military intervention. b. Such indigenous resources as are developed will be used to prepare for and justify this intervention, and thereafter to facilitate and support it.[24]

Taylor stressed the "indigenous resources" so the military and the CIA would shy away from using American resources as much as possible. The memo exemplified the Kennedy position on Cuba. It was critical that these men use American forces sparingly. Further, it is evidence that the administration was watching every angle in an effort to avoid another Bay of Pigs.

Taylor went on to say that the operation would be reviewed at the end of the various phases, and if overt military measures were needed, then they would be considered. He never committed to any American involvement other than collecting "hard intelligence on the target area." At the end of the memo, Taylor stressed that while Lansdale was in charge of the operation, he was required to report to the Special Group Augmented, which was chaired by Taylor. In addition, he referred to the attorney general as a member whom the operation must report to in the same vein as the Joint Chiefs of Staff. The Special Group Augmented, he wrote, "is responsible for providing policy guidance to the project, for approving important operations and for monitoring progress." In this memo, Taylor took away any assumption that the United States was committed to using military forces in Cuba. Further, it emphasized the need for more intelligence and presidential oversight. Kennedy had planted the right man to oversee the American military complex. Taylor's intimate knowledge of the military combined with his loyalty to JFK gave the president a keen advisor at a pivotal time.

On 31 May 1962, Robert Kennedy asked the Special Group (Augmented) to propose "what would be an appropriate course of action for the United States to take in the event that the Soviets establish a military base in Cuba."[25] This was an important question on a variety of levels. If the Soviets put bases in Cuba, then it meant larger economic and military support. In short it demonstrated Soviet commitment to the island. General Lansdale wrote, "Since the Special Group (Augmented) has assumed that overt U.S. military force will have to be used to end Communist control of Cuba, Mr. Kennedy's question is particularly pertinent." He went on to say,

> For should the Soviets choose to exercise their option of establishing a military base under a Soviet flag in Cuba, it is possible that this would act to prevent any future U.S. decision to intervene with U.S. military force, just as the Soviets have refrained from applying military force against countries on which U.S. bases are established.[26]

This question raised awareness that if the United States did not act before there were bases in Cuba, it might never have an opportunity to put forces on the island. Cuba would become, like West Berlin for the European Alliance, a symbol for the Communist Bloc. As with Berlin, if the United States attacked this symbol it could mean war. This demonstrates the complex nature of Mongoose as well as RFK's role in posing policy questions in meetings regarding the operation. Indeed, he was intimately involved in issues surrounding Cuba and the Soviet Union. However, according to Aleksandr Fursenko and Timothy Naftali, "Few people in the group took the question seriously; the possibility was considered 'too remote to waste time on.' Khrushchev just didn't want to invest that much in Castro."[27]

John McCone recorded in an 18 July 1962 memo a discussion between himself and Robert Kennedy. Over dinner, the two men discussed various issues, and eventually came to Mongoose. "The Cuban situation," he wrote, "was reviewed in considerable detail." He said that Robert Kennedy expressed

> the opinion that the last six months' effort had been worthwhile inasmuch as we had gained a very substantial amount of intelligence which was lacking, but that the effort was disappointing inasmuch as the program had not advanced to the point we had hoped.[28]

Clearly, the operation had not had the effect RFK had wanted, which implies that JFK was hoping for more as well. Robert Kennedy "urged intensified effort but seemed inclined to let the situation 'worsen' before recommending drastic action." They went on to discuss who would take over the Cuban government; "however, there was no specific recommendation as to whom we should support or who represented the most dynamic leadership of the Cuban group."[29]

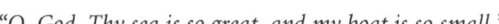

"O, God, Thy sea is so great, and my boat is so small."

John Kennedy hoped to change not only America's direction, but also how the government shaped events. Robert Kennedy was a big piece of JFK's vision for the New Frontier. After the Bay of Pigs, JFK looked to Robert Kennedy as a confidant. His younger brother's unbiased attitude was exactly what the president needed when posed with difficult questions. Bobby asked the hard questions and established a level of presidential oversight in military matters. The Bay of Pigs taught John Kennedy that the military knew of only one way to conduct foreign relations: war.

Robert Kennedy had been a pivotal player in constructing the Kennedy administration. He had worked on the campaign and advised the president on cabinet appointments. Indeed, Robert Kennedy had spent more time with JFK than anyone in the cabinet in both a personal and professional capacity. When it came to seeing issues at different levels, there was not a single other person whom the president could trust implicitly. This was the relationship that JFK needed to challenge the status quo. Robert Kennedy was seen as a person who had JFK's full attention. Their relationship was not fraught with the same vicious political implications as others in the cabinet. John Kennedy's desk had a plaque engraved with the Breton Fisherman's prayer. It read "O, God, Thy sea is so great, and my boat is so small." Perhaps JFK saw the problems he faced as great as the ocean, and he needed a captain to steer the way to port. Bobby Kennedy was that captain.

With Robert Kennedy came a shift in how the White House operated. Eisenhower had had a much different approach than Kennedy. This new liberal method worried the people who had previously worked with Eisenhower. The people who it affected most were the military, as they came in with the administration. Robert Kennedy played a significant role in determining military policy. He was a part of the commission that dissected the Bay of Pigs, and subsequently, as a result, served on the Special Group Augmented. The group focused on unseating Castro through a variety of methods. Robert Kennedy was the epitome of a New Frontiersman and only in his thirties. He would have a chance to affect policy for years to come.

Robert Kennedy had argued that were it not for Cuba, the president would have sent troops to Laos and Vietnam. The ultimate lesson that the Kennedys learned from the Bay of Pigs was to ask questions and not take for granted that the military always knew what they were doing. Military experience no longer impressed the Kennedy brothers and they were not unwilling to question tactics or strategy. Both brothers recognized that lack of communication and poor intelligence contributed to failure at the Bay of Pigs. In this vein, NSAM 55 and 57 were meant to reshape the Joint Chiefs of Staff and the CIA. These new provisions gave presidential oversight to operations that had once worked alone, which translated into Robert Kennedy's getting involved on many levels.

While the main function of the attorney general is to advise the president on domestic legal matters, when it came to a foreign-policy crisis situation RFK had many roles. He did not believe that the National Security Council was a good tool for handling issues. "The National Security Council is worthless as far as dealing with any problems," he said in 1965. "I mean you've got to make up your mind and then get the concurrence of the [NSC]."[30] RFK wanted to have solutions not only for the NSC, but also for his older brother. As a result he looked to Maxwell Taylor as someone who could help with the divide between the president and the military. "Maxwell Taylor — he made such a big difference," Robert Kennedy said. "He had some sense. He could see the whole perspective." Taylor represented what he had expected from the Joint Chiefs as outlined in NSAM 55. They were more than advisors on the military. JFK did not know Taylor other than from his books and distinguished military record. Robert Kennedy brought this man to the Kennedy White House. JFK's trust in his brother changed the direction of the government in the form of Taylor.

This time in American history was arguably the most dangerous. Robert Kennedy helped the president use any and all resources to stave off conflict. His communication with Georgi Bolshakov and efforts with counter-insurgency are examples that he looked to new methods to change the world. Berlin's reaction to RFK is evidence that he was seen a person who could foster great change in a volatile time. Moreover, it was that forward thinking that moved America away from nuclear weapons and into the embrace of more conventional methods to combat the communist threat.

The CIA was intimately involved in actions all over the world. Most prominently, however, its work in Cuba served to increase the tension between the United States and the Soviet Union. Indeed, it may have contributed to Castro's seeing a need for larger Soviet assistance. The CIA's unorthodox methods hurt any hopes for true diplomacy. That being said, Robert Kennedy's efforts to promote insurrection with Operation Mongoose contributed to this tense relationship.

Operation Mongoose is a clear example of how Robert Kennedy was a major player in the foreign-policy team. This effort, though fruitless, demonstrated the faith that JFK had in his younger brother and Maxwell Taylor. While the people involved in this endeavor were a part of the military complex that Kennedy did not trust, his brother was there to provide the oversight JFK did not have in the Bay of Pigs. JFK's reluctance to commit U.S. forces in this operation was largely due to Bobby's advice. All evidence points to JFK's looking to his brother for advice on matters such as these. His newfound trust in Maxwell Taylor only reinforces this notion. Taylor's memo reinforcing the president's position to General Lansdale points to a clear decision to wait and understand the issues before putting soldiers into harm's way. Taylor was the man whom Kennedy relied on for real military advice without an agenda.

Robert Kennedy's role in advisement is different from the role of those already examined in this study. He was someone that JFK relied on to tell him the truth, while protecting the legacy of the administration. In many ways,

Part Four. Brother's Keeper

Bobby was John Kennedy's keeper. His father and JFK wanted RFK in this role to watch out for the president. After the Bay of Pigs, which was the low point of the administration, JFK looked to his brother for help. That was the main reason he appointed him to the role of attorney general. This relationship was very important and was brought to new heights at the end of 1961, going into 1962. It would take on a whole new level in October 1962.

Part Five

"Dogs of War": McNamara, the Joint Chiefs and the American Military Complex

9

Whiz Kid and War Hero

"It did not stop Communist political and military aggression."

After the Bay of Pigs, Robert McNamara went to President Kennedy and said, "Mr. President, I know where I was when you made the decision to launch the invasion. I was in a room where, with one exception, all of your advisors—including me—recommended you proceed." He went on to say, "I am fully prepared to go on T.V. and say so." McNamara recalled that Kennedy replied, "I'm grateful to you for your willingness to assume part of the responsibility. But I am the president. I did not have to do what all of you recommended. I did it."[1] This is a clear example of both McNamara's loyalty to JFK and his intelligence to recognize that he was wrong. He would make a similar gesture to the people of the United States when he published his memoir, *In Retrospect: The Tragedies and Lessons of Vietnam*, except there was no president to shoulder the burden of defeat. The issues in Southeast Asia during the Kennedy years are a prelude to the larger conflict that would develop under Lyndon Johnson and Richard Nixon. The beginning of that conflict lay in the groundwork McNamara and Maxwell Taylor created when they were trying to respond to the Sino-Soviet threat around the world.

Robert McNamara had been described by Robert Kennedy as "head and shoulders" above everyone else. The former Ford Motor Company president had taken the Department of Defense and changed it to meet the new policy of flexible response. In a 1964 interview with Arthur Schlesinger, McNamara described this transition. He began by stating that the policy of massive retaliation "reflected President Eisenhower's belief that fiscal security was the true foundation of military security and his belief that fiscal security was threatened by further increases in the total budget, particularly further increases in the defense budget." He went on to state, "Eisenhower appeared to believe in—and in any event his fiscal limitations on the defense budget forced—complete reliance upon nuclear weapons."[2] This entangled the Defense and Treasury departments. Ironically, it perpetuated the "military-industrial complex" that Eisenhower warned against in his farewell address.

132

McNamara went on to say that this policy did not have the impact that the Eisenhower administration had intended. "I think the important point to recognize with respect to such a policy is that it did not stop Communist political and military aggression." He went on to emphasize, "It did not even stop such aggression during the period when the United States had a clear or near nuclear monopoly, i.e., the ten or fifteen years following the end of World War II." He determined, "Such a policy was never credible. [Especially] after the United States had failed to use nuclear weapons in the Korean War." Most notably, McNamara believed that the "the Soviets did not believe that the United States would respond to minor acts of aggression — however you wish to define minor — with a nuclear response."[3] These minor acts of aggression defined the Cold War. There was never a point where war was declared, so there was no proper method under Eisenhower to fight this war. Massive retaliation handcuffed the United States. There were few options to combat the rise of communism short of nuclear war. McNamara saw this philosophy as tantamount to failure. The United States needed options, and flexible response provided them. It also, however, may have given birth to the Vietnam War. McNamara went on to say that because the Soviet Union "didn't believe we would respond to minor acts of aggression with a nuclear response, they continued to apply pressures on Berlin, on Southeast Asia, and elsewhere in the world." He argued that Eisenhower's approach was inept and characterized it as a "bankrupt strategy."[4]

With these factors in mind, McNamara took the resources of the government and prepared the New Frontier to wage war in a different manner. He said that one of the first acts of the Kennedy administration was to make "a shift from a complete and sole reliance on massive retaliation with strategic nuclear weapons to a controlled, flexible response tailored to the level of the political or military aggression to which it was responding."[5] This, according to McNamara, was a crucial maneuver for the new president. He argued,

> It was this decision which, in my opinion, removed the fetters from our foreign policy, it was this decision which provided for our foreign policy a solid base of military power, and it was this early decision of President Kennedy which permitted such responses to Soviet aggression as that of the United States in the Cuban missile crisis of 1962.[6]

McNamara was a crucial part of this transition. He said that if the United States had continued under Eisenhower's policy it "would not have had enough forces to carry out a successful invasion of Cuba if that should have proved necessary in the missile crisis of October 1962." Further, the United States "would never have been willing to undertake such a blockade had we not had the capability to follow it, if necessary, with an invasion." According to McNamara, there were large issues that needed a remedy quickly. Khrushchev's "Wars of Liberation" speech demanded new thinking on Kennedy's part. It also meant that the United States needed to take inventory of how it fought communism and of its current capabilities, and make some serious decisions.

McNamara said in 1964 that the list of "deficiencies" was long, but he gave Schlesinger a few examples to illustrate what he was saying. "In January of 1961 we had only two-thirds of the required number of armored personnel carriers and only 46 percent of the self-propelled howitzers required." Additionally, the United States "had only 15 percent of the authorized number — the required number — of recoilless rifles…. At the time of the Cuban missile crisis we were still short."[7] Since World War II, military strategy had depended on control of the air. McNamara said, "Perhaps even more important, however, than the deficiencies in the aircraft themselves was the almost complete lack of supplies of modern non-nuclear ordnance." The United States had depended on the threat of nuclear war to deter its enemies. "This [deficiency with the Air Force] meant, in effect, the air force would have been unable to provide any meaningful tactical air support for the army in the event of a non-nuclear limited war."[8] Under Eisenhower, conventional war was not an option. Not only were troop sizes and equipment out of date but "our airlift capability at the time," he said, "was so inadequate it would have taken nearly two months to airlift one infantry division and its equipment to Southeast Asia — a period of time completely unacceptable in relation to the contingency war plans then on the books."[9] Within the first thirty days McNamara and Kennedy addressed these concerns with additions to the budget. Robert McNamara was the "Whiz Kid" that John Kennedy needed to accomplish a transition from threatening nuclear war to fostering peace. That said, their intentions to give the United States options other than nuclear war could have led them deeper into the quagmire of these small wars. Indeed, Vietnam was born at the threshold of this new philosophy to increase conventional warfare.

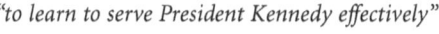

"to learn to serve President Kennedy effectively"

McNamara had mentioned in his interview with Schlesinger that Maxwell Taylor had described the problems with the Eisenhower doctrine in his book *The Uncertain Trumpet*. Taylor was a war hero who, after the Bay of Pigs, came into the Kennedy White House and initiated change. McNamara argued that the Bay of Pigs was chiefly driven by the fact that "most of the senior advisors had been in office less than ninety days." The other issue that drove this decision was that "each of the senior advisors believed they were following a well-established plan and policy developed by the previous administration." Indeed, it may also point to the lack of confidence in JFK. Finally, "the weaknesses of the operational plan were not disclosed to the policy advisors. That is to say, there had been poor staff analysis of the plan — poor staff analysis both by the CIA staff and by the Joint Staff."[10] Maxwell Taylor had just finished dissecting this debacle and his insight was invaluable.

Maxwell Taylor wrote in his memoirs that when he came to Washington at the behest of the president he "was ushered into the Oval Room and there met President Kennedy, Vice-President Johnson, and McGeorge Bundy along with a few other officials who drifted in and out. I sensed an air which I had know from my military past — that of a command post that had been overrun by the enemy." He wrote, "There were the same glazed eyes, subdued voices, and slow speech that I remembered observing in commanders routed at the Battle of the Bulge.... This new administration had, indeed, engaged in its first bloody action and was learning the sting of defeat."[11] This war veteran was exactly what the administration needed to help JFK undertake the military changes that he and McNamara wanted to initiate. In addition, it was a new mind for JFK to use in decision-making. Taylor was a war hero and widely respected.

Taylor remarked in his memoirs that the Bay of Pigs was a "blundering use of national power in support of a questionable national interest."[12] He argued that one factor which hurt the operation was Kennedy's insistence on keeping the operation covert. "This fixation on covertness exercised a baneful influence on the operational plan from start to finish, often causing changes detrimental from start to finish."[13] Taylor's commission on the Bay of Pigs was the beginning of his involvement with the administration. The president asked him to "take a look at all our practices and programs in the area of the military and paramilitary, guerrilla and anti-guerrilla activities which fall short of outright war."[14] Taylor was given Robert Kennedy, Admiral Arleigh Burke from the Joint Chiefs of Staff, and Allen Dulles of the Central Intelligence Agency to assist him in this endeavor. Taylor said,

> It was quite clear I had been given associates each of whom had a special interest in the outcome of the investigation. Robert Kennedy could be counted on to look after the interests of the President while Burke and Dulles, representing two organizations deeply involved in the operation, would see that no injustice was done to the Chiefs of Staff or the CIA.[15]

The result of this inquiry led Taylor to take a role in the administration at the behest of both Robert Kennedy and the president. Having turned down the director of the CIA, his title would be Military Representative to the President until he was appointed chairman of the Joint Chiefs of Staff in October 1962.

Taylor respected the importance of the director of the CIA, but did not want that position. However, he wrote in his memoirs, "I had given my life to the military profession and, if there was any way in which that experience might assist [President Kennedy], I would be happy to put it at his disposal."[16] Taylor was a soldier and, like others in the administration, believed that this was a tumultuous time for the United States. It needed good people to serve and Taylor would never shirk that responsibility. On 26 June 1961 Taylor took the position in the Kennedy White House.

His role, according to JFK, would be that "of a staff officer to advise and assist [the president] with military matters that reached him as Commander in Chief." Interestingly, he was supplementing the chairman of the Joint Chiefs, who were the primary military advisors for the president. While General Lemnitzer had been friends with Taylor since West Point and had no issue with the position, it was a clear message from Kennedy that he did not trust the Chiefs. Taylor told Lemnitzer "not to view [his] responsibilities as competitive with the Chiefs and [he] did not intend to serve as a White House roadblock to their recommendations." Lemnitzer promised he would do as much possible to "prevent anyone from driving a wedge between us." Taylor's other function was to advise on "fields of intelligence and cold war planning, with particular attention to Berlin and Southeast Asia."[17] There were others who resisted this change in the advisor infrastructure.

Robert McNamara, according to Taylor, "seemed to have no misgivings about my assignment." However, Taylor argued that for McGeorge Bundy this new position "proved to be a more sensitive matter." Taylor argued that Bundy was "able, aggressive, and highly self confident."[18] He went on to say,

> The duties of his office had never been accurately defined but depended largely on what Bundy felt needed to be done. My interests in the field of intelligence, Berlin and Southeast Asia cut sharply across many of the activities which Bundy had been directing, and his initial reaction to me was one of considerable unhappiness.[19]

Taylor said that, over time, they were able to work out an arrangement that suited them both. He emphasized, "The heart of my new business was to learn to serve President Kennedy effectively."[20] Taylor analyzed how the staff operated for the president, but turned to JFK's most trusted advisor for help.

"As I mediated on ways and means to serve President Kennedy," he wrote, "I often sought advice from Bob Kennedy as to what was feasible and what was incompatible with the President's natural way of doing business." Once again, Robert Kennedy played a role in both a crucial appointment and how information was streamlined to the president. Where Bundy served JFK early in the administration, RFK evolved into a stalwart advisor. Taylor did his best to advise the president on issues so when he entered a cabinet meeting he was "thoroughly briefed and ready to resolve problems awaiting him."[21] Taylor was asked by JFK to form the Special Group (C.I.), which focused on counter-insurgency forces. Taylor emphasized, as did McNamara and RFK, that President Kennedy was concerned about the 6 January 1961 "wars of liberation" speech from Khrushchev. Indeed, that speech set off a very powerful inaugural address, having a similar effect on policy as had the Bay of Pigs. It geared the new administration to be reactive rather than proactive. This plagued the New Frontier and stymied any efforts at détente. According to Taylor, "This was a new technique which Khrushchev in Russia, Mao in China, and Ho Chi Minh in North Vietnam united in proclaiming as the preferred means for the future expansion of militant communism." Taylor went on to say that the military believed it would go beyond Asia and into Latin America and Africa. "This was a threat which President Kennedy perceived and against which he wished to erect defenses."[22] The CIA and the Joint Chiefs of staff wanted a single body to deal with these measures. In January 1962, Taylor established the Special Group Counterinsurgency (CI) "to assure the ability to use all available resources, when and as directed by the President, in preventing and resisting subversive insurgency and related forms of indirect aggression in friendly countries." Taylor was the chairman of this group. He said that this group was "unique" because it gave top-level people an opportunity to meet and get the government moving on an issue. "The presence of Bob Kennedy on the committee, with his energy and interest in its work, was another force which vitalized the membership and guaranteed unusually candid testimony on the part of those called before the group." He observed, "Bob was a bit rough on evasive witnesses."[23]

"...rests with the people and government of that country."

The Soviet Union posed the greatest threat to the United States. Robert McNamara said, "Having spent three years [in the military] helping turn back German and Japanese aggression only to witness the Soviet takeover of Eastern Europe following the war, I accepted the idea advanced by George F. Kennan ... that the West, led by the United States, must guard against Communist expansion through a policy of containment." Indeed, many New Frontiersmen were reared on Kennan's philosophy and believed in it. McNamara believed that "the Soviets and Chinese were cooperating in trying to extend their hegemony."[24] These beliefs led McNamara to look at Vietnam, not as an attempt by Ho Chi Minh to nationalize their government, but as another battle in the Cold War with the Soviet Union. McNamara saw the Viet-Cong as "signs of a unified communist drive for hegemony in Asia."[25] He said that two developments had "reinforced" his way of thinking on Vietnam: "the intensification of relations between Cuba and the Soviets, and a new wave of Soviet provocations in Berlin." He concluded, "Both seemed to underscore the aggressive intent of communist policy. In that context, the danger of Vietnam's loss and, through falling dominoes, the loss of Southeast Asia made it seem reasonable to expand the U.S. effort in Vietnam." With these ideas in mind the United States was attempting to push back the communist threat in Southeast Asia, not only in Cuba and Berlin. With Laos discussed at Vienna and mostly settled, this brought a heightened sense of an issue in Vietnam and brought the problem closer to the Kennedy White House.

General Taylor also had ideas on how to handle this threat to the United States. McNamara acknowledged in his memoir, "We knew very little about the region. We lacked experience dealing with crises." Cuba and Berlin among others "clamored" for the administration's attention.[26] Maxwell Taylor argued that Kennedy "repeatedly emphasized his desire to utilize the situation in Vietnam to study and test the techniques and equipment related to counterinsurgency, and hence, he insisted that we expose our most promising officers to experience of service there."[27] Taylor said that Kennedy "directed that Army colonels eligible for promotion to brigadier general be rotated through Vietnam on short orientation tours."[28] In May 1955 Ngo Dinh Diem took control of the South Vietnamese. Backed by the United States, he stopped the elections that were a part of the Geneva Accords the previous year. The U.S. and other SEATO allies were afraid of Ho Chi Minh's popularity and believed that the North would win in an election.[29] Diem's government had major problems in maintaining stability, barely surviving several coup attempts. JFK inherited those issues from the Eisenhower administration. George Herring argues that Kennedy's response to the problems in Vietnam was a far cry from his rhetoric on the subject: "In settling the major policy issues, he was cautious rather than bold, hesitant rather than decisive, and improvisational rather then carefully calculated."[30] Indeed, there were many in the administration that wanted Kennedy to act.

In October 1961, Walt Rostow wrote to JFK, "We are deeply committed to Viet-Nam: if the situation deteriorates, we will have to go in; the situation is, in fact, actively deteriorating." Rostow believed that it was "essential that Generals Taylor and Lansdale take a good hard look at Viet-Nam on the ground soon."[31] When he first looked at the issues in Vietnam, Lansdale believed, "The Key to success lay in the support of the people. Without them there could be 'no political base for supporting the fight.'"[32] Kennedy needed to make a decision on the issues in Vietnam. Indeed, this was an issue linked to the overall strategy of fighting communism. With this in mind, he sent Taylor and Rostow to see what major issues plagued the Diem regime in South Vietnam.

In a 13 October 1961 letter, Kennedy asked Taylor to travel to Saigon and assess the situation in South Vietnam "particularly as it concerns the threat to the internal security and defense of that country and the adjacent areas." Kennedy said that after he consulted with the other American military leaders in the region, he wanted to hear Taylor's "views on the courses of action which our government might take at this juncture to avoid a further deterioration in the situation in South Vietnam and eventually to contain and eliminate the threat to its independence." Kennedy stressed in the letter that his assessment should "bear in mind" that the sole responsibility for South Vietnam "rests with the people and government of that country."[33] Kennedy stressed the importance of the military but also emphasized that the "political, social and economic elements are equally important."[34] This letter is evidence that Kennedy saw the issues in South Vietnam belonging to the people of that country. Taylor wrote, "The President made it abundantly clear in private discussions that he fervently hoped that the necessary military force could be provided by the Vietnamese without the need to introduce U.S. ground troops into combat."[35]

Taylor's mission to Saigon provided advice for the president and his defense team. Whether JFK planned to take that advice was a matter of great significance for his administration and the history of the United States.

The United States was not prepared to confront issues other than a communist threat. This was a perfect example where the Kennedy administration did not understand the issues within a region. That ignorance led the United States to begin its involvement in Vietnam. The administration's embrace of flexible response, the existence of threats to Berlin, and its view of the movement in Vietnam as communist rather than nationalist led the United States into the war. Both Robert McNamara and Maxwell Taylor had limited knowledge of how to confront the communist threat in Southeast Asia. Moreover, the CIA created further problems when it was unable to ascertain the issue prevalent in the Chinese-Soviet rift. Had the Kennedy administration known about this problem, they might have been hesitant to offer aid in a situation of which they had limited knowledge. The lessons from the Bay of Pigs led JFK to send Taylor and others to Saigon, but it did not help him see that the way to address issues in the world did not always fall under Kennan's policy of containment. Indeed, American presidents need to look at every region they plan to send military troops with great detail and scrutiny. Ho Chi Minh was a nationalistic leader much like George Washington. While communism played a role in the rise of this leader, it was not at the heart of his ideology. Had they identified this movement accurately, there might not have been a larger conflict.

"What the U.S. does or fails to do will be decisive to the end result."

Taylor wrote in his memoir that when he began this tour of Vietnam there were many tragedies that had befallen the country. There were floods in the Mekong Delta, destroying crops, livestock and housing. In addition there was a murder of a well-known officer by the Vietcong. He argued, "It was no exaggeration to say that the entire country was suffering from the collapse of national morale — an obvious fact which made a strong impression on the members of our mission."[36] Taylor went on to visit with Ngo Dinh Diem as well as many other military personnel to assess their ability to defend the coast as well as the mainland. He argues in his memoir, "I agreed completely with President Kennedy that we Americans should do nothing for Vietnam which the Vietnamese could do for themselves."[37] There were discussions for a SEATO force to assist in the fighting as well as U.S. ground troops.

After an extensive visit, Taylor's conclusions were outlined in a report to the president. Before he left Vietnam he wrote Kennedy a letter outlining some initial observations as a "cover" to the report. "We stressed that we had no illusions as to the finality of our recommendations," he remembered in his memoir. "We were merely sure that they represented actions that should be taken in light of our current knowledge of the situation in Southeast Asia." He also said, "We expressed our deep conviction that the time might come ... when we would be obliged to attack the source of guerrilla aggression in North Vietnam." He concluded in this letter that their "mission was leaving Southeast Asia feeling that the United States had a serious problem, but that the situation was by no means hopeless."[38]

Taylor came to three conclusions in his report. The first conclusion was, "Communist strategy aims to gain control of Southeast Asia by methods of subversion and guerrilla war which by-pass conventional U.S. and indigenous strength on the ground." With regard to this issue, "The interim Communist goal — en route to total take-over — appears to be a neutral Southeast Asia, detached from U.S. protection. This strategy is well on the way to success in Vietnam." His second conclusion was, "In Vietnam (and Southeast Asia) there is a double crisis in confidence: doubt that U.S. is determined to save Southeast Asia; doubt that Diem's methods can frustrate and defeat Communist purposes and methods." This doubt was something that the North could capitalize on. He emphasized, "The Vietnamese (and Southeast Asians) will undoubtedly draw — rightly or wrongly — definitive conclusions in coming weeks and months concerning the probable outcome and will adjust their behavior accordingly." Most importantly, he said, "What the U.S. does or fails to do will be decisive to the end result." Finally, his third conclusion stated,

> The Vietnamese Government is caught in interlocking circles of bad tactics and bad administrative arrangements which pin their forces on the defensive in ways which permit a relatively small Viet-Cong force (about one-tenth the size of the GVN regulars) to create conditions of frustration and terror certain to lead to a political crisis, if a positive turning point is not soon achieved.[39]

He followed these three conclusions with recommendations to help the South Vietnamese in their fight with the North. He wanted to avoid "further deterioration" to this situation in South Vietnam and guarantee the country's independence.

Taylor acknowledged that the tragedies in Vietnam were larger than the conflict with the Vietcong. The flood, which set the tone for the visit, needed to be dealt with, and he argued that this, as much as the Vietcong situation, was something that the United States needed to fix. Taylor said,

> In resisting the increasing aggressions of the Viet-Cong and in repairing the ravages of the Delta flood which, in combination threaten the lives of its citizens and the security of the country, the U.S. Government offer to join the [Government of Vietnam] in a massive joint effort as a part of a mobilization of [Government of Vietnam] resources to cope with both the Viet-Cong (VC) and the ravages of the flood.

He went on to say that U.S. personnel should take an active role in this process "going beyond the advisory role which they have observed in the past."[40] Indeed, this implied that the United States would be sending in ground troops as well as more supplies to assist in this endeavor. Taylor outlined the specifics in the subsequent section of the report.

The eight recommendations would help the government of South Vietnam in many ways. Taylor argued in the first three for "administrative personnel," "improvement of the military-political Intelligence system," and an assessment of "the social, political, intelligence, and military factors bearing on the prosecution of the counterinsurgency." In his fourth and fifth recommendation he said, "A joint effort will be made to free the Army for mobile, offensive operations" and assistance in "effecting surveillance and control over the coastal waters and inland waterways." Both of these recommendations involved U.S. forces and equipment. The greatest involvement, however, came with the seventh recommendation, which stated, "The U.S. Government will offer to introduce into South Vietnam a military Task Force to operate under U.S. control." Taylor outlined the Task Force's responsibility as being to

> a. Provide a U.S. military presence capable of raising national morale and of showing to Southeast Asia the seriousness of the U.S. intent to resist a Communist take-over; b. Conduct logistical operations in support of military and flood relief operations; c. Conduct such combat operations as are necessary for self-defense and for the security of the area in which they are stationed; d. Provide an emergency reserve to back up the Armed Forces of the GVN in the case of a heightened military crisis; e. Act as an advance party of such additional forces as may be introduced if CINCPAC or SEATO contingency plans are invoked.

This is clear evidence that Taylor expected the United States to take an active role in Vietnam. Lawrence Freedman writes, "If the Taylor-Rostow report had been intended to galvanize the American government into action, initially it seemed to have succeeded. Momentum was building up behind a step change in the character of the American contribution to the South's war effort."[41] McNamara had specific ideas for John Kennedy in an 8 November 1961 memo.

The "basic issue" of the Taylor report, according to McNamara, was whether the United States should "commit itself to the clear objective of preventing the fall of South Vietnam to Communism" and "support this commitment by necessary immediate military actions and preparations for possible later actions."[42] He stated in this memo that McNamara, Roswell Gilpatric (deputy secretary of Defense), and the Joint Chiefs all agreed, "The fall of South Vietnam to Communism would lead to the fairly rapid extension of Communist control, or complete accommodation to Communism, in the rest of mainland Southeast Asia and in Indonesia. The strategic implications worldwide, particularly in the Orient, would be extremely serious." McNamara wrote,

> The introduction of a U.S. force of the magnitude of an initial 8,000 men in a flood relief context will be of great help to Diem. However, it will not convince the other side (whether the shots are called from Moscow, Peiping, or Hanoi) that we mean business. Moreover, it probably will not tip the scales decisively. We would be almost certain to get increasingly mired down in an inconclusive struggle.[43]

In addition to this point he stated, "The other side can be convinced we mean business only if we accompany the initial force introduction by a clear commitment to the full objective stated above, accompanied by a warning through some channel to Hanoi that continued support of the Viet Cong will lead to punitive retaliation against North Vietnam."[44]

The main concern for many in the Kennedy White House was perception. It did not matter who was "calling the shots" as long as the rest of the world saw that the United States was standing firm against communism. The "punitive retaliation" that McNamara referred to in his memo would involve almost 8,000 American servicemen. In hindsight he has acknowledged that his advice to the president had been flawed. McNamara concluded, "We do not believe major units of U.S. forces should be introduced into South Vietnam unless we are willing to make an affirmative decision on the issue stated at the start of this memorandum." He also emphasized to JFK, "We are inclined to recommend that we do commit the U.S. to the clear objective of preventing the fall of South Vietnam to Communism and that we support this commitment by the necessary military actions." McNamara, however, would look at this situation again and offer different advice to the president.

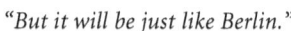

"But it will be just like Berlin."

McNamara wrote in his memoirs, "As soon as I sent the memo to the White House, I started worrying that we had been too hasty in our advice to the President." He went on to say that he had looked into Vietnam further and the more he looked, "the more the complexity of the situation and the uncertainties of our ability to deal with it by military means became apparent."[45] With this in mind, McNamara consulted with Dean Rusk, who felt similarly on this issue, and they sent a second joint memo to the president on 11 November 1961. According to McNamara, they concluded in that memo, "If there is a strong South Vietnamese effort, [U.S. Combat troops] may not be needed; if there is not such an effort, U.S. forces could not accomplish their mission in the midst of an apathetic or hostile population."[46] Walt Rostow knew that this second memo was going to Kennedy. Being one of the principle architects of the report, he had his own opinion on the situation in Vietnam.

Rostow started his memo of 11 November by saying, "I appreciate, of course, the difficulty of the decision and the reasons for reserving this move; but I should like to set out as clearly as I can the reasons for placing some minimal U.S. ground force in Viet Nam as part of the initial package." He went on to state, "This problem has been bedeviled by confusion about the various things a U.S. force could initially accomplish: from fighting in the paddies and jungles (which no one proposes), to guarding engineer units. To simplify the matter, I shall make the case for placing immediately a U.S. (or SEATO) force of (say) 5,000 men on the 17th Parallel." He said, "From the point of view of Southeast Asia, this is the gut issue and gut decision they are awaiting." Rostow holds nothing back as he claimed,

> Without the troop commitment, the Communists (who have been reading of our fears of white men in Asia and of Nehru's line on Ho Chi Minh) will believe they still have plenty of room for maneuver and to continue infiltration. An ambiguous signal to them is dangerous; and, whatever the rhetoric, they will interpret our policy by deeds, not words. The deeds proposed are, indeed, ambiguous.[47]

Rostow's hard line on communism was not a rarity in military circles. This is evidence of the pressure Kennedy faced to maintain a strong stance against communist aggression. These memos, however, demonstrate the division within the Kennedy White House over Vietnam and how to respond to the communist threat. This division was all the more apparent during the preceding Bay of Pigs debacle and the subsequent Cuban Missile Crisis. Indeed, it illuminated the complexities inherent in such a move of American forces to another part of the world.

Arthur Schlesinger wrote, "The Taylor-Rostow report was a careful and thoughtful document, and the president read it with interest.... He did not, however, like the proposal of a direct American military commitment." Kennedy said to Schlesinger in early November, "They want a force of American troops.... They say it is necessary to in order to restore confidence and maintain morale." Kennedy was suspicious of any military proposal that involved military force. This was largely the byproduct of the failed Bay of Pigs invasion, which would dictate the remainder of his presidency. Kennedy went on to say:

> But it will be just like Berlin. The troops will march in; the bands will play; the crowds will cheer; and in four days everyone will have forgotten. Then we will have to send in more troops. It's like taking a drink. The effect wears off and you have to take another.[48]

Schlesinger concluded that the war in Vietnam, according to Kennedy could only be won "so long as it was their war." Nevertheless Kennedy could not ignore the failure of the Diem regime in that region and he needed to act in an effort to bring stability back the region. On the heels of the Bay of Pigs and at the height of the Berlin crisis, Kennedy could not risk looking soft in the face of Soviet posturing. "The President," Schlesinger argued, "unquestionably felt that an American retreat in Asia might upset the whole world balance. In December he ordered the build up to begin."[49]

Kennedy's actions are evidence of his respect and confidence in Maxwell Taylor and Walt Rostow. He took into account McNamara and Rusk's perspective, but ultimately it was his decision to make — not theirs. The Vietnam issue gave rise to a new confidence in Kennedy. While he was not afraid to challenge the Joint Chiefs and look toward peace instead of war, he was also not afraid to use the military where he saw it was necessary. He saw the Vietnam conflict as another Cold War front that could not be ignored. Indeed, it was a battle that needed attention. However, Kennedy and the subsequent administration under Johnson ignored one key factor when making decisions in this area. The war belonged to the South Vietnamese, not the United States. Kennedy's advisors also argued that Diem needed strength in the region for the South Vietnamese to win against the North. The efforts of the United States, however, were aimed at strengthening U.S. forces in the region and not Diem's.

10

The Joint Chiefs of Staff

"We could sink a boatload of Cubans en route to Florida (real or simulated)."

Since the Second World War no other part of the United States government has been so entrenched in war-making than the Joint Chiefs of Staff. Like Washington's war council, this group has been presented with dangerous situations that more than likely meant Americans were going to lose their life. At times, as in the days of Washington, the success of the nation lay in question should they fail. Largely as a result of military strategy during World War II, their current chain of command was established with the National Security Act of 1947. They are a part of the largest military planning body for the United States in the National Security Council. By themselves they constitute the second largest military planning body.

The role of the Joint Chiefs is to advise the president and the secretary of defense. Since their inception, they have been at the helm of every major decision that brought America into global politics and economics. Their actions have led American forces into Korea, Vietnam, Latin America, the Persian Gulf, Iraq and Afghanistan, to name a few. The focus of this chapter is to ascertain the extent of influence that the Joint Chiefs of Staff had over the presidency of John F. Kennedy. Since this period of the Cold War was arguably the most dangerous, it is necessary that we examine the role the American military complex played in maintaining peace or pushing for war. This study has already examined the Bay of Pigs and its impact on presidential decision-making. The goal of this chapter is to see how Kennedy transformed his relationship with the Joint Chiefs to include the lessons he learned from the Bay of Pigs. Nuclear war was a reality in 1962. How did the Joint Chiefs plan to use that arsenal to defend American shores? Was their advice sound or did it resemble the Cold War posturing that nearly brought the Soviet Union and the United States to all-out nuclear war? Finally, how did John Kennedy use their advice?

General Lyman Lemnitzer had served the military with distinction and was a decorated World War II hero. In 1960, he was appointed chairman of the Joint Chiefs of Staff, and he presided over the Bay of Pigs and the 1961 Berlin

Crisis. In early 2007, before his death, Arthur Schlesinger told David Talbot, for his book *Brothers: The Hidden History of the Kennedy Years*, "After the Bay of Pigs, Kennedy had contempt for the Joint Chiefs." Schlesinger recalled:

> I remember going into his office in the spring of 1961, where he waved some cables at me from General Lyman Lemnitzer, chairman of the Joint Chiefs, who was then in Laos on an inspection tour. And Kennedy said, "If it hadn't been for the Bay of Pigs, I might have been impressed by this."[1]

Schlesinger argued that JFK's status as a war hero gave him latitude to contradict and question the Joint Chiefs. "He dismissed them as a bunch of old men. He thought Lemnitzer was a dope."[2] Kennedy's disdain was obvious to military circles when he brought in Maxwell Taylor as a military representative. H.R. McMaster argues, "Aware of Taylor's views [regarding flexible response] ... General Lemnitzer, had been less than enthusiastic about Taylor's appointment as military representative of the president."[3] McMaster went on to argue that Kennedy "was not only dissatisfied with the Joint Chief's advice but also frustrated by his inability to establish with them the kind of friendly rapport that he enjoyed with the rest of his staff and with many of his cabinet officials." Indeed, after the Bay of Pigs, Kennedy was looking for new methods to tackle the military issues that the nation faced at that dangerous time in the Cold War. Lemnitzer, however, presented an idea to Kennedy that some argue led to his subsequent removal from the chairman position.

Lemnitzer was obsessed with Cuba and wanted to use any method possible to attack the island and kill Castro. Lemnitzer and the Joint Chiefs of Staff presented a memo to Robert McNamara on 13 March 1962 giving methods in which they could create "legitimate provocations as the basis for U.S. military intervention in Cuba."[4] Some argue that this memo led JFK to replace Lemnitzer with Taylor in September 1962. The Joint Chiefs argued that a series of coordinated terrorist attacks by the CIA would be conducted and blamed on Castro. Lemnitzer wrote to McNamara, "A series of well coordinated incidents will be planned to take place in and around Guantanamo to give genuine appearance of being done by hostile Cuban forces." The Chiefs posed ideas ranging from "starting riots outside the base main gate" to "blow up ammunition inside the base; start fires" to "Sink ship near harbor entrance. Conduct funerals for mock-victims." The response from the United States would be "executing offensive operations to secure water and power supplies." Finally, the Joint Chiefs could initiate a "large scale military operation." They did not stop there.

Another recommendation involved a "Remember the Maine" incident, which could be contrived in different forms. "We could blow up a U.S. ship in Guantanamo Bay and blame Cuba.... We could develop a Communist Cuban terror campaign in the Miami area, in other Florida cities and even Washington." They went on to say,

> The terror campaign could be pointed at Cuban refugees seeking haven in the United States. We could sink a boatload of Cubans en route to Florida (real or simulated). We could foster attempts on lives of Cuban refugees in the United States even to extent of wounding in instances to be widely publicized.[5]

They even considered creating an incident "which will make it appear that Communist Cuban MIGs have destroyed a USAF aircraft over international waters in an unprovoked attack."[6] The proposals of these actions are evidence that the Joint Chiefs were desperate and wanted a military solution on Cuba. That the Joint Chiefs attempted to foster terrorist attacks on innocent people points to the clandestine nature of the military during this period. It also points to how the military believed that American exceptionalism gave them the right to engage in such actions. Indeed, the Chiefs' advice demonstrates their inability to see new world problems and apply imaginative solutions. Instead, they resorted to the same tactics that brought the CIA to new heights in the 1950s. The Kennedy White House was about looking outside the realm of this strategy.

Operation Northwoods, as it was called, was brought to the president's attention on 16 March 1962. According to David Talbot, there is no clear record of how McNamara reacted to this proposal. When he asked McNamara about it, his response that he had "zero recollection of it." McNamara was certain that he would have "rejected it" and characterized it as "stupid."[7] This proposal would prove to be the downfall for Lemnitzer in the Kennedy White House. Kennedy wanted to steer the military clear of any major covert action that could imply American involvement in Cuba. In that meeting on 16 March 1962, the president made this very clear to the Joint Chiefs as they outlined their proposal for Operation Mongoose. Northwoods was a part of Mongoose, and Lemnitzer wanted it known to Kennedy that this needed to be seen as a viable option.

According to Talbot, "Lemnitzer could not restrain himself. He jumped at that moment to run Operation Northwoods up the flagpole." While the general left out the majority of the gruesome details that were in the memo to McNamara, JFK was not happy, and he wanted to make it clear that this was not an option. He looked at Lemnizter and said "bluntly that we were not discussing the use of military force."[8] This man was leaning too hard on JFK. Nevertheless, the Kennedy White House was fostered on different principles than the Joint Chiefs, who were mostly reared with war in mind. Indeed, Kennedy wanted to pick his military advisors much like he did his cabinet. As he outlined in NSAM 55, he wanted the Joint Chiefs to serve as advisors, not policy makers. These men went beyond advising and tried to coerce the president into using military force through bully tactics.

Lemnitzer was sent to Europe to command NATO, succeeding General Norstad. Maxwell Taylor was appointed the next chair of the Joint Chiefs. He said in his memoirs, "In retrospect, I think that these changes were probably in the interest of both NATO and the president." Next to replacing Allen Dulles, this act was by far one of the most daring that Kennedy had made since coming to the White House. By replacing Lemnitzer, a man who wanted to see military action in Cuba, Kennedy sent a message to the Pentagon that this president was going to think beyond military action in foreign policy. Moreover, it cleared the way for a man he trusted in an important advisory position. Kennedy finally had his own chairman. It was very much the sweeping away of old ideas and ushering in solutions for the new world that Kennedy had argued in his inaugural. Indeed his choice of Taylor was another example of how he wanted people close to him whom he could trust. Taylor would play a pivotal role in the Cuban Missile Crisis. He already had the trust of Bobby Kennedy, which was tantamount to being in the inner circle at Hyannis Port. Maxwell Taylor was a man who would put his vision on the military affairs of the United States. He would, however, encounter resistance from others in his own staff.

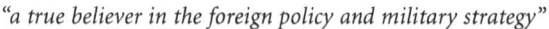

"a true believer in the foreign policy and military strategy"

As military representative Maxwell Taylor examined the issues with the Bay of Pigs and Southeast Asia. He established a rapport with President Kennedy and RFK through this role and looked to be the natural successor to Lemnitzer. Indeed, Taylor himself said, "Presidents have always wanted to pick their own Chiefs, a practice that has much to commend it."[9] The chairman of the Joint Chiefs was an issue with Kennedy. He never felt especially in tune with Lyman Lemnizter and wanted to establish a better system of cooperation with the Joint Chiefs of Staff. The tenuous position of the United States and its allies during the Cold War emphasized the need to have flexible thinking individuals in positions that could affect the outcome of an exchange with the Soviet Union. Lemnizter, as well as others in the military infrastructure, represented a different philosophy on how to approach the Soviets. Kennedy looked to other methods of response to the Soviet threat that did not involve the military — especially nuclear weapons.

Maxwell Taylor understood that the relationship between the Chiefs and the president was important. He argued, "With the opportunity to observe the problems of a President at closer range, I have come to understand the importance of an intimate, easy relationship, born of friendship and mutual regard, between the President and the Chiefs." He went on to emphasize the role of the chairman as "particularly important," as he worked closely with the president and the secretary of defense. "The Chairman should be a true believer in the foreign policy and military strategy of the administration which he serves."[10] In the case of Lyman Lemnitzer, this was not true. Lemnitzer was appointed by Eisenhower and served with the philosophy of massive retaliation in mind. Kennedy wanted to move away from this approach and embrace the notion of flexible response, which was a Taylor brainchild shunned by the Pentagon. Kennedy's insistence on looking to other methods of responding to Soviet aggression is what sets him apart from other presidents in the same scenario. He was committed to finding other alternatives to war. As a matter of fact, he clearly wanted to steer the administration away from the use of nuclear weapons altogether and usher in an initiative of nuclear disarmament. He could not, however, move in this direction without an ally in the Joint Chiefs. Maxwell Taylor was that person he needed to bridge the divide.

When Kennedy addressed West Point in June 1962, he commented to the graduating cadets in a commencement speech: "You will need to understand the importance of military power and also the limits of military power. ... Above all, you will have a responsibility to deter war as well as fight it."[11] This comment describes the kind of soldier Kennedy wanted to follow his lead in the world: not a warrior for war's sake, but a warrior for peace to avoid the devastating effects of war. Cold Warriors needed to understand the issues and ideology before they fought a war. It was what JFK's generation did in the Second World War. It is also something that has been lost since the Vietnam War.

Taylor remembered leaving the White House as a military representative and taking a new position in what he termed the "bear pit of the Pentagon."[12] One of the last things he did was "pay a farewell call on President Kennedy." Taylor said that there were many changes he had to embrace with his move to the Pentagon, but of all those changes the one which he would "feel most was the daily loss of association with [Kennedy]." Taylor went on to say that he "told him that I hoped to retain as much as possible of this closeness in my new assignment and was pleased when he invited me to telephone him directly whenever it seemed necessary."[13] This is an example of the relationship that these two men had when it came to matters of government. Additionally, this was the type of relationship that Kennedy wanted to foster in the White House. Most importantly, Taylor's memory of this event exemplified how he felt about JFK. That speaks to the depth of the relationship between these two men and emphasized the role this man played in presidential decision-making. Clearly, Kennedy would listen to this man over other bellicose military men.

On the day of his swearing in as chair of the Joint Chiefs, Taylor met with reporters who wanted to know if he was the "the man on horseback arriving to take over." He went from there to the "Tank," a term used in the Pentagon for the conference room where the Joint Chiefs met. "We had all known each other before so that there was little to say except to express our hope and intention to work effectively together in the cause of national security."[14] He said that the issues awaiting him as he took this office were "Cuba, Berlin, NATO, Southeast Asia, arms control, a nuclear test ban treaty, structure of the Armed Forces, and the defense budget." The admission of the issues which plagued the Joint Chiefs points to the complexity of the Cold War during Kennedy's time in the White House. At the forefront of those issues was Cuba.

"I don't want that man near me again."

In the Second World War, Curtis LeMay organized an attack on Tokyo that involved incendiary bombs destroying the city and its inhabitants. Robert McNamara was then a young officer under his command and very impressed with the outcome of the operation. LeMay said later, "We burned up nearly sixteen square miles of Tokyo." He went on to say, "There were more casualties than in any other military action in the history of the world."[15] The zealous approach to war was typical of LeMay. The character of Jack D. Ripper in "Dr. Strangelove" was crafted around his persona. John Kennedy did not work well with Curtis LeMay. LeMay's perspectives on war give insight into how some in military circles believed the Cold War should be fought. After all, if he was so far on the outer fringe, why didn't Kennedy remove him from his post? The general had the support of people who believed the United States needed to do more with the Cold War. LeMay is an example of the warmongering that Kennedy had to deal with when approaching foreign policy with peaceful measures instead of war.

David Talbot describes Curtis LeMay as a "cigar chomping, notoriously gung-ho Air Force Chief." He quotes LeMay as saying, "Everyone that came in with the Kennedy administration ... were the most egotistical people I ever saw in my life." LeMay went on to say, "They had no faith in the military; they had no respect for the military at all. They felt that the Harvard Business school method of solving problems would solve any problem in the world."[16] Indeed, Kennedy approached problems with new methods and thinking that were contrary to the Joint Chiefs. Kennedy saw world issues as complex and looked at them as layers rather than black-and-white situations that required action. Indeed, the relationships with the Soviet Union, European allies and Southeast Asia were very complex. These issues needed a fresh perspective. LeMay, on the other hand, saw the conflict with the Soviet Union as black and white. The best way to deal with the Soviet Union, according to LeMay, was through nuclear weapons. Clearly, Kennedy would not get his advice from the general.

LeMay was always at odds with the Kennedy administration. During David Talbot's interview with Robert McNamara, the former secretary of defense said,

> LeMay's view was very simple. He thought the West and, the United States in particular, was going to fight a nuclear war with the Soviet Union, and he was absolutely certain of that. Therefore he believed that we should fight it sooner rather than later, when we had greater advantage in nuclear power, and it would result in fewer casualties in the United States.[17]

Curtis LeMay was not the same general as Maxwell Taylor. Many in military circles saw a nuclear exchange in evitable. After all if history is the benchmark, humankind has been creating weapons, stockpiling them, and unleashing them on each other since the beginning of recorded history. From a military perspective, why would anyone think differently about nuclear weapons? Ironically, LeMay had command responsibility of both the Hiroshima and Nagasaki bombings. Ernest May and Philip Zelikow argue that his attitude toward those bombing was "dismissive. He rejected the notion," they wrote, "that they were somehow special, morally or otherwise." Furthermore, they quoted LeMay as saying, "The assumption seems to be that it is more wicked to kill people with a nuclear bomb, than to kill people by busting their heads with rocks."[18] Curtis LeMay was a principal player in the military planning of the Kennedy White House. He was in command of the Air Force, the forward unit that would be used in a nuclear exchange, and he could not distinguish between a rock and a nuclear warhead.

It has been argued that John Kennedy "despised" LeMay. On one of the many occasions that Kennedy walked away from the general he commented, "I don't want that man near me again." Roswell Gilpatric said once that Kennedy had "a kind of fit" if LeMay came up in conversation.[19] As a matter of fact, in the summer of 1961 Lemnitzer and LeMay wanted authorization to use nuclear weapons to defend Berlin or Southeast Asia. Kennedy walked out of the meeting saying, "These people are crazy." He looked into the cabinet room filled with military personnel and said to no one specifically, "I told you to keep them away from me."[20] Kennedy wanted to use diplomacy or any other method before he pulled the trigger on America's nuclear arsenal. That was not to say that Kennedy was afraid to use force, or that he was a coward, as some claimed.

Despite the fact that Kennedy could not stand LeMay, Schlesinger quotes Kennedy as saying to Hugh Sidey, "It's good to have men like Curtis LeMay ... commanding troops once you decide to go in." He went on to say, "But these men aren't the only ones you should listen to when you decide whether to go in or not. I like having LeMay head of the Air Force. Everybody knows how he feels. That's a good thing."[21] That said, when *Seven Days in May*, a film depicting the Pentagon overthrowing the president, debuted, Kennedy remarked, "It's possible. It could happen in this country, but the conditions would have to be just right."[22] The Joint Chiefs of Staff were Kennedy's principal military advisors. Kennedy needed them when he wanted to assert himself. Indeed, Kennedy explored military options in many instances throughout his presidency. However, he had the forbearance and leadership to look at other options before he put American soldiers in harm's way. LeMay was a warmonger, there was not doubt about that. By replacing Lemnitzer with Taylor, Kennedy was able to get one less zealot in the Joint Chiefs. In addition, Kennedy was able to analyze each situation very carefully. The Bay of Pigs taught him to question his military advisors. It also taught him to rely on the men he put in positions of leadership. Robert McNamara became one of those people. Without him, the Kennedy presidency would have been much different.

"the statutory obligation to serve as the principal military advisors"

James McPherson argued in *Tried by War: Abraham Lincoln as Commander in Chief* that although Lincoln never read Carl von Clausewitz's *On War*, "his actions were a consummate expression of Clausewitz's central argument: 'The political objective is the goal, war is a means of reaching it, and means can never be considered in isolation from their purpose.... Therefore it is clear that war should never be thought of as something autonomous but always as an instrument of policy.'" McPherson went on to say, "Some Professional army officers did in fact tend to think of war as 'something autonomous' and deplored the intrusion of politics into military matters." Lincoln, he argued, "could never ignore the political context in which decisions about military strategy were made." McPherson wrote, "In a highly politicized democratic society where the mobilization of a volunteer army was channeled through state governments, political considerations inevitably shaped the scope and timing of military strategy and even of operations."[23] While McPherson was speaking in terms of the Civil War and the threatened republic, John Kennedy had to deal with the European alliance and a threat of a nuclear exchange, not to mention that there would be American soldiers put in harm's way in the event of a war. Lincoln had to deal with matters of states, while Kennedy dealt with matters of nations. In Kennedy's time, the Joint Chiefs of Staff did not consider those aspects.

What the Joint Chiefs of Staff failed to recognize under Lemnitzer was that they were instruments of policy for the president of the United States. John Kennedy and his advisors whom he trusted considered every option before going to the final option — nuclear war. Article II Section 2 of the Constitution clearly states that the president "may require the Opinion, in writing, of the principal Officer in each of the executive Departments, upon any Subject relating to the Duties of their respective Offices." It does not state in the Constitution that the president must make that advice policy. Nor does it say anywhere that the president should defer to the military for advice on such matters. On the contrary, it outlined the president's role as Commander in Chief.

Robert McNamara was part of Kennedy's inner circle, which included Robert Kennedy and Maxwell Taylor. McNamara's role as secretary of defense gave him authority over the chiefs and their ability to wield the instrument of warfare. His uncanny relationship with Kennedy made him less likely to take the military advice at face value. Indeed, the Bay of Pigs fiasco affected him as much as it did Kennedy. Maxwell Taylor had a new outlook on the role that the Joint Chiefs would play in the administration, but he wanted to establish a few things with his new boss. He had McNamara in mind when he was thinking of taking the position. Taylor said that before he took the role as chairman of the Joint Chiefs, "I called on McNamara and asked him frankly about his attitude toward my proposed appointment. As he seemed genuinely pleased at the prospect, I proceeded to discuss specifics which worried me." Taylor went on to say that he "had got the impression that the so-called Whiz Kids, the young and bright civilian assistants who McNamara brought in, had been allowed to swamp the Joint Chiefs with requests for studies to the point that their effectiveness had become seriously impaired." Taylor and McNamara agreed that the chairman would have the final say on the demands placed on the Joint Chiefs, except when a written request came from McNamara.[24] Taylor was aware of the role McNamara played in checking the military. The constitution makes it clear the people would have control of the military through the Executive branch, which they elect.

Taylor brought the subject of the Whiz Kids up a second time, saying that there were rumors that this bunch had "taken over much of the advisory role of the Joint Chiefs of Staff." He went on to emphasize to McNamara that he

> recognized his right, indeed his duty, to seek advice from many quarters and that he could turn to whomever he liked.... The Joint Chiefs of Staff, however, had the statutory obligation to serve as the principal military advisors to him, the National Security Council, and the President, and [Taylor] asked his help to assure that they were always given full opportunity to discharge this obligation. They could not and did not expect that their advice would always be accepted but it should always be heard.[25]

McNamara was in full agreement with him, and Taylor said that in his tenure as chairman they always operated in "accordance with these understandings." Taylor, unlike his predecessor or others in the Joint Chiefs of Staff, recognized that the military was an instrument, not a policy maker. The president had the final say in matters that dealt with the military. Clearly, from the exchange, McNamara's influence was well known and even seen as intrusive. Taylor understood McNamara's role, but more importantly he was invested in Kennedy's success.

Robert McNamara and Maxwell Taylor were the cogs that kept the Joint Chiefs operating effectively throughout the Kennedy administration. Both men played prominent roles in the Cuban Missile Crisis and had a strong relationship with both John and Robert Kennedy. In order to truly affect policy it was clear that advisors must appeal to both Kennedys, as the elder Kennedy relied on his brother more often after the Bay of Pigs. McNamara and Taylor had that influence. Indeed, McNamara's relationship with Taylor was already much better than it was with Leminizter. David Talbot argues, "Like the president, McNamara regarded Lemnitzer with barely disguised contempt." A Lemnitzer aide said, "McNamara's arrogance was astonishing. He gave General Lemnitzer very short shrift and treated him like a school-boy. The general almost stood at attention when he came into the room. Everything was 'yes sir,' and 'no sir.'"[26] McNamara and Taylor worked well together. This camaraderie is exactly what Kennedy needed heading into October 1962.

Robert McNamara had a good deal of respect for Maxwell Taylor. As the chairman respected the defense secretary's duty to look for various forms of advice in an effort to counsel the president, McNamara held Taylor in high esteem. In his memoirs McNamara characterized Taylor as "scholarly" and "intellectual."[27] It went beyond that. They were frequently travel partners and clearly had a great deal of respect for each other's opinions on matters. There was collaboration between these two men that was lost with Lemnitzer. This relationship would prove crucial in the coming months for the president and the country.

The American Military Complex

Robert McNamara came into the administration ready and willing to make changes to the policy of massive retaliation and to infuse notions of flexible response. He found major problems with spending large amounts of money and resources on a military apparatus that would never be used. Indeed, if it were used the final result could well be the end of civilization. Logically, he felt that the Cold War could be fought with conventional warfare on smaller fronts. This "Whiz Kid" came into his position and utilized statistical analysis to determine what was effective. The Soviet Union and the United States had been posturing toward war since the end of the Second World War. McNamara and Kennedy saw nuclear weapons as a waste of resources. Within the first thirty days, Kennedy adjusted the budget to work on this deficiency of conventional forces. In addition, this need for conventional forces would help the president foster a counter–insurgency program. So much did Kennedy believe in this program that he had his brother overseeing its progress. This transition from massive retaliation to flexible response can be seen in both the counter–insurgency measures and the appointment of Maxwell Taylor as military representative.

Maxwell Taylor was a man whom Kennedy relied on to help him make military decisions. After the Bay of Pigs Kennedy was disenchanted with the Joint Chiefs and others in the military establishment. He wanted to look at problems with fresh ideas. Maxwell Taylor had helped Bobby Kennedy dissect the Bay of Pigs affair. This coalition fostered a lasting relationship not only with the attorney general, but also with John Kennedy. The president was always looking for someone who he trusted in making these military decisions. He had a tough time with the Joint Chiefs under Lemnitzer and struggled with the intelligence establishment. Taylor was someone JFK respected and whose points of view he could trust in a crisis situation. The result of the Bay of Pigs investigation brought Taylor into a distinguished group that helped Kennedy foster his Soviet policy. Taylor, McNamara, Robert Kennedy and Bundy were four people whom the president would listen very closely to in the cabinet room during those long days and nights in October 1962. Clearly Kennedy saw a gap in the CIA position, as Taylor was offered that first. Once he refused, Kennedy still kept him on to help him with the Joint Chiefs, creating a tense situation with then-chairman of the Joint Chiefs, Lyman Lemnitzer.

The emboldened Kennedy made decisions in 1962 that would redefine his presidency. The previous year, Kennedy had been careful not to make waves and took most advice from the Joint Chiefs. But the Bay of Pigs changed everything. Kennedy knew that his name would be in the history books in the end, and it was important that he made decisions. His forbearance on issues after the Bay of Pigs showed his tenacious approach to leadership as well as his willingness to search for peaceful measures when dealing with the Soviet Union. While both McNamara and Bundy took some issue with Taylor's role as military representative, they clearly got over it. The three of them would be the backbone of a foreign policy team that Kennedy trusted and relied on through important decisions for the next year. The decisions included the Cuban Missile Crisis and the Berlin trip, which is considered by many a turning point not as much for Kennedy as for the Cold War.

Beyond Berlin and Cuba, Southeast Asia became a battleground in the Cold War. The threat of communism from the forces of Ho Chi Minh in the North gave pause to the military advisors in Kennedy's administration. McNamara believed that Kennan's principles should be applied in this situation and every effort should be made to contain the communism in the North. However, McNamara also acknowledged that they knew very little about the movement in North Vietnam and that it was much more complicated than originally thought. However, military thinking had been addressing issues like Vietnam with the principles used to fight similar situations since the Second World War. While Ho Chi Minh's movement was linked to the Soviets, it also had strong elements of nationalism, which was a defining factor in that war. Taylor's trip to Saigon was Kennedy's attempt to get a perspective on this situation. While Taylor expected the United States to play a role in the developing issues in Vietnam, Kennedy was reluctant to provide a strong military presence in that region.

Kennedy's forbearance to hold off both Walt Rostow and Maxwell Taylor is an example of where his leadership style was moving. Toward the end of 1961, we see Kennedy with new confidence on military matters. The Bay of Pigs shaped this man into a different president who was suspicious of the military. Moreover, he consistently looked at every alternative to sending in troops. Kennedy concluded in 1961 that the Vietnamese could only win the war if they claimed it as theirs. With that in mind, however, he could not ignore the events in Vietnam. They were in a bad situation not only from pressure in the North, but also from an inept government that was still trying to find their voice. This issue would plague the South for the rest of the war.

The Joint Chiefs of Staff were the principle military advisors to the president. Kennedy, however, had a tenuous relationship with these men — particularly Lyman Lemnitzer and Curtis LeMay. Cuba was a constant thorn in these relationships, and the Joint Chiefs wanted to force Castro out of power. Operation Mongoose is an example of this effort. The Joint Chiefs implemented much of their plan for Cuba in 1962. Operation Northwoods, a radical operation that aimed at using a terror campaign in parts of Florida and blaming the Cubans, was one of the approaches to this situation that angered Kennedy.

In the wake of this proposal, Kennedy made a move to change his military advisors by moving Lemnitzer to command NATO and bringing in Maxwell Taylor as his chairman of the Joint Chiefs. Kennedy's move in this case proves that he was intent on getting the old approach to the Soviets out of the White House. While he was not unwilling to use military action, Kennedy wanted to embrace diplomatic and peaceful measures first. Lemnitzer saw the enemy and wanted to attack first and ask questions later. This transition was the last piece of the puzzle that Kennedy needed to address foreign policy concerns. By appointing Maxwell Taylor chairman, Kennedy gained allies in the military. Taylor, Bundy, McNamara, and Robert Kennedy were now all in positions to help Kennedy make important decisions when it came to the security of the United States. Bundy and McNamara had already been in these positions for the previous year. But since the Bay of Pigs, Robert Kennedy and Maxwell Taylor came into the decision-making circle and were a part of this cabinet of peace that Kennedy was trying to foster. Indeed, the four men were Kennedy's kitchen cabinet.

Part Six

Waiting for the Enemy to Blink: Perspectives on the Cuban Missile Crisis

11

Preparing for a Storm

"What other aggressive steps could be taken"

A lot has been written on the Cuban Missile Crisis. This study will not attempt to add to the plethora of material surrounding those thirteen days in October. It was clearly the most dangerous time in the history of the United States. The United States and the Soviet Union were on the brink of destroying not only themselves, but also the world. There are very few chapters in the history of the world as perilous as this one. With that in mind, this study examines the people who guided John Kennedy in decision-making. While there are studies that approach this subject with a broad brush, this one looks at the individuals who comprised Kennedy's kitchen cabinet: McGeorge Bundy, Robert McNamara, Robert Kennedy, Ted Sorenson and Maxwell Taylor. Each person played a significant role in this crisis. The examination of memoranda and primary source material that follow analyzes how these men made a difference in presidential decision-making. Since this was such a dangerous time, it is important that we examine how these men counseled the person who held the burden of choosing to use military force, which could potentially lead to a nuclear exchange.

Before he took over as chairman of the Joint Chiefs, Maxwell Taylor commented on Operation Mongoose in his role as military representative and as chair of the Special Group (Augmented). In a 17 August 1962 memo Taylor said that Phase One, the collecting of hard intelligence on Cuba, was complete but had varied results.

> The responsible agencies have worked vigorously to accomplish this objective, generating the largest intelligence effort directed at any Soviet Bloc country and attacking the target country broadly across the political, economic and psychological fronts. However, in spite of some progress in intelligence collection, the Special Group (Augmented) does not feel that the information obtained has been adequate to assess accurately the internal conditions. Nevertheless, from what we know we perceive no likelihood of an overthrow of the government by internal means and without the direct use of U.S. military force.[1]

11. Preparing for a Storm 159

Taylor wanted to take a more aggressive approach to the Cuban situation. He wrote that after looking at Operation Mongoose the Special Group (Augmented) came up with an alternative plan. Knowing that Kennedy did not want to commit military forces in the region, he said, "We have ruled out those which would commit us to deliberate military intervention although we recognize that an unanticipated revolt might at any time force a decision for or against the support of such a revolt by U.S. forces." He went on to say, "For the coming period, we favor a somewhat more aggressive program than the one carried on in Phase I, wherein we continue to press for intelligence, attempt to hurt the local regime as much as possible on the economic front and work further to discredit the regime locally and abroad."[2] General Lansdale approved of this measure and attached the guidelines to the memo. The fact that the group was leaning away from initiating a revolt or even the very aggressive Northwoods plan is evidence that Taylor was making headway on a different approach to the travails of the Cold War. That being said, the United States was watching a slow buildup of forces in Cuba.

There were consistent intelligence reports on the situation in Cuba. While there were most likely holes in some aspects of it, it seems clear that in this situation the CIA did an exemplary job of discovering a threat to the United States. On 21 August 1962, Robert McNamara, Robert Kennedy, Dean Rusk, Maxwell Taylor, McGeorge Bundy, Lyman Lemnitzer, Alexis Johnson and John McCone met in Rusk's office to discuss intelligence findings at the time. McCone argued that "the extent of the Soviet supply operations was much greater than had been reported [previously]." He went on to say that "there were indications that construction work was undertaken by Soviet personnel." There was agreement in the room that "the situation was critical." These men also discussed the "various courses of action open to [them] in case the Soviets place MRBM missiles on Cuban territory." Among those options were "discussion of blockades of Soviet and Bloc shipping into Cuba or alternatively a total blockade of Cuba."[3] The men in the room discussed this issue further. Chief among the men who debated these circumstances and possible U.S. response were those closest to Kennedy.

McGeorge Bundy, Robert McNamara, and Robert Kennedy had specific points to make in this meeting. First the memo, prepared by John McCone, stated, "Throughout these discussions, it was abundantly clear that in the minds of State, and Mr. Bundy, speaking for the White House, there is a very definite inter-relationship between Cuba and other trouble spots, such as Berlin." They said:

> It was felt that a blockade of Cuba would automatically bring about a blockade of Berlin; that drastic action on a missile site or other military installation of the Soviets in Cuba would bring about similar action by the Soviets with respect to our bases and numerous missile sites, particularly Turkey and southern Italy. Also, there is a reluctance, as previously, to the commitment of military forces because of the task

involved and also because of retaliatory actions of the Soviets elsewhere throughout the world.[4]

McNamara wanted to look at other options, having "strong feelings that we should take every possible aggressive action in the fields of intelligence, sabotage and guerrilla warfare, utilizing Cubans and do such other things as might be indicated to divide the Castro regime." McCone said those things could be done. Robert Kennedy "queried the meeting as to what other aggressive steps could be taken, questioning the feasibility of provoking an action against Guantanamo which would permit us to retaliate, or involving a third country in some way." Finally, Bundy believed, "All overt actions would involve serious consequences throughout the world and therefore our operations must be covert at this time, although we should expect a high degree of attribution."[5] There was no agreement on a course of action; however, they did agree that the president should review the situation and make a decision.

At the 23 August 1962 meeting with the president, the White House explored their options for the recent buildup in Cuba. The meeting started with McCone advising the president on the aforementioned meeting and intelligence. Kennedy wanted further analysis on "the number and type of Soviet and Oriental personnel imported into Cuba; quantity and type of equipment and its probable use." Most interesting in this meeting was that Kennedy asked if they "should make a statement in advance of our position, should the Soviets install missiles and alternative actions open to [them] in such event." Kennedy was already looking to solve this issue with "alternative" methods, which exemplified his commitment to wait before the administration used the military. In addition, JFK "raised question of what we could do against Soviet missile sites in Cuba. Could [they] take them out by air or would ground offensive be necessary or alternatively could they be destroyed by a substantial guerrilla effort." Finally, the president asked what the United States would do if these issues in Cuba prompted a Berlin crisis. After the meeting, McCone privately told Robert Kennedy, "Cuba was [the] most serious problem."[6] As a result of the meeting, Kennedy issued NSAM No. 181 to clarify their response to the military buildup in Cuba.

Kennedy directed that the situation be explored using a variety of methods. Kennedy wanted the people in the administration to explore the following: what action they should take to get the Jupiter missiles out of Turkey, what information should be made abroad regarding these actions, and whether there should be an "organized effort" to bring this information to the NATO allies. In addition the memo stated that several studies would be completed:

> An analysis should be prepared of the probable military, political and psychological impact of the establishment in Cuba of either surface-to-air missiles or surface-to-surface missiles which could reach the U.S...; A study should be made of the advantages and disadvantages of making a statement that the U.S. would not tolerate the establishment of military forces (missile or air, or both?) which might launch a nuclear

attack from Cuba against the U.S...; A study should be made of the various military alternatives which might be adopted in executing a decision to eliminate any installations in Cuba capable of launching nuclear attack on the U.S. What would be the pros and cons, for example, of pinpoint attack, general counter-force attack, and outright invasion; A study should be made of the advantages and disadvantages of action to liberate Cuba by blockade or invasion or other action beyond Mongoose B plus, in the context of an aggravated Berlin crisis.[7]

These measures were a strong indicator that Kennedy was comfortable with his advisory situation as well as his ability to analyze the situation in Cuba. They are direct and clear orders to explore every alternative in the region. Moreover, they demonstrate that when the president was confronted with the actual crisis, he was ready to act and trusted the people who were giving him advice, which was not the case with the Bay of Pigs.

Bundy made it clear in a 31 August memorandum to Kennedy how he thought the administration should approach the problem: "We probably should make it plain during next week that while the activities in Cuba are further evidence of Castro's sell-out to the Soviets, they do not pose any new active threat to us or to the hemisphere." In addition he argued that the administration "should distinguish these activities from any form of aggressive action, or any activity which could aggressively threaten us or any other American state. We should make it plain that we know exactly what is going on and will continue to be able to watch it from inside and outside Cuba." According to Bundy, "This is less a matter of the Monroe Doctrine than one of elemental national security." He went on to say, "It is not the same as missiles in Turkey. It is like the Soviet attitude toward the Black Sea or the Baltic states. In domestic politics, again, we need to draw this same sharp distinction between what is now going on and what we would not tolerate."[8] Bundy's assessment focused on national security. These acts by the Soviets gave the United States the right to defend itself from aggressive actions. Indeed, he felt it should be made plain to the Soviet Union that the United States knew of their actions and would respond accordingly if necessary. It was time for JFK to make that clear to the Soviets and the world.

"The Castro regime will not be allowed to export its aggressive purposes."

John Kennedy followed up the NSAM with a statement at a news conference on 4 September 1962. In this statement, issued by Pierre Salinger, Kennedy stated that Americans and friends in this hemisphere had been concerned over the "recent moves by the Soviet Union to bolster the military power of the Castro regime in Cuba." Kennedy's statement went on to emphasize that there was in fact intelligence linking the Soviets to the buildup of offensive weapons in

Cuba. However, he also stated that there were no organized combat forces or military bases provided by Russia or other Soviet bloc countries, "Were it to be otherwise, the gravest issues would arise."[9]

Kennedy had a lot to consider when giving this statement. "The Cuban question," he wrote, "must be considered as a part of the worldwide challenge posed by Communist threats to the peace. It must be dealt with as a part of that larger issue as well as in the context of the special relationships which have long characterized the inter–American system." Not only did JFK want to send a message to Europe, he also wanted Latin America to hear that he was unwilling to acquiesce to a Soviet presence in the region. "It continues to be the policy of the United States that the Castro regime will not be allowed to export its aggressive purposes by force or the threat of force. It will be prevented by whatever means may be necessary from taking action against any part of the Western Hemisphere."[10] Theodore Sorensen, the author of JFK's statement and special counsel to the president, met with the Soviet ambassador two days later to discuss these issues.

On 6 September 1962, Sorensen and Anatoly F. Dobrynin, Soviet ambassador, met at the Soviet embassy. Khrushchev had asked Dobrynin to covey the following to Sorensen: "Nothing will be undertaken before the American Congressional elections [on November 6] that would complicate the international situation or aggravate the tension in the relations between our two countries." In addition, Khrushchev was coming to speak at the United Nations, arguing that he did not "wish to become involved in our internal political affairs." Sorensen appreciated the message, but let the ambassador know that "recent Soviet actions in Cuba had already caused considerable political turmoil — that this was a far more difficult problem for the administration politically because of the frustrations felt by many Americans over the Cuban situation." He went on to say, "The Chairman's message therefore seemed both hollow and tardy." Dobrynin said that he had tried to reach Sorensen earlier, before the Cuban issue "became so hot." Sorensen did not let the ambassador or his boss off the hook. He said that Kennedy understood that Khrushchev would not want to give the president's political opponents any grounds for attack. JFK regarded the Cuban action "as something of a deliberate and personal affront." He went on to say, "Given the current situation in Berlin and elsewhere, the President could hardly be expected to take a very accommodating attitude in the months ahead." Dobrynin said he would report the conversation to the chairman, but left saying that the Soviets had "done nothing new or extraordinary in Cuba."[11] A Kennedy cabinet member would further the intrigue as he spoke with Khrushchev in his villa at Petsunda in the Soviet Union.

On 6 September 1962, Secretary of Interior Stewart Udall met with Khrushchev in Russia and discussed the situation with the United States and Cuba. "Now as to Cuba," the chairman said, "here is an area that could really lead to some unexpected consequences." Indeed, Khrushchev had discussed with Andrei Gromyko on 20 May 1962 at the Kremlin the possibility of sending nuclear missiles to Cuba.[12] This man knew exactly how dangerous the situation could become in that area of the world, because he was about to turn up the heat. He argued that when "Castro [came] to us for aid, we [gave] him what he need[ed] for defense." Khrushchev stressed, "But only for defense." He emphasized that if the United States ever attacked Cuba, it would change the situation. Khrushchev complained about some in Congress who were calling for an invasion of Cuba. In turn, the chairman made it clear to Udall, "If you attack Cuba, then we will attack one of the countries next to us where you have placed your bases." Udall responded by saying that Kennedy made the military decisions for the United States. At the time, Kennedy was getting a great deal of strife from members of Congress who believed that JFK needed to be more aggressive.

"These congressmen do not see with their eyes, but with their asses. All they can see is what is behind," Khrushchev said. This exchange is evidence that Khrushchev believed he was covert enough to deny any offensive weapons in the region to a member of Kennedy's cabinet, when in fact he had already discussed putting weapons in Cuba. While Udall made it clear that JFK was the commander in chief, Khrushchev continued to play a game with Udall, blaming some in Congress for the hostilities between the nations. He even went as far to say that the United States was no longer the strongest nation in the world. He said, "The President knows and understands this."[13] This furthers the notion that Khrushchev did not believe Kennedy to be as strong as other presidents. Khrushchev gave Udall misinformation in the hopes of leading Kennedy astray. He thought he was still dealing with the man he had met in Vienna. Kennedy, however, had matured since then and was ready for Khrushchev's game.

In an effort to appease hardliners in Congress and make his intentions clear, on 13 September 1962, Kennedy gave a press conference regarding the buildup in Cuba. "There has been a great deal of talk on the situation in Cuba in recent days both in the communist camp and in our own," Kennedy said, but insisted, "It was Mr. Castro and his supporters who were in trouble. In the last year his regime has been increasingly isolated from this hemisphere." Kennedy went on to state that Castro did not invoke the same fear as previously and had mismanaged the Cuban economic system. Moreover, Cuba's industries were stagnant and its agriculture declining. "His followers," Kennedy said, "are beginning to see that their revolution has been betrayed. So it is not surprising that in a frantic effort to bolster his regime he should try to arouse the Cuban people by charges of an imminent American invasion, and commit himself still further to a Soviet takeover in the hope of preventing his own collapse." Kennedy addressed the Republicans in Congress who were bent on invading Cuba, saying that it was "regrettable that loose talk about such action in this country might serve to give a thin color of legitimacy to the communist pretense that such a threat exists." However, JFK made it clear to the Soviets and the world, "If at any time the communist build up in Cuba were to endanger or interfere with our security in any way ... then this country will do whatever must be done to protect its own security and that of its allies."[14] JFK emphasized that the United States would do everything in its power to keep from getting to this point. He went on to say that the only people talking about the invasion were in Havana and Moscow. He also said that American people would, in light of the nuclear age, "keep both their nerve and their head." In answering questions from the press, Kennedy said that if offensive weapons were in Cuba it would change the "nature of the threat." He answered another question involving the Monroe Doctrine and its influence on these matters. Kennedy said, once again, that if Cuba possessed "a capacity to carry out offensive actions against the United States ... the United States would act."[15] Kennedy took Bundy's advice from the 31 August memo stressing national security over the Monroe Doctrine. These words, however, came back to haunt JFK when he was trying to preserve a peaceful solution to the crisis.

Khrushchev sent a message to Kennedy on 28 September 1962 because he was upset that Kennedy had called up 150,000 reservists on 7 September. Khrushchev claimed, "We haven't done anything that could give a pretext for that. We did not carry out any mobilization, and did not make any threats." Khrushchev went on to say, "I must tell you straightforwardly, Mr. President, that your statement with threats against Cuba is just an inconceivable step." Khrushchev said, "Under present circumstances, when there exist thermonuclear weapons, your request to the Congress for an authority to call up 150,000 reservists is not only a step making the atmosphere red-hot, it is already a dangerous sign that you want to pour oil in the flame, to extinguish that red-hot glow by mobilizing new military contingents."[16] Khrushchev went on to discuss how the Senate played a role in this crisis. "Very serious consequences," he wrote, "may have the resolution adopted by the U.S. Senate on the Cuban question. The contents of that resolution gives ground to draw a conclusion that the U.S. is evidently ready to assume responsibility for unleashing thermonuclear war."[17]

Khrushchev said that he hoped to "normalize" the relations of the two countries. He said that this could only happen if the United States recognized international law and did not interfere in the domestic affairs of other nations. "How can one, especially under these circumstances, consider it to be one's right to attack another country merely because its government and internal order are not to your liking?" Khrushchev said, "If we conduct such a policy, where this will lead to — to world war." On this topic he concluded, "The most reasonable and the only right policy in our time if we want to ensure peace and to live in peace is the policy of coexistence. And coexistence is first of all recognizing for every people the right to choose its socio-political system and non-interference by states into internal affairs of others."[18]

11. Preparing for a Storm

"It was a hell of a secret."

The Cuban Missile Crisis was not something that snuck up on the administration. Kennedy's advisors had been watching the island, looking for offensive weapons. Indeed, Kennedy's kitchen cabinet members had been communicating with one another on these issues. At this point, Kennedy had created the dream team he had envisioned from day one. There were varying opinions from people who he trusted. This was critical as he moved into the most dangerous time in the Cold War. On 2 October 1962, McNamara sent a memo to Maxwell Taylor regarding situations in Cuba. McNamara wrote that in a meeting on 1 October with the Joint Chiefs, "the question arose as to the contingencies under which military action against Cuba may be necessary and toward which our military planning should be oriented." Among those possible situations was tying Cuba to Berlin and "evidence that the Castro regime has permitted the positioning of bloc offensive weapon systems on Cuban soil or in Cuban harbors." McNamara asked Taylor for the Joint Chiefs views on three questions pertaining to these issues: "(a) The operational plans considered appropriate for each contingency. (b) The preparatory actions which should now and progressively in the future be undertaken to improve U.S. readiness to execute these plans. (c) The consequences of the actions on the availability of forces and on our logistics posture to deal with threats in other areas, i.e. Berlin, Southeast Asia, etc."[19] McNamara was acutely aware of the problems that Cuba might cause if they were able to get offensive weapons on the island. Moreover, he was already looking for options if they did.

On 4 October 1962, Robert Kennedy chaired a meeting on Operation Mongoose. In this meeting, Robert Kennedy said that he spoke with the president about Cuba and expressed how JFK was "dissatisfied with lack of action in the sabotage field." He went on to say that "nothing was moving forward, [and] commented that one effort attempted had failed, expressed general concern over developing situation." John McCone, CIA director, said that the first phase was intelligence gathering, which had been going well. Further, McCone said that there was hesitancy in some part of Washington regarding any further intervention.

Robert Kennedy took "sharp exception" to that comment, "stating the Special Group had not withheld approval on any specified actions to his knowledge, but to the contrary had urged and insisted upon action by the Lansdale operating organization."[20] Both sides eventually decided to move forward. This exchange is an example of how there was a lack of communication between the intelligence community and the White House. It is also another example of how Kennedy's advisors were pushing the envelope on Cuba. It is difficult to say John Kennedy was looking for peace all the time. He looked to secure the United

States, satisfy the European alliance, and hold off Khrushchev. Cuba was a pawn in this struggle. While the Kennedys wanted to avoid Operation Northwoods, they realized that military options might be necessary. Boosting conventional forces and moving to a flexible response are evidence of their attitude.

On 5 October 1962, it was John McCone that was concerned over action in Cuba. In a meeting with McGeorge Bundy, McCone expressed some issues with the progress on Cuba. McCone "felt it most probable that Soviet-Castro operations would end up with an established offensive capability in Cuba including MRBMs. McCone stated he thought this a probability rather than a mere possibility."[21] Bundy, however, "took issue stating that he felt the Soviets would not go that far, that he was satisfied that no offensive capability would be installed in Cuba because of its world-wide effects and therefore seemed relaxed over the fact that the Intelligence Community cannot produce hard information on this important subject." Perhaps it was Kennedy's reluctance to get too involved militarily, but in this case the kitchen cabinet was off mark. As a matter of fact, "McCone said that Bundy's viewpoint was reflected by many in the Intelligence Community, perhaps a majority, but he just did not agree and furthermore did not think the United States could afford to take such a risk."[22] This exchange demonstrates that while there was no clear consensus on how to handle Cuba, the people in the administration were talking about the problems and proposing solutions. Indeed, the fact they had proposed the scenario is evidence that they had a clear picture of Soviet intentions in the hemisphere.

The meeting continued with Bundy stating that "it was agreed that the whole Government policy with reference to Cuba must be resolved promptly as basic to further actions on our part." He went on to say that "we should either make a judgment that we would have to go in militarily (which seemed to him intolerable) or alternatively we would have to learn to live with Castro, and his Cuba and adjust our policies accordingly." McCone followed up with hopes of potential NSC meetings like Eisenhower. Bundy, however, "rejected the idea of regular NSC meetings stating that every President has to organize his Government as he desires and that the Eisenhower pattern was not necessarily adaptable to the Kennedy type of administration."[23] This was, of course, an issue Bundy had brought to JFK on the heels of the Bay of the Pigs. The two men, however, agreed to have occasional meetings in an effort to "review specific estimates or other intelligence situations." While they disagreed on their approach to Cuba, Bundy and McCone had common ground and learned to work with each other. Kennedy's reluctance to commit a full military force in the region did not mean he did not want progress on Cuba. He wanted the intelligence community to look at new methods in an effort to avoid a larger conflict.

On 11 October 1962, McCone met with Kennedy and Bundy. McCone had shown the president photos of crates, which presumably carried IL 28s, Soviet medium bombers, going to Cuba. Kennedy requested that "such information be withheld at least until after [the November congressional] elections as if the information got into the press, a new and more violent Cuban issue would be injected into the congressional campaign and this would seriously affect his independence of action." Indeed, Kennedy continued to battle varied opinions from both his allies abroad and Congress at home. When McCone told him that these photographs could not be restricted, Kennedy asked if the wording on them could "indicate a probability rather than an actuality." In the future he wanted such information "suppressed." When the conversation finished they determined the future protocol. Already expecting a backlash JFK said, "We'll have to do something drastic about Cuba."[24] Indeed it would not be long before he would have to take drastic measures to ensure peace.

Ironically, it was Bundy who would inform Kennedy of the MRBMs in Cuba. A 14 October 1962 U-2 reconnaissance flight discovered three MRBM sites in San Cristobal, in Pinar del Rio province. The following day a fourth one was found near the same region. In addition two IRBM sites were discovered at Guanajay. John McCone informed Bundy of these missiles on 15 October at 8:30 pm. Bundy wrote in a memo to Kennedy the following year, "This was very big news, and its validity would need to be demonstrated clearly to you and others before action could be taken. The blow-ups and other elements of such a presentation would not be ready before morning. I was satisfied that the word was going out quietly to those with an immediate need to know. The one obvious operational need was for more photography, and that was in hand." He went on to say, "It was a hell of a secret, and it must remain one until you had a chance to deal with it. Thus everything should go on as nearly normally as possible, in particular there should be no hastily summoned meeting Monday night." Finally, Bundy said, "I had heard that you were tired.... So I decided that a quiet evening and a night of sleep were the best preparation you could have in the light of what would face you in the next days. I would, I think, decide the same again unless you tell me different."[25]

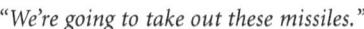

"We're going to take out these missiles."

Robert Kennedy wrote in his memoir of the crisis, *Thirteen Days*, that on 16 October 1962, President Kennedy had called him down to the Oval Office. "He said only that we were facing great trouble." The president told his brother of the U-2 spy planes and the photography that was discovered. Robert Kennedy characterized this crisis as a confrontation "which brought the world to the abyss of nuclear destruction and the end of mankind."[26] He said that when he and others met in the cabinet room not too long after this encounter with his brother, "the dominant feeling was stunned surprise. No one had expected or anticipated that the Russians would deploy surface-to-surface ballistic missiles in Cuba."[27] The administration moved into two distinct camps—hawks and doves. The hawks wanted to attack Cuba immediately, while the doves wanted to look for alternative measures. Arthur Schlesinger argues that Robert Kennedy was a dove from the start.[28] "I could not accept the idea that the United States would rain bombs on Cuba, killing thousands and thousands of civilians in a surprise attack." He went on to say, "Maybe the alternatives were not very palatable, but I simply did not see how we could accept that course of action for our country."[29] Robert Kennedy's perspective was important and would play a huge role in the events subsequent to the discovery of the missiles in Cuba.

On 16 October 1962, the EXCOMM (Executive Committee) of the National Security Council met to determine what course of action the administration would take with regard to these missiles in Cuba. Ted Sorensen wrote that at this first meeting,

> we were advised that the missiles themselves were not in place and no threat had yet been uttered by Khrushchev. Nonetheless the sudden secret initiation of those missile sites represented a dire warning, a warning that Kennedy immediately decided to take seriously and formulate a counter plan.[30]

Sorensen would also play an integral role as an advisor to Kennedy during this crisis. He was a dove and struggled with the idea that a wrong move on the part of either side could result in a nuclear exchange. Before the meeting began, John Kennedy's five-year-old daughter, Caroline, came running into a somber faced room of what Robert Kennedy called men who were "of the highest intelligence, industrious, courageous, and dedicated to their country's well being."[31] President Kennedy immediately smiled and asked Caroline if she had been eating candy. The five-year-old gave no reply. Kennedy smiled again and said, "Answer me. Yes, no or maybe." He put his arm around her shoulders and left the room. He returned without the same smile.[32]

President Kennedy was briefed on the missiles and the photographs at the 11:50 A.M. meeting on 16 October 1962. Robert McNamara was concerned that the missiles were ready for deployment against the United States. "This is important," he said, "as it relates to whether these, today, are ready to fire." He turned to Kennedy and said, "Mr. President. It seems almost impossible to me that they would be ready to fire with nuclear warheads on the site without even a fence around it." McNamara, like Robert Kennedy and Ted Sorenson, was a dove and favored a blockade from the beginning. The difference between him and those other two was that he had to work with the Joint Chiefs of Staff. Further, military options were an important avenue to consider. McNamara may have wanted to be a dove, but his role as secretary of defense made it impossible to fully embrace the concept. The national security of the United States was his charge, and he was not the type of person to shirk his duty.

Maxwell Taylor responded as a military man would and should respond in this situation, saying, "However, there is no feeling that they can't fire from this kind of field position very quickly, isn't that true?"[33] Taylor was hawkish in his approach to this situation. This is one of the more interesting facets of the relationship between Kennedy and the advisors on whom he depended in situations like this. Indeed, Kennedy himself wavered back and forth on a military strike on Cuba. The president never made it clear which camp he favored, which was an important move. If he needed to order the strikes, the military wanted a leader with conviction at the helm.

This was a difficult position for Kennedy on many levels. If Kennedy fully embraced the doves, then he would alienate the Joint Chiefs of Staff and other principal people in government. Conversely, any all-out embrace of a military strike would embolden those same military-thinking individuals and bring doubt to his commitment to peace. McNamara reasserted his reasoning on a strike by saying, "The question is one of readiness to fire, and this is highly critical in forming our plans. The time between today and the time when the readiness-to-fire capability is a very important thing."[34] McNamara knew that any military strike could result in the Cubans' launching nuclear weapons at the United States.

Dean Rusk played an interesting role on the first day of this crisis. While on other occasions the president was not keen on his advice, it was clear that Kennedy wanted to hear from everyone. His approach is a stark difference from the earlier crisis of the administration at the Bay of Pigs or even his performance at the Vienna summit. While the Berlin crisis in late 1961 gave him confidence in his decision-making skills, the kitchen cabinet that he had created since then gave him the infrastructure he needed to handle these situations.

"Mr. President, this is, of course, a very serious development. It's one that we, all of us, had not really believed the Soviets could carry this far," Rusk said. Rusk's advice was very lucid and to the point. He gave the president many alternatives to attack this problem. "Now, I do think we have to set in motion a chain of events that will eliminate this base. I don't think we can sit still," Rusk said, "The question becomes whether we do it by sudden, unannounced strike of some sort, or we build up the crisis to the point where the other side has to consider very seriously about giving in, or even the Cubans themselves take some, take some action on this." Very astutely, Rusk said, "The thing that I'm, of course, very conscious of is that there is no such thing, I think, as unilateral action by the United States."[35] The last comment spoke to U.S. commitment in Berlin. Rusk was already supposing that any act would affect the U.S.'s relationship with its European allies. Rusk leaned toward a strike, but was not steadfast on his feelings. He concluded his comments saying, "I think we'll be facing a situation that could well lead to general war."[36]

McNamara and Taylor played a big role in this meeting. Their willingness to share their perspectives on the situation in this venue is evidence of their comfort with Kennedy. McNamara said, "There are a number of unknowns in this situation I want to comment upon." McNamara was very vocal on his view that no decision should be made without the right information. "Before commenting on either the unknowns or outlining some military alternative, there are two propositions I would suggest that we ought to accept as foundations for our further thinking." First and foremost, McNamara wanted to be clear that any strikes they made against the island needed to take place before these missile sites became operational. Second, any air strike needed to be directed not only at the missile sites, but also the airfields and any hidden aircraft at the time. After the air strikes he said that they should be prepared for "an invasion, both by air and by sea." He was commenting on the military capabilities and the reasoning behind such action.

Taylor reasserted what McNamara outlined and also stated, "We must do a good job the first time we go in there, pushing 100 percent just as far, as closely as we can with our strike." He went on to advise the president, "The decision can be made as we're mobilizing, with the air strike, as to whether we invade or not. I think that's the hardest question militarily in the whole business, and one which we should look at very closely before we get our feet in that deep mud in Cuba."[37] Both McNamara and Taylor acknowledged that this action would have overarching effects. Moreover, it seemed that based on the best advice at this point, on the morning after discovery, the administration was moving toward invading Cuba. McNamara wanted to know the location of any nuclear warheads on the island, because he knew that they could potentially be used against the invasion.

There was some discussion of diplomacy at this first meeting. This was where the division between hawk and dove was apparent. Some in the group suggested that they reach out to the Organization of American States and NATO, but it was Bundy who said, "The amount of noise we would get from our allies, saying that they can live with MRBMs, why can't we? The division in the alliance. The certainty that the Germans would feel that we are jeopardizing Berlin because of our concern over Cuba." He went on to say that the "prospect of that pattern is not an appetizing one."[38] Bundy pointed out that the diplomacy of involving the allies was very complex, while Rusk had said earlier that the United States could not make any unilateral action because of their relationships with other nations. These were concerns that they would look at for the next twelve days in an effort to stave off war with a diplomatic rather than military solution. Kennedy asked some important questions in this situation that speak to his calm demeanor.

Kennedy turned to Taylor, whom he had just appointed chairman of the Joint Chiefs, and asked, "How effective can the take-out be, do they think?" Taylor replied, "It'll never be 100 percent, Mr. President, we know. We hope to take out the vast majority in the first strike, but this is not just one thing — one strike, one day." Taylor argued that action would consist of a "continuous air attack for whatever necessary, whenever we discover a target." When asked by Bundy if the U.S. could handle the "military problem" and keep the strikes to what caused the action instead of a continuous attack, Taylor responded by saying, "I would think we should be in a position to invade at any time, if we so desired."[39] Taylor promoted using conventional warfare, because that was the premise of flexible response. Instead of scaring the Soviets with a threat of nuclear war, the United States would use conventional forces. The room moved toward air strikes.

President Kennedy at this point summarized the potential options in this situation. There was the initial strike on just the three bases; the broader strike, according to McNamara, which included airfields and SAM sites; and also doing both of those while launching a blockade. In addition, he said, "The fourth question is the degree of consultation." He said that the British would most likely object and that the United States would "just have to decide to do it." Indeed the administration was gearing up for the war Rusk said could happen. Even Robert Kennedy questioned why they should wait seven days to introduce troops. He wanted to invade five days after the air strike. The attorney general argued, "The United States is going to be under such pressure by everybody not to do anything. And there's going to be pressure on the Russians to do something against us. If you could get it in, get it started so that there wasn't any turning back."[40] Since the majority of the people in the room looked on the invasion as the only way to approach this crisis, one must ask how they moved to the alternative solution of a blockade. Perhaps it was the initial shock guiding this dialogue. Indeed, the men in the room shouldered heavy burdens.

John F. Kennedy did not believe on this first day that the situation would result in a nuclear war. He said, "I would think you'd have to assume they'd be using iron bombs and not nuclear weapons. Because, obviously, why would the Soviets permit nuclear war to begin under that sort of half-assed way." McNamara agreed and said, "I think that's reasonable." As a matter of fact, Kennedy said, "I think we ought to, beginning right now, be preparing to. Because that's what we're going to do anyway. We're certainly going to do number one. We're going to take out these missiles." He went on to say that the real question involved what he referred to as "number two, which would be a general air strike. That we're not ready to say, but we should be in preparation for it. The third is the general invasion. At least we're going to number one. So it seems to be we don't have to wait very long. We ought to be making those preparations."[41]

The group decided to meet at 6:30 pm and broke up. The morning session had brought good ideas to the table, but the group could not move away from an air strike. Robert Kennedy, however, met with the Mongoose group and discussed options for speeding up the operation in Cuba.

*"I don't know quite what kind of world
we live in after we've struck Cuba."*

At 2:30 P.M. on 16 October, Robert Kennedy met with the Operation Mongoose committee. He "opened the meeting by expressing the 'general dissatisfaction of the President' with Operation Mongoose. He pointed out that the Operation had been under way for a year, that the results were discouraging, that there had been no acts of sabotage, and that even the one which had been attempted had failed twice." He then "spoke of the weekly meetings of top officials on this problem and again noted the small accomplishments despite the fact that Secretaries Rusk and McNamara, General Taylor, McGeorge Bundy, and he personally had all been charged by the President with finding a solution." Bobby Kennedy said that since this had been unsuccessful he was going to give Operation Mongoose more "personal attention."[42] He told the group that they were going to meet every day at 9:30 A.M. This meeting is an example of how Robert Kennedy was his brother's keeper on these matters. He tried to take some control of the situation that was beyond his scope. In this circumstance, he was attempting to affect the situation with the authority he had. Moreover, he had a great deal of influence in these situations, as people saw him as the direct representative for his brother. While he was very quiet in that first meeting with Kennedy's advisors, he was very vocal in this arena, which points to his desire to affect the outcome of the situation on his terms. The EXCOMM group, however, still had much to look at on that first day of the crisis.

At the 6:30 EXCOMM meeting there was little discussed that was new since the earlier meeting. It was clear, however, that the group had a much better grasp of the situation and had started to think of how their actions could change the world. Above all, this meeting illuminated Robert McNamara's position as a dove and his ability to see the situation from many aspects, which helped Kennedy in the long run. It was McNamara who pointed out to Kennedy that to take only the missiles out was not what the Joint Chiefs wanted to do. Taylor emphasized that by saying, "It would be a mistake to take this very narrow selective target because it invited reprisal attacks and may be detrimental."[43] McNamara, however, presented a new idea that he believed the group should consider.

Robert McNamara outlined three courses of action to the group. The first was a political and diplomatic route. He called this the "political course of action." In this scenario, the administration would approach Khrushchev, Castro and U.S. allies. He felt that it might lead to "no satisfactory result" and it killed any notion of a military attack. With that in mind, it left this course as something they could not explore. His second option, however, involved a blockade of Cuba. He argued that it was "in between the military course ... and the political course of action." This action, he said, "would involve [a] declaration of open surveillance: a statement that we would immediately impose a blockade against offensive weapons entering Cuba." In addition, he said that the United States "would be prepared to immediately attack the Soviet Union in the event that Cuba made any offensive move against this country." It was Bundy who asked, "Attack who?" McNamara responded coolly, "The Soviet Union."[44] McNamara went on to describe the third alternative, which was military action directed against Cuba. "It seems to me," he said, "almost certain that any one of these forms of direct military action will lead to a Soviet military response of some type, some place in the world." He went on to say, "It may well be worth the price. Perhaps we should pay that."[45] McNamara's cool, calculated assessment of U.S. options brought into focus Kennedy's choices for response. While there were complex layers within these solutions, his simplistic, acute description was what Kennedy needed to see the crisis clearly. JFK weighed these options very carefully, but it remained clear from these transcripts of the first day, that he was leaning toward a strike and calculating how he could lay the blame on Khrushchev.

Referring to Khrushchev, Kennedy said, "But he's initiated the danger, really, hasn't he? He's the one that's playing at God, not us."[46] The group wanted to find a way out of this situation, and the momentum continued to involve military action. Lines were being drawn. Bundy asked, "What is the strategic impact on the position of the United States of MRBMs in Cuba? How gravely does this change the strategic balance?" McNamara responded that the Joint Chiefs said "substantially." His own view was "Not at all."[47] Of course the Joint Chiefs of Staff would see it as substantial change. In the wake of the Bay of Pigs, a "soft" response to Soviet threats in Berlin, and weak reaction in Vietnam, the Chiefs wanted those missiles away from American soil. Each situation that the administration had endured played a role for those men in the cabinet room — including JFK. Principal advisors to the president disagreed on their approach to a situation that would have long-lasting effects on the nation and the world. Taylor responded to this by saying, "I think it was cold-blooded from their point of view, Mr. President." He went on, "You're quite right in saying that these are just a few more missiles targeted on the United States. However, they can become a very, rather important, adjunct and reinforcement to the strike capability of the Soviet Union." He finished by saying, "We have no idea how far they will go." Kennedy agreed. He said that if they did not attack these bases because it was "too much of gamble," then they would build up those bases over time and "squeeze us on Berlin."[48]

Bundy said, once again, "If this thing goes on, an attack on Cuba becomes general war." The figures presented at the meeting pointed toward a larger conflict. Indeed, Taylor said that the invasion called for a quarter of a million troops to take the island. Kennedy made it clear that nuclear war was something that could happen despite whether nuclear missiles were in Cuba or not.

"What difference does it make?" he said, "They've got enough to blow us up now anyway." JFK said, "After all, this is a political struggle as much as military."[49] While Kennedy leaned toward taking only the missiles out of the equation, McNamara posed to the group things that they were not considering. McNamara said, "I don't believe we have considered the consequences of any of these actions satisfactorily. And because we haven't considered the consequences, I'm not sure we're taking all the action we ought to take now to minimize those."[50] McNamara, once again, was cautious about committing his position to a military strike. History is wrought with situations where leaders jump into battle, only to find out there other aspects worth considering.

McNamara's point, at this juncture, was one that many in the room considered for the rest of the crisis—including JFK. While President Kennedy did not express it in this meeting, subsequent actions are evidence that he considered McNamara's statement that "I don't know quite what kind of world we live in after we've struck Cuba, and we've started it." This statement implies that the true blame for all-out nuclear war was the United States. It invoked Lincoln's phrase in the second inaugural that while one side would make war, the other side would accept war. The responsibility of the men in that room was to do anything possible not to accept war in the nuclear age. From then on in the meeting, contrary to the Joint Chief's recommendation, Kennedy looked to focus on a limited strike in an effort to keep it from becoming a global struggle. As a matter of fact he said to Taylor, "Let's not let the Chiefs knock us out of this one."[51] McNamara went on to assert his point of view that the consequences for this attack should be worked out on paper. In fact, Bundy said, "Our [principal] problem is to try and imaginatively to think what the world would be like if we do this, and what it will be like if we don't, if we fail in what we do."[52] Where the group had been leaning toward a military strike, McNamara's point opened up new dialogue and explored alternative options available.

The EXCOMM looked at various options to diffuse the situation, including sending RFK as an envoy to Dobrynin, extrapolating what would happen if the Soviets put offensive weapons in Cuba, and looking at the calendar to ascertain if the Soviets had made this move in conjunction with JFK's 4 September and 13 September statements. It was when Kennedy left, however, that the notion of a blockade was explored once more by McNamara with Bundy. "It seems to me that there are major alternatives here that I don't think we discussed fully enough today." McNamara went on to mention the "political approach" to Bundy once again and said, "Once you start this ... approach, I don't think you're gonna have any opportunity for a military operation." Clearly, the defense secretary was leaning toward a non-military solution. He said that he had phrased this idea "improperly" before and that they needed to consider the "results that we're causing for mankind."[53] McNamara then mentioned a blockade as something to consider. He said to Bundy that they could "blockade offensive weapons." When asked how to accomplish this feat, he replied that "we search every ship." McNamara went on to say "in any case that's an alternative. I'd liked to see it expressed and discussed."[54]

Kennedy's advisors were somewhat surprised by the developments in Cuba. With the exception of McCone, none believed that the Soviets would make such an aggressive move against the United States. On several occasions, during the discussion on that first day, Kennedy wondered why the Soviets would do such a thing. While McNamara initially looked to the military option, it was clear that by the end of the first day he was thinking of the ramifications of such a truculent act. Indeed, his questions may have given others in the cabinet room pause, forcing them to choose a side in this confrontation with the Soviets. Kennedy, however, would not only use the men in that room.

12

Brinkmanship in the Kennedy White House

"I think it's a hell of a burden to carry."

The discourse that ensued over the next twelve days was unparalleled in United States history. The men who advised Kennedy were among the most intelligent of the time. This chapter will look at the major turning points in that dialogue, not in an effort to assess the crisis but to ascertain the impact these men had on Kennedy's decisions. There are many studies that dissect the many facets of this period in history. However, a close examination at the transcripts and memorandum from important moments may give insight into who had the largest impact on Kennedy. Bundy and McNamara were men who helped with the Bay of Pigs. In the end, both men had different views on which course the United States should take in this Cuban crisis. These were men whom the president trusted. The administration seemed poised to strike Cuba. With that in mind, what led Kennedy to favor a blockade?

At the military level, Maxwell Taylor was someone Kennedy brought in specifically because he did not trust the Joint Chiefs of Staff after the Bay of Pigs. The chairman of the Joint Chiefs favored an air strike and invasion to get the missiles out of Cuba. Indeed, the Joint Chiefs did not waver on this. What gave JFK the forbearance to defy such authoritative military figures? Moreover, he seemingly trusted Taylor. Why did he choose to ignore that advice?

Kennedy operated on his own terms throughout the Cuban Missile Crisis. While many offered advice, he chose the path America would embrace. It was a very presidential moment for a man who stumbled his first year in office. Robert Kennedy, on the other hand, favored a blockade, and he had a great deal of influence over his brother. Indeed, RFK did not go very far from his brother during this ordeal. After all, the elder Kennedy had wanted his brother by his side since the Bay of Pigs. Neither Taylor nor RFK were a factor in decisions that led to failure at the Bay of Pigs, unlike Bundy and McNamara.

12. Brinkmanship in the Kennedy White House

McGeorge Bundy, Robert McNamara, Maxwell Taylor and Bobby Kennedy were among the few that enjoyed implicit trust and respect from JFK, yet they were divided down the middle. Since there was no prevailing attitude among Kennedy's kitchen cabinet, the prospect of nuclear war guided Kennedy's decisions. Of all the dilemmas and suppositions none gave JFK more pause than the prospect of a nuclear exchange, which he called a "prime failure." With that in mind, after the first day, when people "cooled down" somewhat, reality set in. The term "general war" had been referred to several times. In 1962 general war meant a nuclear exchange, which would kill millions of people around the world. This act would pale in comparison to those lost in World War II. Kennedy was obsessed with miscalculation causing a nuclear exchange. He had come close the previous year in Berlin and did not want to tempt fate twice in his presidency.

John Kennedy looked at every possible alternative before he came to the conclusion that a blockade was the way to approach this problem with the Soviets. By Thursday 18 October, the Joint Chiefs of Staff unanimously favored air strikes followed by an invasion of Cuba. The U-2 spy photography found more missile sites, which, combined with the presence of offensive weapons in Cuba, elevated such a truculent stance by the Joint Chiefs. While Bundy was still wavering at this point, the next day he would move into the hawk camp, presenting an outline of air strike and invasion. They would refer to it as the "Bundy plan."

While McNamara went along with the Chiefs to a degree, he had one issue that he was not willing to risk. At this meeting, McNamara said, "All of these cases are premised on the assumption there are no operational nuclear weapons there." He went on, "If there's any possibility of that I would strongly recommend that these plans be modified substantially." McNamara acknowledged, in a break with his military colleagues, that his "personal views are not shared with the Chiefs."[1] The defense secretary said, in his opinion, this was not a military problem; "it's a political problem. It's a problem of holding the alliance together. It's a problem of properly conditioning Khrushchev for our future moves." All of these issues, combined with the "domestic public," McNamara argued, required "action that, in my opinion, the shift in military balance does not require."[2]

Taylor refined his position, making it clear that "a totally diplomatic action … will not stop a threat of this kind from building up."[3] Llewellyn Thompson had made it to this meeting. As discussed earlier, he had knowledge of Khrushchev like none in the room. McNamara argued in the documentary *Fog of War* that empathy should be a factor when looking at foreign affairs. His contention was that among the men in the room, Thompson was able to empathize with Khrushchev, which made his advice crucial. When asked by Bundy what Thompson preferred, his reply was blockade. "I think it's very highly doubtful," Thompson said, "that the Russians would resist a blockade against military weapons, particularly offensive ones, if that was the way we pitched it before the world." RFK at this point had been leaning toward a blockade and said that the president had not heard this idea. JFK commented that this plan "would not take these missiles that they now have out, or the planes that they now have out."[4] In addition to those aspects, Thompson confirmed that the Soviets would move on Berlin. With all the talk on this second day, the one thing that pushed Kennedy to favor blockade was a discussion of general war and its ramifications.

Bundy and McNamara had differing views on a solution. McNamara posed to the group that if there was a strike without "preliminary discussions" with Khrushchev regarding potential Soviet casualties, there might be problems. McNamara said, "We're using napalm, 750-pound bombs. This is an extensive strike we're talking about." Bundy replied, "Well, I hope it is." Dismissing the comment, McNamara said, "I think we must assume we'll kill several hundred Soviet citizens. Having killed ... Soviet citizens, what kind of response does Khrushchev have open to him?" He said, "It seems to me that it must be a strong response, and I think we should expect that. And, therefore, the question really is: Are we willing to pay some kind of rather substantial price to eliminate these missiles? I think the price is going to be too high."[5] The group discussed the possibility of losing Berlin as a price to pay to have these missiles removed, which had implications not only to American prestige in the world, but also to the relationship the nation had with its allies. McNamara asked what they meant by taking Berlin. It was clear that if United States troops were "overrun" by the Soviets in Berlin, it would lead to, according to Taylor, "general war." JFK clarified by saying, "You mean a nuclear exchange?"[6] There was agreement throughout the room. Nuclear war permeated JFK's thoughts. Indeed, this question to clarify the comment points to JFK's lucidity and concern about a nuclear exchange.

JFK wanted to avoid any nuclear exchange. Upon hearing the men in the room discuss a nuclear exchange in such an obtuse manner, he asked more questions regarding the alliance and other alternative options available. He was afraid that the alliance with NATO and other European countries would "disintegrate." Kennedy was under pressure from allied nations to maintain a presence in Berlin. If he made any decisions to surrender that ground, then it might hurt an already strained alliance. "Now the question really is," Kennedy said, "what action we take which lessens the chances of a nuclear exchange, which obviously is the prime failure — that's obvious to us — and at the same time, maintain some degree of solidarity with our allies." A moment later, JFK asked, "Now, to declare a blockade on Cuba, do we have to declare war on Cuba?" There was confusion in the room to his question, and Kennedy spoke above the men. "I think we shouldn't assume we have to declare war." He went on to say, "We do the message to Khrushchev and tell him that if work continues, et cetera, et cetera. At the same time, launch the blockade. If the work still continues, that we go in and take them out." There was more discussion on the prospect of strike versus blockade, but it remained clear that Kennedy wanted to know more about a blockade. Robert Kennedy asked, "What kind of country are we," if they went ahead with a strike. He said, "Now in the interest of time, we do that to a small country. I think it's a hell of burden to carry."[7]

In the end, there still was not a consensus for blockade or air strike. Thus far, JFK had heard from McNamara, Thompson, Bundy, Taylor and his brother, and they all had differing opinions on a solution. Later that day, Kennedy met with Dean Acheson, who agreed with the Chiefs to strike the missile sites and follow up with an invasion. That night he met with the Soviet foreign minister, Andrei Gromyko. Kennedy brought up Cuba early in the conversation, but the ambassador insisted that any assistance to Cuba had been for defensive reasons.

According to minutes that were kept of the meeting, "The President said that in order to be clear on this Cuban problem he wanted to state the following: The U.S. had no intention of invading Cuba. Introduction last July of intensive armaments had complicated the situation and created grave danger." He went on to read his press statements from 4 September. "He noted that the Attorney General had discussed the Cuban situation with Ambassador Dobrynin so that the latter must be aware of what it was. The President again recalled his Indianapolis speech of last Sunday and said that we were basing our present attitude on facts as they had been described by Mr. Gromyko; our presumption was that the armaments supplied by USSR were defensive."[8] It was after this meeting that former secretary of defense Robert Lovett was called in to the Oval Office.

Kennedy told Lovett he had never been told as many "barefaced lies" as in that short period of time. "All during his denial that the Russians had any missiles or weapons, or anything else in Cuba," Kennedy said, "I had the low level pictures in the center drawer of my desk, and it was an enormous temptation to show them to him."[9] Sorensen wrote that Kennedy wanted to meet at 9:00 that night to discuss this meeting with Gromyko. Sorenson contends, "The blockade course was now advocated by a majority."[10] Indeed, that night George Ball claimed, "It was at that meeting [with advisors after the Gromyko meeting] that the President sort of ... tentatively indicated: 'Let's think in terms of a blockade that I can announce next Monday.'"[11] Kennedy himself said in a recorded memo that night, "The consensus was that we should go ahead with the blockade beginning on Sunday night." He went on to say, "I was most anxious that we not have to announce a state of war existing, because it would obviously be bad to have the word go out that we were having a war rather than it was a limited blockade for a limited purpose."[12] Kennedy had clearly made up his mind. His next step was to present his decision to both the American people and the American military complex.

"I think we ought to think of why the Russians did this."

Despite the fact that this was a military problem, the only member of the Joint Chiefs present at these discussions was Maxwell Taylor, a trusted Kennedy advisor. On 19 October at 9:45, Kennedy briefed the Joint Chiefs of Staff on his decision to employ a blockade. Taylor was for an air strike, followed by an invasion. "I think the benefit this morning, Mr. President, would be for you to hear the other Chiefs' comments, either on our basic, what I call the military plan, or how they would see the blockade plan." JFK summarized what he saw as the major issues up to that point. "First," he said, "I think we ought to think of why the Russians did this." He went on, "If we attack Cuban missiles, or Cuba, in any way, it gives them a clear line to take Berlin.... We would be regarded as the trigger-happy Americans who lost Berlin. We would have no support among our allies.... They don't give a damn about Cuba. But they do care about Berlin and about their security." In addition to that, Kennedy said, "There's bound to be reprisal from the Soviet Union, there always is—[of] their just going in and taking Berlin by force. Which leaves me only one alternative, which is to fire nuclear weapons—which is a hell of an alternative—and begin a nuclear exchange with all this happening." Finally Kennedy said,

> So I don't think we've got any satisfactory alternatives. Whether we balance off that, our problem is not merely Cuba but it is also Berlin. And when we recognize the importance of Berlin to Europe, and recognize the importance of our allies to us, that's what made this thing to be dilemma for three days. Otherwise, our answer would be quite easy.[13]

The situation was multilayered in that if attacking Cuba meant a reciprocal attack on Berlin, then it meant further action from the United States. In this event, the only alternative planned was a nuclear exchange—leading to a possible World War III. For some, however, it was not that complicated.

Curtis LeMay reacted to Kennedy's comments by saying, "I'd emphasize, a little strongly perhaps, that we don't have any choice except direct military action." He went on to say, "As for the Berlin situation, I don't share your view that if we knock off Cuba, they're going to knock off Berlin." Kennedy asked what LeMay believed their reply would be. "I don't think they're going to make any reply if we tell them that the Berlin situation is just like it's always been." LeMay concluded: "So I see no other solution. This blockade and political action, I see leading into war. I don't see any other solution. It will lead right into war. This is almost as bad as the appeasement at Munich."[14] Kennedy must have sat there holding his temper, as this was an obvious comment against his father, who was a proponent of the Munich decision before World War II. The rest of the chiefs followed LeMay with similar arguments, though not as abrasive.

12. Brinkmanship in the Kennedy White House 181

Kennedy asked questions and tried to empathize with the Chiefs' perspectives. LeMay, however, finally said, "I think that a blockade, and political talk, would be considered by a lot of our friends and neutrals as being a pretty weak response to this. And I'm sure a lot of our own citizens would feel that way, too. You're in a pretty bad fix Mr. President." Kennedy replied, "What did you say?" "You're in a pretty bad fix," LeMay repeated. Kennedy retorted, "Well, you're in there with me. Personally."[15] There was strained laughter to this comment, but the fact remained that the president was, once again, at odds with his principal military advisors. JFK finally said, "I appreciate your views. These are unsatisfactory alternatives. The obvious argument for blockade was [that] what we want to do is to avoid, if we can, nuclear war by escalation or imbalance." He added, "[Gromyko and those] people last night were so remote from reality there's no telling what the response." The meeting broke up and Kennedy left the room. General Shoup, of the Marines, said to LeMay, "You pulled the rug right our from under him. Goddamn." LeMay laughed, and looking for more, said, "Jesus Christ. What the hell do you mean?" Shoup said that Kennedy finally had gotten around the word "escalation." He went on, "That's the only goddamn thing that's in the whole trick. Go in and out and every goddamn one. Escalation, that's it. Somebody's got to keep them from doing the goddamn thing piecemeal. That's our problem." The Joint Chiefs wanted to move on this issue and attack Cuba. Moreover, they wanted to hit everything. Shoup said that they should "do the son of a bitch and do it right, and quit friggin' around."[16]

During planning for Operation Mongoose, the president and Robert Kennedy reinforced to the military the idea that they did not want any overt acts. The military's proposal for Operation Northwoods was an example of how fixated they were on removing Castro. Kennedy continued with a calculated approach. He assessed each issue as it was presented and did not jump into a decision. The Joint Chiefs' ardent position did not sway Kennedy. The lines were being drawn and, although they would change frequently throughout the crisis, the next night, the EXCOMM members made some decisions as to where they stood.

On the afternoon of 20 October, Kennedy met with most of the principal advisors in an NSC meeting. According to the notes from the meeting, the group identified more MRBM sites as well as two IRBM sites. While they could not confirm the presence of nuclear warheads at this point, they were able to ascertain that eight MRBMs could be fired on that day. The flights had covered 95 percent of the islands, and it was believed that they knew of all the missiles.[17] As the meeting progressed McNamara informed the president that there "were differences among his advisors which had resulted in the drafting of alternative courses of action." The minutes of the 505th National Security Council gives a description of how Kennedy's advisors chose their positions. "Secretary McNamara, for one, described his view as the 'blockade route.' This route was aimed at preventing any addition to the strategic missiles already deployed to Cuba and at eventually eliminating these missiles. He said to do this we should institute a blockade of Cuba and be prepared to take armed action in specified instances."[18] Kennedy was given a paper by Ted Sorensen describing the "blockade route" to read. This alternative had a military flair to it:

> He said we would have to be prepared to accept the withdrawal of United States strategic missiles from Turkey and Italy and possibly agreement to limit our use of Guantanamo to a specified limited time. He added that we could obtain the removal of the missiles from Cuba only if we were prepared to offer something in return during negotiations. He opposed as too risky the suggestion that we should issue an ultimatum to the effect that we would order an air attack on Cuba if the missiles were not removed. He said he was prepared to tell Khrushchev we consider the missiles in Cuba as Soviet missiles and that if they were used against us, we would retaliate by launching missiles against the USSR.[19]

Clearly, this was a scenario that Kennedy did not want, but the military people in the group needed to see evidence in writing that JFK would consider military action in addition to the blockade. It was a ploy, by McNamara and others, to get a peaceful and diplomatic start to the solution.

The disadvantages, according to McNamara, were that this route would take a long time to eliminate the missiles, would result in political trouble in the United States, and would cause the world position of the United States to appear weak. The advantages, however, were the following:

> It would cause us the least trouble with our allies; 2. It avoids any surprise air attack on Cuba, which is contrary to our tradition; 3. It is the only military course of action compatible with our position as a leader of the free world; 4. It avoids a sudden military move which might provoke a response from the USSR which could result in escalating actions leading to general war.[20]

General Taylor did not share McNamara's perspective. He "reported that the Joint Chiefs of Staff favor an air strike on Tuesday when United States forces could be in a state of readiness. He said he did not share Secretary McNamara's fear that if we used nuclear weapons in Cuba, nuclear weapons would be used against us." While the group went back and forth on this, JFK worried about the presence of these missiles in Cuba. Rusk and Ball believed that a blockade would hurt Cuba's ability to get these missiles ready. Robert Kennedy agreed with Taylor that it might be the last chance to get rid of the both the missiles and Castro. Sorensen disagreed with the attorney general. There were no tape recordings of this meeting, only minutes. This exchange of ideas was the essence of decision-making in this crisis.

Bundy handed the president a copy of the air strike option, then called the "Bundy plan." Bundy, the Joint Chiefs, Secretary Dillon and CIA director John McCone supported this plan. McNamara argued that this scenario did not guarantee getting all the missiles. He explained, "Those missiles not destroyed could be fired from mobile launchers not destroyed." There was a discussion about the planes in Cuba, but JFK wanted to be sure that there was a distinction made: He "stated flatly that the Soviet planes in Cuba did not concern him particularly. He said we must be prepared to live with the Soviet threat as represented by Soviet bombers." He went on to clarify that "the existence of strategic missiles in Cuba had an entirely different impact throughout Latin America. In his view the existence of fifty planes in Cuba did not affect the balance of power, but the missiles already in Cuba were an entirely different matter."[21] Robert Kennedy had said very little at this point, but would eventually offer his thoughts.

According to the notes, Robert Kennedy "said that in his opinion a combination of the blockade route and the air strike route was very attractive to him. He felt we should first institute the blockade. In the event that the Soviets continued to build up the missile capability in Cuba, then we should inform the Russians that we would destroy the missiles, the launchers, and the missile sites." Clearly, RFK had seen that any other course would lead to larger implications for the United State and the world. "If the Russians did not halt the development of the missile capability," he added, "then we would proceed to make an air strike. The advantage of proceeding in this way ... was that we would get away from the Pearl Harbor surprise attack aspect of the air strike route."[22] This last piece was something that Robert Kennedy argued in his own memoir as an issue that bothered him. It was not in the American tradition to make a sneak attack against an opponent. It speaks to his thinking at the time. He was looking at world opinion as well as domestic.

Maxwell Taylor went on to argue that a blockade would not solve the problem of the missile threat. McNamara said that if the military went ahead with the strike, it would result in "several thousand Russians being killed, chaos in Cuba, and efforts to overthrow the Castro government. In his view the probability was high that an air strike would lead inevitably to an invasion." He went on to say that "he doubted that the Soviets would take an air strike on Cuba without resorting to a very major response. In such an event, the United States would lose control of the situation which could escalate to general war."[23] JFK agreed that an air strike would mean a strong Soviet response, which might implicate Berlin. Kennedy, at this point, had made up his mind. He wanted to gauge where everyone else was—especially the military. Adlai Stevenson famously suggested that the United States give up Guantanamo as well as the missiles in Turkey. He was sharply rejected by JFK and others as the move pointed to appeasement. By the end of the meeting, JFK agreed to a blockade and took actions necessary for an air strike.

It was a tense meeting with sharp distinctions among the people in the room. When Taylor returned to the Pentagon he remarked, "This was not one of our better days." He also said that JFK said to Taylor, "I know you and your colleagues are unhappy with this decision, but I trust that you will support me in this decision." Taylor told JFK that they would.[24] This meeting is also a good example as to what Kennedy had in front of him to make this decision. While it is somewhat clear that he had leaned to a blockade the night before, his questions still signified that he believed it could lead to war. In addition, these meetings over the four days examined here show a John Kennedy much different than the one at Vienna or in the room when the news of the Bay of Pigs came in. This JFK was cool and calculating; moreover, he was able to ask important questions while considering the allies and the American people. His style in these meetings was to listen, not talk over the group. Indeed, it was an exemplary performance of leadership under stressful situations. Also, his strong position with the Joint Chiefs demonstrates that he was not afraid to stand up to the military advisors. Indeed, Kennedy was trying to maintain peace in the world. After this crisis, it would be the goal for the rest of his administration.

"I'm in favor ... of an invasion, and an all-out one, and as quickly as possible."

On 22 October, Kennedy prepared to give his speech to the American people that night. Before making the speech he briefed congressional leadership on the situation and his course of action. Among the twenty statesmen in the cabinet room were Senator Richard Russell, a democrat from Georgia and chair of the Armed Services Committee, and Senator William Fulbright, chairman of the Foreign Relations Committee. Both Russell and Fulbright were very respected for their views on foreign affairs. Their perspectives were important to JFK. The people in the room knew that something was happening, as the president requested time on the networks to speak to Americans. This is another opportunity to see how Kennedy took yet another perspective, this time from congress, and used it for decision-making during crisis. While there was a lot said in this meeting, Russell and Fulbright were the most outspoken on their points of view.

McCone briefed the members of congress on the facts of the situation, while some of the members asked probing questions. In addition to McCone, Kennedy brought in Thompson to explain his discussions with Khrushchev and how this move related to Berlin. After McNamara gave his presentation to the group Kennedy asked them for their opinions. However, before McNamara could brief them, Russell jumped in with his opinion commenting on the blockade. "We're either a first class power or we're not," Russell said. He went on to say, "You have warned these people time and again, in the most eloquent speeches I have read since Woodrow Wilson, that's what would happen if there was an offensive capability created in Cuba. They can't say they're not on notice." Russell was very pessimistic in his assessment of the future of Berlin, saying, "The time is going to come, Mr. President, when you're going to have to take this step in

Berlin and Korea and Washington, D.C., and Winder, Georgia, for the nuclear war. I don't know whether Khrushchev will launch a nuclear war over Cuba or not."[25] Kennedy interrupted Russell, saying that he wanted them to hear McNamara's assessment. Indeed, JFK was getting agitated with the congressional leadership. He had been working this problem for a great deal of time. They were already second-guessing his decisions after a few minutes in the room.

After McNamara explained the aspects of the blockade, Russell chimed in again, asking to complete his statement. "My position," he said, "is that these people have been warned." Kennedy explained the issues of moving the military into position prior to the invasion. It was not that they were not preparing for a war. Indeed, Kennedy said that the United States could invade in 24 to 48 hours. He responded further to Russell directly, saying, "In order to invade Cuba as we attempt this buildup of force, one of the reasons why we've been concerned this week is we wanted to know all the sites. We wanted to know the firing position of these missiles." He furthered this issue by saying, "If we go into Cuba we have to all realize that we are taking a chance that these missiles, which are ready to be fired, won't be fired. So that's a gamble that we should take. In any case we are prepared to take it. The fact is that that is one hell of a gamble, but I think we are going to have to assume that." Kennedy brought in McNamara's concern of those missiles being ready to fire on the U.S. Kennedy was fearful of the war this would cause. If he miscalculated the intentions of the people operating those missiles, it could lead to World War III. After devouring *The Guns of August* that past year, it was his greatest fear. He went on in an attempt to assuage the men's anxiety toward his action, saying that they should meet again in 48 hours to decide if they should "take the risk of going in there, under the conditions we have described."[26]

It seemed a given that Berlin was an issue in this scenario. His point in his retort to Senator Russell said, "We have a prospect, if the Soviet Union, as a reprisal, should grab Berlin in the morning, which they could do within a couple of hours. Our war plan at that point has been to fire our nuclear weapons at them." Russell finally said, after a few more comments, that he was done. Kennedy asserted that he realized that he asked for their opinions, "But it's a very difficult problem that we're faced with. I'll just tell you that. It's a very difficult choice that we're faced with together." Before Kennedy could finish Russell said, "Oh, my God, I know that. A war, our destiny, will hinge on it. But it's coming someday Mr. President. Will it ever be under more auspicious circumstances."[27] This speaks to the times that these men made decisions. These were Cold Warriors and believed that a confrontation was inevitable. According to their mindset, war with the Russians was inescapable, and it would be beneficial to have it on their terms. Kennedy was under pressure from members of his own party to act on this threat. He believed that the act they wanted would lead to nuclear war, which was a "prime failure." Indeed, it would have meant the end of civilization, as they knew it. In addition, Kennedy's reference to their opinions was a clear indicator that at that point, he had had enough of their posturing. He saw this decision as much more complicated than they thought. However, the transcripts from the first day of the crisis demonstrate that nearly everyone in the room wanted to invade Cuba with at least an air strike. Perhaps Kennedy should have considered that when he asked for their opinions.

Senator Fulbright had reservations as well. He had issues with the fact that Americans would be confronting Russians on these ships when they boarded. "A blockade seems to me the worst alternative," Fulbright said. He saw a distinction between Cuba and the Soviet nation, saying that Cuba was a "sovereign nation" and not even a part of the Warsaw Pact. "I'm in favor, on the basis of this information, of an invasion, and an all-out one, and as quickly as possible."[28] Kennedy listened to his points, but then jumped in with his own perspective. He then said to Fulbright, "The reason we've embarked on the course we have ... is because we don't know where we're going to end up on this matter. Ambassador Thompson has felt very strongly that the Soviet Union would regard, will regard the attack on these SAM sites and missile bases with the killing of 4 or 5,000 Russians as a greater provocation than the stopping of their ships." He went on to say, "We tried to make judgment on a matter about which everyone is uncertain." The exasperated Kennedy said, "But at least — at least it's the best advice we could get. So we start here, we don't know where it's going to take us or where we're going to take ourselves."[29]

Kennedy was so frustrated with this meeting with the congressional leaders that he commented to Ted Sorenson, "If they want this job, they can have it — it's no great joy to me."[30] Robert Dallek writes that Kennedy called the three former presidents for their advice because "he thought they were the only ones who could imagine his burden." JFK told historian David Herbert Donald, "No one has the right to grade a president ... who has not sat in his chair, examined the mail and information that came across his desk, and learned why he made decisions."[31] Privately, Kennedy said to Kenneth O'Donnell that the congressional leaders were saying, "Oh, sure, we support you Mister President, but it's your decision, not ours, and if it goes wrong, we'll knock your block off."[32] Kennedy also said later, "The trouble is that when you get a group of Senators together, they are always dominated by the man who takes the boldest and strongest line.... After Russell spoke, no one wanted to take issue with him."[33] Despite the heavy criticism, Kennedy went on television and outlined to the nation both the threat and the course of action. Afterward, he had Harold Macmillan on the phone to dissect the speech. It was the first time, since the crisis, that he had spoken to the man. They exchanged letters regarding the incident, but the British prime minister had his opinion of the course as well.

When Kennedy had visited Britain on his trip to Europe, Macmillan and he got along well. They corresponded on other matters, which included the Berlin crisis a year earlier. Macmillan supported Kennedy and his endeavors in foreign policy. Kennedy started the phone conversation by explaining how he needed to do something in the face of such posturing by the Soviet Union. "Our strong feeling was that after my statements to them against bringing missiles in, after their frequent statements that they weren't, the fact that this was done in a wholly clandestine way would have left us in November, when Mr. Khrushchev was planning to come over." Macmillan acknowledged that he understood that, but had a few reservations. "What's worrying me is how do you see the way out of this? What are you going to do with the blockade? Are you going to occupy Cuba and have done with it or is it just going to drag on?"[34] Macmillan asked further questions just short of second guessing Kennedy's actions. "What worries me, I'll be frank with you, [is] having a sort of dragging-on position. If you occupied Cuba, that's one thing. In my long experience we've always found that our weakness has been when we've not acted with sufficient strength to start with." Kennedy responded by saying that the response was "not complete force." But he emphasized, "Our action is obviously moderated by the realization that we could move very quickly into a world war over this, or to a nuclear war, or to lose Berlin, and that's why we've taken the course we've taken. Even though, as I say, it doesn't represent any final answer."[35] Macmillan finished the call by saying to Kennedy, "You must have had a very hard time. I feel sorry for you and all the troubles. I've been through them. I only want to tell you how much we feel for you."[36] With that, the two leaders ended their conversation.

Kennedy was under a great deal of pressure from home and abroad to take an aggressive stance against Cuba. While Macmillan did support his decision, he did so with reservations. His decision to make the announcement and implement the blockade was a triumph for Kennedy. It was the first time in his presidency that he did something that was uniquely his from the start to the end. The Bay of Pigs and Berlin crises were inherited from previous presidencies. While it is clear that Cuba is related to both of those issues, the context and players of this crisis belonged to Kennedy. His decision was all the more important for him as it would define his presidency. This was the ultimate test for a leader—to look war in the face and wait for the other side to make the first move. Indeed, his move was as pivotal for his presidency as the men on Breeds Hill waiting to see the whites of their opponents' eyes. Like those patriots, had he done anything else, there is no telling what the end result would be.

"His face seemed drawn, his eyes pained, almost gray."

Americans did not panic, but they did prepare. The shelves of grocery stores went bare as people waited for the next move by the Soviets. Walter Cronkite led the media as they tried to decipher what was happening in Washington and Moscow. JFK moved the Defense Condition level to 3 in an effort to prepare for the military and send a message to Khrushchev that he meant business. Meanwhile, the president's EXCOMM team continued to meet and discuss their options. On 23 October, they received the reply from Khrushchev. In this response the Soviet premier argued, "I should say frankly that measures outlined in your statement represent a serious threat to peace and security of peoples." He claimed, "Armaments now on Cuba, regardless of classification to which they belong, are destined exclusively for defensive purposes, in order to secure Cuban Republic from attack of aggressor." He went on to say further, "I hope that Government of United States will show prudence and renounce actions pursued by you, which could lead to catastrophic consequences for peace throughout world."[37] Aleksandr Fursenko and Timothy Naftali argue that Khrushchev wanted to take a less aggressive stance in his private correspondence with Kennedy than he did in public. They also wrote, "[Khrushchev] was not inclined to test the U.S. blockade for two reasons. Besides wanting to avoid a confrontation that might escalate, he did not want to give the United States the opportunity to capture any of the strategic technology loaded on some of the ships."[38] Later that night Robert Kennedy met with Dobrynin at the Russian embassy. When Robert Kennedy asked Dobrynin about the presence of missiles in Cuba, the ambassador replied that "there were no missiles in Cuba; that this was what Khrushchev had said."[39] On the way out Bobby looked back at Dobrynin and said, "I don't know how all this will end, but we intend to stop your ships."[40] The day after the speech was mild compared to what was ahead.

Robert Kennedy said that the morning meeting on 24 October, in addition to the one on 27 October, "seemed the most trying, the most difficult, and the most filled with tension." He sat across from JFK as the Russian ships approached the quarantine line. He wrote, "This was the moment we had prepared for, which we hoped would never come. The danger and concern that we all felt hung like a cloud over us all and particularly over the President." One of the first issues that Kennedy had to deal with was a Soviet submarine that moved in between the *Gagarin* and the *Komiles*, two Soviet ships. An American carrier, the *Essex*, was to signal the submarine to surface, and if it refused, send depth charges into the water. Robert Kennedy described the president in the midst of this tense situation: "I think these few minutes were the time of gravest concern for the President." He went on to write,

> [JFK's] hand went up to his face and covered his mouth. He opened and closed his fist. His face seemed drawn, his eyes pained, almost gray. We stared at each other across the table. For a few fleeting seconds, it was almost as though no one else was there and he no longer President. Inexplicably, I thought of when he was ill and almost died; when he lost a child; when we learned our oldest brother had been killed; of personal times of strain and hurt.[41]

Indeed, this was a difficult moment for JFK's presidency. All the advice and decisions were being put to the test. Kennedy was ready to act on Berlin when

12. Brinkmanship in the Kennedy White House

reports came in that Russian ships were stopped "dead in the water." Kennedy made sure that the *Essex* did not attack the submarine. Rusk famously said to Bundy, "We're eyeball to eyeball, and I think the other fellow just blinked."[42] The drama continued to unfold at the United Nations where Adlai Stevenson, ambassador to the United Nations, asked the stone faced Valerian Zorin, the Soviet ambassador, if the Russians had put offensive weapons in Cuba. "Don't wait for the translation," Stevenson said; "Yes or no." Zorin said that he was not in an "American courtroom," but Stevenson retorted, "You are in the court of world opinion right now!" Zorin said that Stevenson would get his answer in due time. The sly politician said, "I am prepared to wait for my answer until Hell freezes over, if that's your decision."[43]

This was captivating the world and Kennedy was at the center. U Thant, secretary-general of the United Nations, asked Kennedy to bring back the quarantine line and to try to talk to Khrushchev about the situation in Cuba. While both sides contemplated their next move, the United Sates enforced the quarantine line and even boarded a Soviet-chartered Lebanese ship on the morning of 26 October.[44] That night, Kennedy spoke with Macmillan. Kennedy was hoping that some political arrangement would present itself the next morning. JFK acknowledged, "If at the end of 48 hours we were getting no place, and the missile sites continue to be constructed, then we are going to be faced with some hard decisions." Macmillan said that those "hard decisions" would "have their effect on Berlin, as well as on Cuba."[45] Kennedy was only two hours from receiving a reply from Khrushchev, and those hard decisions would occupy the most dangerous day of the crisis.

On 26 October, Kennedy received word from Khrushchev. In substance, the Soviet premier pledged to dismantle the weapons in Cuba if the United States guaranteed not to invade the island. Khrushchev wrote that he wanted to avoid war: "War is our enemy and a calamity for all the peoples." He went on to say, "But if indeed war should break out, then it would not be in our power to stop it, for such is the logic of war. I have participated in two wars and know that war ends when it has rolled through cities and villages, everywhere sowing death and destruction."[46] The letter was very emotional and seemed by many in the administration to be a first draft, written by a person under heavy stress. In fact, Llewellyn Thompson believed that Khrushchev had written it "in a state of near panic without consultation."[47] Khrushchev said that he felt he could talk to Kennedy in this manner because of their discussions at Vienna. "We quarrel with you, we have differences on ideological questions. But our view of the world consists in this, that ideological questions, as well as economic problems, should be solved not by military means, they must be solved on the basis of peaceful competition,"[48] Khrushchev wrote. Indeed, this letter invoked a peaceful measure as a solution instead of war. Khrushchev said he was willing to work with U Thant at the United Nations and broker a deal to end the confrontation.

Khrushchev made his position very clear when he wrote, "If assurances were given by the President and the Government of the United States that the U.S.A. itself would not participate in an attack on Cuba and would restrain others from actions of this sort, if you would recall your fleet, this would immediately change everything."[49] He said that he did not speak for Castro. This letter ended with Khrushchev saying,

> If, however, you have not lost your self-control and sensibly conceive what this might lead to, then, Mr. President, we and you ought not now to pull on the ends of the rope in which you have tied the knot of war, because the more the two of us pull, the tighter that knot will be tied.[50]

Khrushchev's metaphor was typical of his correspondence with Kennedy. In their private correspondence he consistently used such language. To emphasize the point, he went on to say, "And a moment may come when that knot will be tied so tight that even he who tied it will not have the strength to untie it, and then it will be necessary to cut that knot, and what that would mean is not for me to explain to you, because you yourself understand perfectly of what terrible forces our countries dispose."[51] Prior to the crisis, Kennedy and Khrushchev had entered into a back-channel correspondence with each other. It was possible that Khrushchev believed he was communicating with Kennedy from that perspective with this letter. There was no mention of the missiles in Turkey, only that the United States promised not to attack Cuba. In fact, Aleksandr Fomin, the KGB station chief in Washington, made contact with the administration through John Scali of ABC news with the same message. The next day, however, there would be a much different letter with a hardline tone.

The largest concern from the EXCOMM group was that this message of 26 October might in fact be a decoy to allow the work on the sites to continue. Indeed, as EXCOMM debated how to respond to the letter of 26 October, another letter came in from Khrushchev which pointed to such a strategy by the Soviets. Kennedy and his team were inclined to accept the letter of 26 October. The second letter, however, made this decision much more complicated. Written as if Khrushchev had never sent the letter the previous night, this letter made it clear that the Soviets wanted more. In addition to a promise not invade Cuba, the Soviet Union wanted nuclear missiles in Turkey dismantled and removed. This move would affect NATO's relationship with the United States and hurt U.S. prestige in the world. If the United States agreed to such an arrangement, they would lose political capital in foreign affairs. "You are disturbed over Cuba," Khrushchev wrote.

> You say that this disturbs you because it is 90 miles by sea from the coast of the United States of America. But Turkey adjoins us; our sentries patrol back and forth and see each other. Do you consider, then, that you have the right to demand security for your own country and the removal of the weapons you call offensive, but do not accord the same right to us? You have placed destructive missile weapons, which you call offen-

sive, in Turkey, literally next to us. How then can recognition of our equal military capacities be reconciled with such unequal relations between our great states? This is irreconcilable.[52]

This letter had a different tone than the first. Many in the group believed that it was the work of the Politburo attempting to get more from the deal.[53] In fact, Scali had relayed a message to Fomin that Kennedy would accept a declaration not to invade Cuba if the Soviets took the missiles out. Did the back-channel communiqué play a role in this new aggressive stance? EXCOMM took the whole day to determine its course of action.

The group started meeting at 10:00 A.M. During that meeting they received word that the second letter from Khrushchev had come in. Thompson said, "My idea is that the letter — the long letter he wrote last night — he wrote himself and sent out without clearance." McNamara followed up: "This really changes the character of the deal we're likely to be able to make." He added, "Our action in the interim must be really to keep the pressure on."[54] The group had not expected a reply so hard on the heels of the first, and it threw them off. At this point in the crisis, they had been working countless hours for nearly twelve days. They could very easily have gone to war. Robert Kennedy brought up the notion of taking the missiles out of Turkey with a few other caveats to satisfy the Turks and NATO. Bundy said that it was "too complicated." Bobby shot back sharply, "Well, I don't think it is."[55] Indeed, tension was high and they were trying to find a creative way to stave off war with the Soviets.

The move by the Soviet Union made it very difficult for the United States to reject the deal presented to them. In addition to sending this message, the Soviets made it public, which put more pressure on Kennedy to make a decision to keep the peace. "There isn't any doubt. Let's not kid ourselves," said Kennedy. "They've got a very good proposal, which is the reason they made it public." Bundy said that this letter was "his own hard-nosed people overruling him, this public one. They didn't like what he said to you last night. Nor would I, if I were a Soviet hard-nose."

The group broke up without a resolution to the matter. They had given Kennedy sound advice thus far. It was clear that Kennedy valued Bundy's advice for invasion but wanted to explore peaceful options. Robert Kennedy and Robert McNamara gave him those peaceful options. Kennedy's kitchen cabinet had been exemplary. The greatest example, however, came in the 4:00 P.M. meeting that same day.

Llewellyn Thompson had been a big contributor to the presidency since before the inauguration. At the 4:00 P.M. meeting, when the United States had exhausted all possible ideas, he proposed that Kennedy ignore the second letter and respond to the first. Kennedy said, "It seems to me ... to be reasonable. We're not going to get these weapons out of Cuba ... by negotiation." Thompson replied, "I don't agree, Mr. President. I think there is still a chance that we get this line going." Kennedy said, "That he'll back down?" Kennedy said that the second letter had become the Soviet Union's "public position." Thompson said, "This is maybe just pressure on us. I mean to accept the other, I mean so far — We'd accepted noninvasion of Cuba." As the group discussed this, he went on, "The important thing for Khrushchev, it seems to me, is to be able to say: 'I saved Cuba. I stopped an invasion.' And he can get away with this if he wants to."[56] While every piece of advice up to that point had been vital in preparing Kennedy to make the right decision, this changed the scenario from grim to hopeful. The key to cooperation with the Soviets lay in a pledge not to invade Cuba. Kennedy remarked, "There's going to be a hell of fight about that." He went on to say, "I don't mind taking it on if we're going to get somewhere.... You don't just talk about an 'agenda of peace.'"[57]

While the group deliberated how to write their response to Khrushchev, a U-2 plane was shot down over Cuba, killing the pilot. The other problem was the notion of trading missiles in Turkey for missiles in Cuba. There was very little to point to in that first letter, other than a pledge not to invade Cuba. The complexities with trading missiles in Turkey point to the NATO relationship. Harold Macmillan had commented during Kennedy's speech, "[Kennedy] may never get rid of Cuban rockets except by trading them for Turkish, Italian or other bases." He went on to say, "Thus Khrushchev will have won his point." In addition, Macmillan commented, "Anything like this deal would do great injury to NATO."[58]

The missiles in Turkey were a factor that Kennedy could not ignore. It was clear that the Soviets demanded reciprocity for removing missiles from Cuba. In contrast, NATO wanted to guarantee its protection through the existence of such weapons. While Kennedy planned to agree to the first letter, he had a difficult time figuring out what to do about Turkey. Dean Rusk suggested that the missiles in Turkey be removed once the crisis had been resolved. Bundy remembered, "It would allow us to respond to Khrushchev's second proposal in a way that he might regard as helpful, while at the same time it did not require us to engage NATO or the Turks in a public trade of 'their' interests for 'ours.'"[59]

The State Department had drafted a letter that "flatly rejected" the Turkish exchange. Robert Kennedy and Ted Sorensen, disagreeing with the "content and tenor" of the State Department letter, wrote the final letter that would be hand delivered to Ambassador Dobrynin by the attorney general.[60] Robert Kennedy met the Russian in his office. He drafted a memo three days later regarding the meeting: "I told him first that we understood that the work was continuing on the Soviet missile bases in Cuba," he wrote. He went on to explain that "in the last two hours we had found that our planes flying over Cuba had been fired upon and that one of our U-2's had been shot down and the pilot killed. I said these men were flying unarmed planes." He said that this was a "serious turn of events" and they had to make a decision in the next 12 to 24 hours. Kennedy complained to Dobrynin that "Mr. Khrushchev and he had misled us. The Soviet Union had secretly established missile bases in Cuba while at the same time proclaiming, privately and publicly, that this would never be done. I said those missile bases had to go and they had to go right away." They needed to have a commitment to remove the missiles by the next day. This was not an ultimatum, according to RFK; it was a "statement of fact." Kennedy said that if the Soviets did not remove the bases, then the United States would. "His country might take retaliatory action but he should understand that before this was over, while there might be dead Americans there would also be dead Russians." Kennedy said that a letter was being transmitted to the Soviet Embassy stating that the Soviets had to remove the missiles and in exchange the United States would pledge not to invade Cuba.

Dobrynin asked about the other letter regarding Turkey. RFK responded "that there could be no quid pro quo—no deal of this kind could be made. This was a matter that had to be considered by NATO and that it was up to NATO to make the decision." He went on to say that "it was completely impossible for NATO to take such a step under the present threatening position of the Soviet Union." A crossed-out sentence in the memo read, "If some time elapsed—and per your instructions, I mentioned four or five months—I said I was sure that these matters could be resolved satisfactory."[61] Of course, this referred to the secret deal that Rusk had suggested he propose to the Soviets, wherein the United States would work with NATO and remove the missiles from Turkey. Aleksandr Fursenko and Timothy Naftali write, "John Kennedy assumed that it was the Turkish offer that had sealed the agreement. Not wishing to let on that he made a last-minute concession, the president and the attorney general confined this knowledge to a small group of advisors."[62] This is another example of how John Kennedy cherished his relationship with certain advisors, particularly his brother.

RFK went on to write, "Per your instructions I repeated that there could be no deal of any kind and that any steps toward easing tensions in other parts of the world largely depended on the Soviet Union and Mr. Khrushchev taking action in Cuba and taking it immediately." He finished by saying that he needed an answer the next day, otherwise there could be "drastic consequences."[63] This was the last communication from the Kennedy White House.

The next day, Khrushchev cabled to tell the United States he agreed to the terms. Nowhere in that memo was the Turkish exchange mentioned. Fursenko and Naftali also wrote that Khrushchev met with Ulbricht on the 27 October. There is no record of what they discussed, only that the East German leader was "satisfied."[64] In fact, Fursenko and Naftali reveal new information that Khrushchev was willing to take the deal without the pledge to dismantle the missiles in Turkey.[65] Nevertheless, Kennedy's kitchen cabinet successfully navigated the president through arguably the most dangerous crisis of the Cold War.

Kennedy Brinkmanship

Cuba had been an issue in American foreign policy since Castro took over the island in 1959. Eisenhower and Kennedy both had varied results when trying to deal with this problem. Kennedy's group of advisors wanted to keep the United States away from war and any direct military involvement, while at the same time demonstrate force in the region. Prior to the Cuban Missile Crisis, Maxwell Taylor gathered as much intelligence as possible for potential military action. Indeed, Taylor's reluctance to embrace the truculent Northwoods Operation is evidence of his desire to look beyond the usual Cold War channels. However, during the crisis, when the United States was presented with the possibility of offensive weapons in Cuba, Taylor did not hesitate to advocate a military solution.

When gathering this intelligence on Cuba, the group was presented with different pieces of information, not knowing how to act. For example, the August memo revealing that Soviet personnel were working on the island was never taken that seriously. The president was informed of this work, but was reluctant to take any overt action that would implicate the United States. As a matter of fact, Bundy said the buildup was nothing to worry about in his 31 August memo. Did Kennedy's kitchen cabinet's disregard for this buildup contribute to the problems they would face in October? While there was a level of disbelief that Khrushchev would be so bold, it was clear from the evidence that Kennedy's advisors reacted according to the information they had. Kennedy's statements of 4 and 13 September outlined his reaction to the buildup in Cuba and sent a message to the Kremlin that Washington was watching. In addition, they made it clear that Kennedy would not permit offensive weapons in the region and detailed his reaction to such acts. Some argued that this was a fine reaction to the events in Cuba, while others wanted more direct action.

The Soviet Union attempted to deceive America on many levels. Ambassador Dobrynin made it clear to Ted Sorensen that the Soviets wanted the elections over before there was any action. Georgi Bolshakov gave no indication to Robert Kennedy of any action. Stewart Udall's conversation with Khrushchev himself gave JFK some solace that any weapons given to Cuba were of a defensive nature. Kennedy was inclined to believe Khrushchev and Dobrynin, but his press conference of 13 September is evidence that he did not trust what they said entirely. With all these factors in mind, the missiles in Cuba were not as much a surprise as some make them out to have been. Kennedy monitored the situation in Cuba very closely. Indeed, his reaction before and during the crisis was a great example of statesmanship. He used many channels to communicate with the Soviets, reacted to intelligence, and issued press statements outlining his position. Khrushchev knew the consequences, which makes him more culpable for threatening the peace. Kennedy's reaction to these nuclear weapons remains one of the most important acts by a president in American

12. Brinkmanship in the Kennedy White House

history. That being said, what role did his advisors play in crafting that reaction?

Memoranda written by McNamara, Taylor and Bundy demonstrate the acute awareness these men had of the developments in Cuba. Robert Kennedy's constant oversight is evidence that JFK was also consistently watching the island. Indeed, John McCone proposed at one of these meetings that that the Soviets might put MRBMs in Cuba and that the United States should have a reaction planned in that instance. While many in intelligence disagreed, thinking that Khrushchev would never be so bold, JFK trusted McCone and his notion was heard. Bundy was among those who did not believe there would be missiles in Cuba, which may explain his determination to strike.

The Cuban Missile Crisis illuminated the role these men played in shaping foreign policy. Indeed, Kennedy's kitchen cabinet had come a long way since the Bay of Pigs. Not only did the cabinet approach crises differently; it also comprised different people who had Kennedy's trust. Robert Kennedy, particularly, played a definitive role during and at the end of the crisis. John Kennedy had more confidence in his team during the Cuban Missile Crisis then he did for the Bay of Pigs. This confidence translated into success. Robert McNamara played a pivotal role in the decision to act on the blockade. Both Kennedys placed his advice above everyone else. While JFK worked this crisis, these men helped him see the broader issues. That Kennedy did not take Bundy or Taylor's advice does not diminish its value. Kennedy went back and forth on the strikes and blockade. His inability to decide immediately is evidence that these men had an impact on JFK.

Kennedy analyzed each piece of evidence before he made a decision. This act in the face of pressure from those within his administration as well as congress to strike the Cubans demonstrates his desire for peace. JFK was committed to peace and did not want to see the United States and Soviet Union embroiled in World War III, which had the potential to significantly alter the state of the world. Kennedy used many minds to make his decision. Dean Acheson and Llewellyn Thompson were called in specially for this crisis, and their advice was held in high value. While Acheson's analysis was contrary to what Kennedy did, it still shows that Kennedy wanted to take every perspective and make the right decision for America.

Kennedy's forbearance in the face of Curtis LeMay and other military men demonstrated he was his own president and not a spokesperson for someone else's agenda. The president's meeting with the Joint Chiefs of Staff on 19 October was a clear example of how far apart the military complex and Kennedy were on these matters. LeMay, in particular, was unrealistic in his assessment of Soviet reaction to American military strikes on Cuba. This relationship is an indicator of the kind of support Kennedy had from the military when making decisions. Indeed, he was much more inclined to take advice from Robert McNamara or even his thirty-six-year-old brother, the latter never having served in a war. This poses an important question for presidential scholars. In peacetime, who should principally advise the president on military matters? Clearly if the United States were at war, men like LeMay were needed to conduct it. Kennedy himself had said he would want LeMay involved if there were another war. In peace, however, those same men could create war rather than avoiding it. It was the only way they knew how to react to danger. Such was the situation for Kennedy. Had he listened to the Joint Chiefs and not questioned their course of action, the United States and the Soviet Union would most likely have been involved in a larger conflict.

John Kennedy took the advice of his closest advisors and made foreign policy decisions that staved off war. He gambled on a diplomatic route that could have had serious consequences for the safety of the United States. Congress wanted him to invade. The Joint Chiefs wanted an invasion. Bundy and Taylor, two men whom he trusted, told Kennedy to strike Cuba. Dean Acheson, a former secretary of state who presided over similar crises with Truman, wanted JFK to strike. NATO was unwilling to budge on the missiles in Turkey. Kennedy's decisions during the crisis were his own, and they made the difference. He had assistance coming to the conclusions; ultimately, however, the burden was his to carry. His decision to acknowledge the first letter from Khrushchev and send Robert Kennedy to meet with Dobrynin was risky. Llewellyn Thompson may have suggested the idea to Kennedy, but there were many others on the table as well. His decision to trade missiles in Turkey months later risked a further deterioration in the relationship with the European alliance. Kennedy's decisions were the determining factors through the whole crisis. His team gave him sound advice from all sides of the issue. Without his advisors he would not have those options to choose from.

It was the men who sat with him to debate these issues that gave Kennedy solutions to these problems. While he was the owner of the decisions, without the constant discourse, which was evident in the transcripts, there would not have been the ideas to solve this problem. While Kennedy acted on these notions, the men who supplied them should be equally commended. McNamara was integral in deciding on a blockade. Robert Kennedy played both an emotional and political role. His presence at the meetings meant a great deal to the embattled president. It was something he did not have during the Bay of Pigs. Finally, Thompson's insight into Khrushchev gave Kennedy the final piece of strategy he needed to bring closure to the crisis. It was the pinnacle of his presidency. He would have other successes, but they would pale in comparison to this one.

Part Seven

"No man is an island, entire of itself": Leading to Peace and Cooperation

13

"A Strategy of Peace"

"I am encouraged by your letter."

Ted Sorensen had been with John Kennedy since his time in the senate. He was very young when he came to work for JFK and soon became one of his closest advisors. Few men in history have written with greater care for the English language than Sorensen. His way with words was on par with that of Abraham Lincoln, who was his own speechwriter. Though Lincoln was prone to using metaphors and biblical references, Sorensen preferred language that was direct and to the point. They both, however, drove their ideas home to their audience. There are hundreds of speeches to examine that could illustrate this quality of writing, which Sorensen produced on a daily basis. When it comes to understanding the Kennedy Doctrine after the Cuban Missile Crisis, the American University commencement on 10 June 1963 is the best gauge. The speech outlined Kennedy's vision for the future. On the heels of such a dangerous time, Kennedy wanted a statement of peace to the world and the Soviets. In addition, he wanted to secure a nuclear test ban treaty. JFK believed that a statement of peace was what Khrushchev needed to commit to such an act.

This study as a whole has been committed to showing how Kennedy's advisors shaped diplomacy. This part examines how Kennedy shaped his public message in the wake of the Cuban Missile Crisis. While Cuba still loomed as an issue for the United States, and there were many in military circles that did not like Kennedy's decision in October 1962, Kennedy was insistent on crafting a message of peace. Indeed, this thinking flew in the face of many in Washington. Kennedy had utilized a back-channel communication after the Berlin crisis in 1961 and often spoke of peace, staying away from the usual Cold War rhetoric. The American University speech was an especially important statement, which was helpful in leading to peaceful relations with the United States and Soviet Union. Sorensen's language captured Kennedy's vision, sending the right message to Moscow and the world.

The Nuclear Test Ban Treaty was something Kennedy had wanted since the Vienna summit. By December 1962 the Soviets had dismantled the offensive weapons in Cuba and were negotiating with the United States on a pledge not to invade Cuba. There seemed to be a cooling in the hostilities between the nations and perhaps an opportunity for a peaceful gesture. Khrushchev wrote to Kennedy on 11 December saying, "It would seem that you and we have come to a final stage in the elimination of tension around Cuba. Our relations are already entering now their normal course since all those means placed by us on Cuban territory which you considered offensive are withdrawn."[1] Despite the fact that Khrushchev blamed "the policy of the United States with regard to Cuba" for the crisis, the letter had an amiable tone. Khrushchev said that although the Soviets had made good on their commitments, the United States had "long term" commitments with their pledge not to invade Cuba. "But it is important to fulfil them and to do everything so that no doubts are sown from the very start."[2] Khrushchev went on to say, "Within a short period of time we and you have lived through a rather acute crisis. The acuteness of it was that we and you were already prepared to fight and this would lead to a thermonuclear war, with all its dreadful consequences." That passage, in particular, is evidence that Khrushchev was well aware of the possible consequences of the crisis. Khrushchev said that the Soviets "being convinced that mankind would never forgive the statesmen who would not exhaust all possibilities to prevent catastrophe, agreed to a compromise."[3]

Khrushchev went on to say that the stability of the entire world depended on how Kennedy would fulfill his commitments. Later on in the letter, however, Khrushchev alluded to a test ban treaty. "Let us, Mr. President, eliminate promptly the consequences of the Cuban crisis and get down to solving other questions, and we have them in number. As far as nuclear test ban this is a minor question on the whole." Khrushchev said that he planned to address the test ban in a confidential letter and said that he hoped "that we will overcome difficulties existing in this question." He went on to conclude, "The problem of disarmament is a different matter, it is a major and difficult question now."[4] The letter affirmed issues on Cuba and Berlin, but it also demonstrated Khrushchev's willingness to look into disarmament. Indeed the possibility of a thermonuclear war and its effects were at the heart of this letter. It was an attempt to rekindle that back-channel correspondence initiated by Robert Kennedy and Georgi Bolshakov only a year prior. Kennedy responded very quickly.

"I was glad to have your message of December 11th," Kennedy wrote in his 14 December reply, "and to know that you believe, as we do, that we have come to a final stage of the Cuban affair between us." Kennedy asserted, "We have never wanted to be driven by the acts of others into war in Cuba." JFK said he agreed with Khrushchev that "the larger part of the crisis was now ended." Kennedy spoke to their confidential channel, saying that he valued it. "I have not concealed from you," he wrote, "the serious disappointment to me that dangerously misleading information should have come through these channels before the recent crisis."[5] He went on to say, "I appreciate your writing me so frankly, and in return I have tried to be as straightforward, for I agree with you that only through such frank exchanges can we better understand our respective points of view." He ended with a reference to the test ban, saying, "I look forward to receiving your confidential letter and proposals on the test ban question, and I think there is every reason to keep working on this problem."[6] Kennedy not only mentioned the test ban but went on to say, "I hope that in your message on this subject you will tell me what you think about the position of the people in Peking on this question." He concluded, "It seems to me very important for both of us that in our efforts to secure an end to nuclear testing we should not overlook this area of the world."[7] Kennedy was concerned about China, and the evident strain in the Soviet-Sino relationship was something that could hurt his efforts at peace.

Khrushchev wrote back within a week. On 19 December he started his letter by saying, "It seems to me, Mr. President, that time has come now to put an end once and for all to nuclear tests, to draw a line through such tests." Khrushchev said, "The Soviet Union does not need war." He said, "Thermonuclear catastrophe will bring enormous losses and sufferings to the American people as well as other peoples on earth." Khrushchev wanted peace and cooperation with the United States. He clearly had this in mind before Kennedy sent his 14 December letter. His allusion to this effort in his 11 December letter is proof. "The main obstacle to an agreement," Khrushchev wrote, "is the demand by the American side of international control and inspection on the territories of nuclear powers over cessation of underground tests."[8] The number of inspections was a major issue in getting the deal passed through the United States Senate. Khrushchev spoke to this, saying, "This circumstance, as we understand, ties you and does not allow you to sign a treaty which would enable all of us to abandon for good the grounds where nuclear weapons are tested." Khrushchev said that if this was the only problem, "then for the noble and humane goal of ceasing nuclear weapons tests we are ready to meet you half way on this question."[9] The letter's tone and message were in keeping with Kennedy's hope for peace.

The Cuban Missile Crisis changed both leaders. In the past, each side had used nuclear war as a means of leverage. The Cuban crisis illustrated that now members of both governments saw nuclear war not as a deterrent, but as a viable option for war. Khrushchev wrote, "With the elimination of the Cuban crisis we relieved mankind of the direct menace of combat use of lethal nuclear weapons that impended over the world."[10] He asked, "Can't we solve a far simpler question.... I think we can and we must do it." This letter exemplified Khrushchev's willingness to meet Kennedy halfway on an agreement. Indeed, these men had the ability to bring peace to a very volatile world, or at least act as the role models for such peace. While there were questions on both sides, it seemed clear that each leader was ready to embrace those questions with solutions. Kennedy responded to Khrushchev in a 28 December letter.

"There appear to be no differences between your views and mine," Kennedy wrote, "regarding the need to eliminate war in this nuclear age."[11] Kennedy proposed, "Perhaps only those who have responsibility for controlling these weapons fully realize the awful devastation their use would bring." Kennedy and Khrushchev's correspondence, originally established in late 1961, finally showed promise of brokering peace. The two leaders had been through a lot up to that point and were weary. "If we are to have peace between systems with far reaching ideological differences, we must find ways for reducing or removing the recurring waves of fear and suspicion which feed on ignorance, misunderstanding or what appear to one side or the other as broken agreements." Kennedy wrote, "To me, the element of assurance is vital to the broader development of peaceful relationships."[12] Kennedy's letter had a clear, hopeful start. These letters demonstrate that Kennedy and Khrushchev wanted to start their relationship anew. While Khrushchev had other pressures with the Chinese, so did Kennedy with the European alliance. In many ways they did in fact hold similar positions with regard to the pressures and considerations they had to factor in when making decisions that affected their country. That being said, Khrushchev and Kennedy had to bridge a gap with regard to the specifics of the test ban treaty.

Khrushchev had reservations about on-site inspections. In the previous letter, Khrushchev had suggested that unmanned stations measure the seismic activity, hence determining if there were a nuclear event in a given region. He proposed three regions in the Soviet Union. Kennedy said that while that was hopeful, they needed to look beyond those three areas. The stations were outside the "areas of highest seismicity" and would not record the "phenomena" in those areas the United States wanted to monitor. "Notwithstanding these problems," JFK wrote, "I am encouraged by your letter. I do not believe that any of the problems which I have raised are insoluble, but they ought to be solved."[13] While Kennedy's letter was positive, Khrushchev replied the next day, saying, "I do not think that in this message I should touch more in detail on the negotiations on disarmament." The sudden shift signified that Khrushchev either did not like JFK's 28 December response or was getting pressure from his hardliners for being too affable on these issues.

"But the next step is up to him."

Fursenko and Naftali write in *Khrushchev's Cold War* that the premier's "debate with the Chinese was playing some role in his willingness to compromise with Kennedy to achieve a test ban agreement."[14] They cite that while confiding in Norman Cousins, the *Saturday Review* editor, Khrushchev said, "The Chinese say I was scared," referring to the Cuban missile crisis. "Of course

I was scared. It would have been insane not to be scared." The historians argue that Kennedy saw the strained relationship between China and the Soviet Union as "the greatest variable in the international system."[15] JFK met with his advisors regarding the test ban on 8 February 1963. At this meeting, he asked McNamara if he would accept six annual inspections, which demonstrates that Kennedy was showing some empathy toward Khrushchev's position. However, Kennedy made it clear to the group that they should "proceed on the assumption that the USSR would cheat." He went on to say in this meeting that "in his opinion, the whole reason for having a test ban, is related to the Chinese situation."[16] Indeed, this situation was complex from all sides. Norman Cousins would get involved again, and play a further role in this path to peace.

JFK wanted some resolution on the test ban but remarked in May 1963 that he was "not hopeful."[17] Kennedy believed that a message of peace could move Khrushchev. JFK had a great deal of confidence in the wake of the Cuban Missile Crisis. Additionally, he had political capital both at home and abroad. These elements may have emboldened his approach to foreign policy. According to Ted Sorensen's book, *Kennedy*, the president decided "without any recommendation from the departments or consultation with the congress" that he was going to send a message of peace to Chairman Khrushchev and the Soviets. Sorensen went on to write, "His motives were many. It was, first of all, an expression of his deep personal concern." Indeed, his calculated decision-making during the missile crisis was evidence that he was willing to look beyond the normal response to the Soviets. Clearly, he was aware of the impact his actions had on the world. With regard to the test-ban treaty, Sorensen said that JFK "thought it desirable to make clear his hopes for East-West agreement as a backdrop to his European trip in June."[18]

This speech would be a defining moment for Kennedy and declare his commitment to peace. Just his insistence on issuing such a statement is solid evidence that after the Cuban Missile Crisis he was ready to look for a peaceful solution to the Cold War. Kennedy had weathered the Bay of Pigs and a Berlin crisis in addition to the missiles in October. He had dealt with more crises than most presidents before or since in such a short period to time. Such intense exposure to these circumstances gave Kennedy a perspective not shared by many world leaders. Khrushchev, in turn, had been through the same crises and others during the previous Eisenhower administration. The premier may have been ready for a change. The Cuban Missile Crisis had scared both sides, and a dramatic event would hopefully propel Kennedy and Khrushchev, as well as their respective governments, to the table for peace. This grand gesture for peace was in tune with New Frontier ideology.

Richard Reeves argues that the road to the American University speech began in April of that year. Norman Cousins, the *Saturday Review* editor, came to the White House and met with Kennedy before his trip to Russia. Cousins was meeting with Khrushchev for an interview and wanted to check in with

Kennedy before he left. Kennedy asked Cousins to communicate that there was an "honest misunderstanding" in these negotiations on a test ban treaty to Khrushchev. Kennedy said that "Khrushchev and I occupy approximately the same political positions inside our governments.... He would like to prevent a nuclear war but is under pressure from his hard-line critics who interpret every move in that direction as appeasement." Kennedy went on to say, "I've got similar problems. The hard liners in the Soviet Union and the United States feed on each other."[19] Once again, Kennedy demonstrated that he was willing to use any method at his disposal to send a message to Khrushchev. On 12 April 1963, Cousins spent time with Khrushchev by the Black Sea.

Sitting in Khrushchev's dacha, Cousins recorded the premier saying that he also needed to persuade before he could govern, and that his position was not a dictatorship. "Frankly," Khrushchev said, "we feel that we were misled. If we change our position at all, it will not be in the direction of making it more generous." Khrushchev went on to say that his atomic scientists and generals were pressing him to allow more tests.[20] He said to Cousins, "You want me to accept President Kennedy's good faith? All right I accept his good faith. You want me to believe that the United States sincerely wants a treaty banning nuclear tests? All right, I believe the United States is sincere." Cousins told Khrushchev that Kennedy was under pressure by the senate, and that they would never accept only three inspections. Khrushchev finally said, "You can tell the President I accept his explanation of an honest misunderstanding and suggest that we get moving. But the next step is up to him."[21] Kennedy's step involved a speech meant to shape the rest of his foreign policy.

"But we have no more urgent task."

John Kennedy was ready to announce his doctrine that involved world peace. He wanted a test ban as a step to this endeavor but recognized that there was more to do beyond that measure. Most importantly, JFK wanted to lead the world away from nuclear confrontation. On 10 June 1963, at the American University commencement, JFK outlined his peace initiative for the rest of the world. Ted Sorensen played a role in shaping the language and vision for this speech. JFK, however, was the spark that lit this effort. Sorensen himself wrote that Kennedy did not consult anyone when he decided to bring this doctrine to the rest of the world. He did not have to. The crises that predated this event were enough to bring him to these conclusions. Kennedy and Khrushchev had flirted with nuclear confrontation twice. The speech was majestic in tone and kept with the New Frontier principles of sacrifice and introspection. Sorensen was a very important piece of crafting this message.

In his book *Counselor: A Life at the Edge of History*, Ted Sorensen outlines his six basic rules for speech writing. Sorensen was more than a speech-writer to Kennedy; he was close and valuable advisor. He was present at most if not all of the EXCOMM meetings. While his advice may not be as obvious from the tapes, he was a factor in many Kennedy decisions. With regard to speech writing, Sorensen argued, "Less is almost always better than more." This philosophy stems from William Strunk Jr. and E.B. White's classic book *Elements of Style*. Sorensen also believed that a good speech-writer must "choose each word as a precision tool." He argues, "In his foreign policy speeches, JFK stayed out of the terminology trap, the common tendency to label groups with names that put them beyond the pale of negotiation, such as 'Communist,' or 'enemy,' or 'evil.'" In this speech Kennedy avoided such labels of the Soviet Union. In fact, he praises the sacrifices the Russian people made in the Second World War. Sorensen said that Kennedy often used metaphors, especially nautical ones.[22] Of the six basic rules, Sorensen employed the third and fourth very effectively in this speech.

"Organize the text to simplify, clarify, emphasize," Sorensen wrote. "A speech should flow from an outline in logical order." He went on to say, "There should be a tightly organized, coherent, and consistent theme." The theme for this address was world peace and how America could lead in that endeavor. "Use variety and literary devices to reinforce memorability, not confuse or distract." Sorensen used "alliteration and repetition" to help make a speech memorable.[23] In addition he used rhyming as well. These were important elements to consider for any speech that dealt with the Cold War. Indeed, his method was very effective. Many of Kennedy's speeches are still quoted today.

Sorensen finished with two equally important rules for speech writing. The first was, "Employ elevated but not grandiose language." This element was integral when looking at an important message, especially those that involved sacrifice for the American people. Sorensen wrote,

> A president who elevates the sights of his countrymen above and beyond the limits of their daily chores ... a president whose words enable the young dreamers of his country to feel that someone is listening who cares—such a president is bound to antagonize some and ultimately disillusion others, but he nevertheless fulfills as he speaks an essential role of national leadership consistent with the Founders' vision of this country as a beacon to the world.[24]

Sorensen said that he and JFK tried to elevate their speeches without patronizing their audience. This was an especially important element at American University, as JFK wanted to convey his notions of peace to not only the college graduates, but also the world. The second important rule stated, "Substantive ideas are the most important part of any speech." What better notion that world peace? "If the ideas are great," wrote Sorensen, "the speech will be great."[25] Kennedy's insistence on a speech to discuss world peace was a momentous opportunity to invoke language that the administration had previously held back due to Cold War posturing.

Wearing a graduation gown on a bright glittering day, speaking from a podium bearing the presidential seal, John Kennedy outlined his vision for the American people. Kennedy started his speech by quoting John Masefield, who said that a university was "a place where those who hate ignorance may strive to know, where those who perceive truth may strive to make others see."[26] Kennedy chose this "time and place to discuss a topic on which ignorance too often abounds and the truth is too rarely perceived — yet it is the most important topic on earth: world peace." The speech illuminated the problems and misconceptions so dangerous in the Cold War, offering solutions. It was a doctrine contrary to the American military complex. Kennedy saw potential in the world that went beyond the crises he endured. Indeed, his cabinet members' resistance to a peaceful solution on Cuba led to an unwavering doctrine of peace, not war. Berlin, Cuba and Southeast Asia had taught him how easy it was to send in military means to combat ideas contrary to the United States. Moreover, they demonstrated how close the world was to a nuclear confrontation, with the United States and the Soviet Union at the center. This speech offered solutions to those "man made" problems.

To start, Kennedy defined the type of peace he hoped to see. "Not a Pax Americana," an allusion to the Romans, "enforced on the world by weapons of war. Not a peace of the grave or the security of the slave." He stated, "I am talking about genuine peace, the kind of peace that makes life on earth worth living, the kind that enables men and nations to grow and to hope and to build a better life for their children." The world he envisioned offered opportunities for all, he said, "not merely peace for Americans but peace for all men and women — not merely peace in our time but peace for all time." According to Kennedy, this peace was necessary in what he termed "the new face of war."

"Total war," he said, "makes no sense in an age when great powers can maintain large and relatively invulnerable nuclear forces and refuse to surrender without resort to those forces." In a nuclear age, total war had changed. It was not an option, considering that the aftermath would have devastating results for the whole world, not only the United States and the Soviet Union. "It makes no sense in an age when the deadly poisons produced by a nuclear exchange would be carried by wind and water and soil and seed to the far corners of the globe and to generations yet unborn." Kennedy went on to say that stockpiling these weapons was no way of assuring peace. "I speak of peace, therefore, as the necessary rational end of rational men." Though his message might fall on deaf ears, he concluded, "we have no more urgent task." After Kennedy defined the kind of peace he hoped to foster and the danger implicit with the arms race, he defined four elements that America needed to consider. According to Kennedy, America must examine its attitudes on peace, the Soviet Union, the Cold War, and peace and freedom at home. This journey was introspective and against the status quo. A nation reared in crisis would have a difficult time embracing peace and stability. Nevertheless, in the wake of the Cuban Missile Crisis, Kennedy made clear his intentions.

"Confident and unafraid, we labor on."

Much as in his inaugural, Kennedy wanted Americans to think about where they stood on the Soviet Union. He wanted them to look at America, and how they could shape the future of the world. He said that the Soviet Union's leaders could "adopt a more enlightened attitude. I hope they do. I believe we can help them do it." He did not lay blame on the Soviets for failure to look at the world's problems in peaceful terms. Instead, he pointed to the United States to lead the way. "But I also believe that we must reexamine our own attitude — as individuals and as a Nation — for our attitude is as essential as theirs." From Kennedy's point of view, world peace was contingent not only on the attitudes of the Soviet people and their leaders, but also on the attitudes of Americans. It was an important lesson.

"First," Kennedy said, "let us examine our attitude toward peace itself. Too many of us think it is impossible. Too many think it unreal. But that is a dangerous, defeatist belief. It leads to the conclusion that war is inevitable — that mankind is doomed — that we are gripped by forces we cannot control." Kennedy was not only asking Americans to reexamine their own attitudes, born in the ashes of the Second World War, but was empowering them to take control of peace, and not let war dictate the world's fate. Kennedy went so far as to invoke the American dream, saying, "Our problems are manmade — therefore, they can be solved by man. And man can be as big as he wants." This was the essence of his speech, empowering the people to look inward and find a way to work out their perceptions of the Soviet Union. However, he was careful not to invoke too much idealism.

"I am not referring to the absolute, infinite concept of universal peace and good will of which some fantasies and fanatics dream." He went on, "Let us focus instead on a more practical, more attainable peace — based not on a sudden revolution in human nature but on a gradual evolution in human institutions — on a series of concrete actions and effective agreements which are in the interest of all concerned." The test ban was an example of these concrete, gradual measures. World peace was not something that happened as an instant, "sudden revolution." Instead it would take time and sacrifice. "Genuine peace must be the product of many nations, the sum of many acts. It must be dynamic, not static, changing to meet the challenge of each new generation. For peace is a process — a way of solving problems." Indeed, he did not believe that the United States would bear the burden; rather, it would lead the world by example. He argued that world peace only meant living together in "mutual tolerance." This peace would enable nations to communicate and live in the world without the prospect of war. "And history teaches us," he said, "that enmities between nations, as between individuals, do not last forever." In 1963 Great Britain was the United States' greatest ally. Less than two hundred years prior, the American colonists had been tearing down a statue of King George to use for musket balls. He concluded, "So let us persevere. Peace need not be impracticable, and war need not be inevitable. By defining our goal more clearly, by making it seem more manageable and less remote, we can help all peoples to see it, to draw hope from it, and to move irresistibly toward it."

"Second," he said, "let us reexamine our attitude toward the Soviet Union." This was a radical stance in a time when such talk was considered appeasement and the United States needed to take a firm, strong stance against the Soviet Union. Kennedy quoted a Soviet text on military strategy which argued that the "American imperialist" was trying to unleash "different types of wars" against the Soviet Union. "Yet it is sad to read these Soviet statements—to realize the extent of the gulf between us." The Kennedy administration contributed to Soviet suspicion of the United States with, among other things, their counter-insurgency program. This speech and the test ban are examples of how they hoped to temper that militant policy. Indeed, Kennedy's own experiences in office illuminated the need for such a policy shift. He said that the example of the Soviet perception was also "a warning to the American people not to fall into the same trap as the Soviets, not to see only a distorted and desperate view of the other side, not to see conflict as inevitable, accommodation as impossible, and communication as nothing more than an exchange of threats." Kennedy wanted the American people to see the Russian people for who they were, not the villains they were made out to be in film and the press. "No government or social system is so evil that its people must be considered as lacking in virtue." He went on to commend the "Russian people for their many achievements—in science and space, in economic and industrial growth, in culture and in acts of courage." This was not the usual Cold War rhetoric. JFK and Ted Sorensen had constructed a speech reintroducing the Russian people to the American people — or so they hoped.

The United States and the Soviet Union had defeated Hitler's Germany in World War II. There was never a time in the history of the world where such an alliance was necessary for the peace. Kennedy wanted to show Khrushchev and the Russians that he knew the sacrifice they made in that war. "Among the many traits the peoples of our two countries have in common, none is stronger than our mutual abhorrence of war. Almost unique, among the major world powers, we have never been at war with each other." He went on to say,

> No nation in the history of battle ever suffered more than the Soviet Union suffered in the course of the Second World War. At least 20 million lost their lives. Countless millions of homes and farms were burned or sacked. A third of the nation's territory, including nearly two thirds of its industrial base, was turned into a wasteland — a loss equivalent to the devastation of this country east of Chicago.

This acknowledgment had great significance. Indeed, there were many in military circles that did not want Kennedy to utter those words. The United States came out of World War II as a much stronger nation, but so did the Soviet Union. Kennedy went on to say that should total war every break out, all that had been built in both nations would be destroyed in the first twenty-four hours. He urged Americans, "So, let us not be blind to our differences—but let us also direct attention to our common interests and to the means by which those differences can be resolved." He concluded with what is the most recognizable passage from this speech: "For, in the final analysis, our most basic common link is that we all inhabit this small planet. We all breathe the same air. We all cherish our children's future. And we are all mortal." This was a doctrine of extraordinary proportions. It is a testament to Kennedy's commitment to peace and Sorensen's ability as a writer. Sorensen employed many of those aforementioned six principles. His language and tone sent a message to the American people that they should all look beyond the usual prejudices and find a common link to the Soviet Union.

JFK went even further with his third point, telling Americans, "Let us reexamine our attitude toward the cold war, remembering that we are not engaged in a debate, seeking to pile up debating points." The world was not something that the United States could control. Despite the fact that presidents prior to Kennedy had attempted to move the world in various directions, he said, "We must deal with the world as it is, and not as it might have been had the history of the last 18 years been different." Kennedy's Cold War policy was moving to one of understanding, empathy. This was a president who finally felt he had enough experience and knowledge to assert his own ideology into foreign affairs. "For we can seek a relaxation of tensions without relaxing our guard. And, for our part, we do not need to use threats to prove that we are resolute." Kennedy believed that there was a way to confront injustice without resorting to nuclear war. In this section of the speech, Kennedy pointed to American actions around the world and characterized them as "peaceful." In addition, he emphasized the importance of the United States' alliance with other nations.

JFK said, "Our commitment to defend Western Europe and West Berlin, for example, stands undiminished because of the identity of our vital interests." While this was an important gesture to the Russian people, he emphasized that the United States would "make no deal with the Soviet Union at the expense of other nations and other peoples, not merely because they are our partners, but also because their interests and ours converge." Again, he mixed the olive branch with the arrows, a common practice in Kennedy's rhetoric. However, it was not done in a truculent, dangerous fashion. His argument was that the nations of the world needed to understand that "mutual tolerance" went both ways. He said that the Soviet Union needed to refrain from imposing their "political and economic" system on others. "For there can be no doubt that, if all nations could refrain from interfering in the self-determination of others, the peace would be much more assured." Kennedy asserted self-determination and also took the opportunity to announce that the United States, Great Britain and the Soviet Union would engage in what he termed "high level" discussions on a test ban treaty. "Our hopes must be tempered with the caution of history — but with our hopes go the hopes of all mankind." Also, JFK pledged that the United States would not conduct nuclear tests in the atmosphere. It was gesture that put action to his words.

He turned from the Cold War to confront the domestic issues at home. Racial segregation was another very important front that both John and Robert Kennedy had been fighting since the beginning of the administration: "Finally, my fellow Americans, let us examine our attitude toward peace and freedom here at home. The quality and spirit of our own society must justify and support our efforts abroad." Sorensen and Kennedy brought the issue back to the American people. They started pointing to what Americans could do for their country, and then urged them to make America the beacon needed to foster such grand change in the world. "And it is the responsibility of all citizens in all sections of this country to respect the rights of all others and to respect the law of the land." He concluded, "All this is not unrelated to world peace." He asked the people: "Is not peace, in the last analysis, basically a matter of human rights — the right to live out our lives without fear of devastation — the right to breathe air as nature provided it — the right of future generations to a healthy existence?" In a nation divided on the issue of segregation, Kennedy was once again going against the status quo, telling Americans that human rights were as important as world peace. It only seems obvious today because Kennedy said it then.

Kennedy concluded the speech by saying that the United States would never start a war. "This generation of Americans has already had enough — more than enough — of war and hate and oppression. We shall be prepared if others wish it. We shall be alert to try to stop it." His final message was not Cold War rhetoric, nor was it an emphasis on the might of the United States. Instead, it asserted his pledge to peace. "But we shall also do our part to build a world of peace where the weak are safe and the strong are just. We are not helpless before that task or hopeless of its success. Confident and unafraid, we labor on — not toward a strategy of annihilation but toward a strategy of peace."

"The impact of the appeal will be felt in many ways."

The day after the speech, the *New York Times* reported, "President Kennedy's effort today to alter the direction of Soviet–United States relations represented his fundamental and long held views on the cold war." Building on principles outlined in his inaugural and an address to the United Nations in 1961, this speech was meant to be a "peace speech." The article said that administration sources confirmed that the test ban treaty did not influence the speech. Instead, the "Soviet agreement provided Mr. Kennedy with an appropriate time and place to do several things he had wanted to do." The article went on to say that Kennedy's speech was "most carefully constructed, in content and tone, in the hope that it would strengthen Mr. Khrushchev in any disposition to resist those who might be urging a tough line."[27]

According to other articles in the *Times*, the speech had further implications in other parts of the world: "The impact of the appeal will be felt in many ways, according to a Latin-American source. He described the speech as extremely significant, well timed, and courageous." The article went on to say, "The President's speech was characterized as 'The Kennedy Doctrine' by an Arab representative who said that there was a great deal of thought behind it."[28] Some in London had called it Kennedy's "greatest speech," and it was published "extensively and prominently" in newspapers.[29] Indeed, this speech had lofty ideas and important principles to dictate the rest of the administration. Had Kennedy not been killed, it would have been the outline for his foreign policy with the Soviet Union. Max Frankel of the *New York Times* also reported that Averell Harriman would lead the United States at the test ban treaty conference, which was to take place in Moscow. The three-power negotiation, which included Britain, was meant to bring closure to nuclear testing. Frankel reported that Harriman was "expected to convey the President's hopes and anxieties not only to the Soviet negotiators but to Premier Khrushchev personally." China's reluctance to enter into such a deal had been a source of tension within the Sino-Soviet relationship. Frankel also wrote, "Generally there was not much optimism in official Washington that the President's conciliation address ... would produce an agreement on the test ban treaty or anything else."[30] In fact, Senator Barry Goldwater, Republican from Arizona, attacked JFK, saying that he was taking a "soft stance" against the communists. In addition, Goldwater and other conservative Republicans in congress opposed this "compromise with the Soviet Union."[31]

Michael Beschloss argues, "This lyrical address was easily the best speech of Kennedy's life. Read three decades later, the words do not exert the power they did at the time. The reason for that power was their startling dissonance with the shrill alarms of the President's first two years in office." Beschloss concluded, "No Cold War President, save Eisenhower after Stalin's death, had so publicly endorsed the need to find a way out of conflict."[32] Aleksandr Fursenko and Timothy Naftali argue, "At the heart of the speech was the issue that had been the centerpiece of his private diplomacy with Moscow for over two years." Indeed, this was an olive branch that would not have come in 1961 or 1962. Only after the two powers had come to the brink and back were they able to extend such possibilities. Fursenko and Naftali went on to say, "The Cuban missile crisis may well have opened Khrushchev's eyes to the dangers of an uncontrolled arms race. But it was John Kennedy's courage in June 1963 that drove Khrushchev to give the White House an arms control agreement, which he knew Kennedy personally desired."[33] Courage was at the heart of the speech. Many in Washington did not approve of such rhetoric, preferring that crisis drive the administration's agenda.

A test ban treaty was signed with Harriman at the helm in Moscow. The British, American and Russian delegates were able to come to an agreement. When the three powers initialed the deal, Harold Macmillan burst into tears as he told his wife. In a phone call to Kennedy, the British prime minister said, "I find myself unable to express my real feelings on the telephone tonight.... I do understand the high degree of courage and faith which you have shown."[34] This arms control agreement, in the wake of the Bay of Pigs, Berlin and the Cuban Missile Crisis, is evidence that Kennedy and his advisors had made it to a new level in the Cold War. They presided in the worst of times, and it seemed that the two nations were finally looking toward détente. While the Chinese and French were still stubborn obstacles to peace, the other three members of the Security Council were in agreement.

At the heart of this success were the words that drove so many to envision peace. Ted Sorensen had as much to do with this new episode in the Cold War as did Kennedy and Khrushchev. Sorensen wrote in this memoirs,

> JFK and I agreed that Woodrow Wilson's call "to make the world safe for democracy"—which sounded like imposing our system on mankind, exactly what he did not want the Communists to do with their system—should be changed to "making the world safe for diversity," thereby envisioning the day when each country, including those within the Communist orbit, would be free to choose its own system.[35]

This speech was not one man's vision, rather a collective vision that involved Sorensen and Kennedy. Once again, for Kennedy and Sorensen peace did not mean imposing American ideology on other nations. It did not mean that the Soviets had to acquiesce to American demands in Europe. World peace meant that every nation should accept each other's differences. It was a message that resonated beyond foreign policy and into the segregated South. After Sorensen wrote the speech, and while Kennedy was on his way to give it, it was shared with Bundy, Rusk and McNamara, who were asked not to circulate it among their departments. Sorensen said Kennedy "knew that the unprecedented message of the speech would set off alarm bells in more bellicose quarters in Washington, possibly producing leaks and political attacks in advance of his talk."[36] Kennedy wanted to exude the same idealism he had before he encountered such crises as Berlin and Cuba. Looking to the future, he tapped Sorensen's ability to use words, shaping his vision for peace in the world. What followed was a trip to Europe and another historic speech that many believed was a turning point in the Cold War.

14

"Ich bin ein Berliner"

"Our unity was forged in a time of danger."

Soon after his "peace speech," Kennedy took a trip to Europe in the hopes of strengthening the United States' relationship with the rest of the West. The strained relationship with France, in particular, was similar to the Soviet relationship with China. De Gaulle did not like the idea that the United States was at the center of power and France was a smaller player in global politics. There was, however, a level of irony in that Kennedy was very popular in France. Frank Costigliola argues, "Even as the Kennedy administration failed to shape Europe's development and stimulated anti–Americanism, many Europeans admired the charismatic President."[1] In addition, de Gaulle created problems for the president by not participating in the limited nuclear test ban treaty, which was signed by Britain, the United States and the Soviet Union. George Ball wrote a briefing memo to Kennedy before he made the trip to Europe entitled "The Mess in Europe and the Meaning of Your Trip." Ball wrote, "Never, at any time since the war—and this is the main point—has Europe been in graver danger of backsliding into the old destructive habits." He continued, "De Gaulle's revival of nationalism threatens to restore the disastrous cycle that has marked modern French history."[2] Ball argued that this was the worst time to undermine American authority in the region, as there would be a shift in power in West Germany. He said that Germany was not "institutionally" tied to the West. "A Germany at large," he wrote, "can be like a canon on shipboard in high sea." Ball said that the Americans still had influence in Berlin, which was a "Soviet hostage, and the German people know that their only defense is the American strength and commitment."[3] This was an important point, and put greater emphasis on Kennedy's trip to Germany.

Kennedy needed to demonstrate to the people in Germany that America was committed to holding its ground in that region. While the "peace speech" brought hope to some in the world, the FRG took it with apprehension and concern. Despite the fact that Kennedy made it clear he would not negotiate the United States' position in Europe, many believed that the U.S would sacrifice its alliance with Europe for its own security. Indeed, at the height of the Cuban Missile Crisis, Kennedy's advisors explored such avenues. Therefore, this feeling of trepidation was not unwarranted, and needed to be addressed by Kennedy if he wanted to maintain a strong relationship with Europe.

The State Department discussed the significance of this trip in a 14 June 1963 memo saying, "While officially labeled an 'informal working visit,' the President's trip to West Germany and Berlin will have many of the trappings of a state visit and can be expected to attract more public attention and interest than any previous visit by a foreign statesman to modern Germany." The memo went on to state that this was such an important visit because it was the first visit by Kennedy since assuming office and only the third by a president; both Truman and Eisenhower had visited Berlin during their presidencies. Another point was, "The visit comes at a time of change and flux in Western Europe when the role and influence of the American President have acquired added significance in German eyes." Furthering that point, the memo said, "The visit comes at an important turning point in modern German history, on the eve of the transition from [Konrad] Adenauer to [Ludwig] Erhard with its obvious relation to the shifting of generations in German political life."[4] The change in leadership only compounded the feelings of foreboding in Germany.

The first of seven broad objectives stated that Kennedy had "to furnish tangible evidence of American good will toward the German people and of our recognition of the increasing importance of the Federal Republic as one of our major allies." The State Department also stated that Kennedy needed "to provide graphic emphasis to the continuing American presence in and responsibility for Europe and to help restore some of the momentum toward European unity and Atlantic interdependence." While there were other objectives, the final one was "to strengthen German-American cooperation, understanding and sense of common purpose at the top level by discussion of current problems of mutual concern."[5] This advice was presented to Kennedy and his advisors as they prepared for their trip abroad. Clearly, this was a defining moment in Kennedy's pursuit of an alliance with Europe. This alliance had been strained in the wake of Soviet and American rhetoric. Indeed, according to the State Department, Kennedy should aim at fostering this relationship with Germany. Ball's memo was right. At the heart of this relationship was how America demonstrated to Germany its steadfastness, halting the Soviet threat. Kennedy and his advisors contemplated giving Berlin to the Soviets during the missile crisis, and did in fact give up missiles in Turkey. Europe needed a strong show of support from Kennedy.

Richard Reeves argues, "The depth of that American influence struck President Kennedy within minutes of stepping off Air Force One in Bonn on the morning of June 23." He went on to write, "In the German capital, and then in Cologne and Frankfurt, the crowds were gigantic, chanting over and over again: 'Kenn-ah-dee! Kenn-ah-dee! Kenn-ah-dee!'"[6] Upon his arrival Kennedy said, "I am grateful for your invitation and I am happy to be here. I have crossed the Atlantic, some 3,500 miles, at a crucial time in the life of the Grand Alliance. Our unity was forged in a time of danger; it must be maintained in a time of peace." He went on to say, "Our Alliance was founded to deter a new war; it must now find the way to a new peace. Our strategy was born in a divided Europe, but it must look to the goal of European unity and an end to the divisions of people and countries." With echoes of his American University speech, Kennedy hoped to win the crowds of Germany. The response told him that he was succeeding. JFK said, "We all know the meaning of freedom and our people are determined upon its peaceful survival and success." This beginning demonstrated that Kennedy was not only in Europe to preserve the "Grand Alliance" but also to promote his new vision of peace. However, he tempered his words with both the olive branch and sword. "So long as our presence is desired and required, our forces and commitments will remain." JFK said. "For your safety is our safety, your liberty is our liberty, and any attack on your soil is an attack upon our own. Out of necessity, as well as sentiment, in our approach to peace as well as war, our fortunes are one."[7] He did not stop there.

At City Hall in Bonn, JFK said, "I can assure you that as long as there are any who join with us, who wish this common effort to continue, the United States will help bear its fair share of the burden in a great half-circle, stretching from Berlin to Saigon," he said at the city hall in Bonn. "We will keep this free world free until the day comes, as Thomas Jefferson predicted it would, that the disease of liberty, which is catching, spreads throughout the world."[8] Indeed, the implication Kennedy conveyed urged a world free from communism and embracing a democratic spirit, something that Jefferson had known. This was exactly what the State Department memo as well as Ball's briefing paper had advised the president. It was also, in a larger sense, evidence of JFK's tenuous position. While he wanted peace, there were realistic obstacles to attaining such goals. Indeed, being a keen student of history, Kennedy was aware of Wilson's failed attempt at the League of Nations. Bearing that in mind and knowing the complexities of Western Europe, this was not the only time that Kennedy would imply such resolve.

"This is a matter of the greatest importance to us and I hope to the people here."

President Kennedy spent a few days in Germany. Following the day of his arrival, Kennedy took questions from reporters at the foreign ministry in Bonn. When asked of the importance that Kennedy placed on the relationship between Germany and the United States, JFK responded, "That relationship is, I think, even more vital today [than in 1945] because while I think the security of Western Europe against military attack is well guaranteed by the efforts that we have all made collectively, I think Western Europe and the United States, and Canada, Great Britain, and the Commonwealth, have a major role in serving as the center or the core of a great effort throughout the world to maintain freedom." Once again, Kennedy stressed the importance of this relationship and how it would serve as security from communist aggression in this region. Though he did not use those words, it was implicit due to the nature of the discussion and the history. He said, "The Federal Republic and Berlin, are in the front lines of this struggle."

A follow-up question addressed some of his remarks from the previous day. One reporter asked JFK about his reaction to some of Adenauer's comments at the airport. According to the reporter, it seemed that the chancellor was concerned that Kennedy's new commitment to peace, as outlined in the American University speech, would hamper his ability to defend Berlin effectively. Kennedy responded, "Most of his remarks were a quotation from a speech which I gave at American University a week ago. He was quoting statements that I had made in regard to our commitment to Western Europe which, of course, is very basic to American policy." He furthered, "I also feel that the effort that we are making is on behalf of freedom and peace. That is the object of our policy, the policy of the United States."[9] Again, Kennedy mixed his message. While it was clear that he was committed to peace, he also had to contend with the European alliance and the unwillingness of its leaders to see peace as anything other than appeasement. In the wake of Hitler and Nazism it seemed to many that confronting aggression was the only policy.

Kennedy was asked why he was willing to make this "entire trip." "Because," he replied, "I regard the relationship between the United States and Western Europe as vital to our security. This is a changing period in the West as well as in the East. We deal with problems of nuclear defense, of monetary policy, of trade policy." He wanted to stress the camaraderie between Western Europe and the United States, as the State Department memo suggested. He went on to comment, "I think it very appropriate that the President of the United States come to Western Europe. This is a matter of the greatest importance to us and I hope to the people here." While Kennedy was walking the tightrope of satisfying the West and keeping a strong stance on the Soviet Union, another reporter wanted to explore his "peace speech."[10]

One reporter asked Kennedy about his comment that the Soviet Union "should let each nation choose its own future so long as that choice does not interfere with the choices of others." This is strong evidence that the American University speech was pervasive overseas as well as to many in Washington. Kennedy said, "What we mean is that we cannot accept with equanimity, nor do we propose to, the Communist takeover of countries which are now free." He went on,

> What we have said is that we accept the principle of self-determination. Governments choose a type of government, if the people choose it. If they have the opportunity to choose another kind, if the one they originally chose is unsatisfactory, then we regard

that as a free matter and we would accept it, regardless of what their choice might be. But what we will not accept is the subversion or an attack upon a free country which threatens, in my opinion, the security of other free countries. I think that is the distinction we have made for a great many years.¹¹

While it was clear that Kennedy wanted peace, this is another example where he wanted to maintain a strong stance on any "subversion" or "attack" on another country. Indeed, he had similar statements in the speech, but never did he mention those words in describing the Soviet threat. Kennedy was politically acute when answering questions in Germany because he had to maintain a strong stance in the face of the West Germans, who, according to Kennedy, had been a part of this struggle since 1945.

Another great example at this conference of such posturing involved East Berlin. Kennedy was asked if he planned to travel to East Berlin since he had a legal right to go. He said no, "Because the trip that we planned is to take us to West Berlin. I don't think that any gesture, however spectacular, of this kind would materially improve the lot of the people of East Berlin. That is why we are not going."¹² Kennedy's reference to East Berliners' "lot" is a clear reference to communism. Indeed, Kennedy skillfully maneuvered through the questions. When asked about de Gaulle, he chose to answer directly. When asked about the pope, he chose to stress that he was going to Italy to meet with the Italian government. These responses are all very reminiscent of the 1960 election, when Kennedy's closest advisors helped him shape an aura of a youthful, independent leader. This exchange was also a great example of the Kennedy wit, which helped him relate to the American people.

"Let them come to Berlin."

Kennedy arrived in West Berlin on 26 June 1963. He made two stops before he made a speech that would be recalled for years to come as a highlight of his presidency. First, Kennedy went to see Checkpoint Charlie, the roadblock separating East from West. Perhaps he wanted to see where conflict almost broke out between the Soviets and the United States during the fall of 1961. Tom Wicker of the *New York Times* wrote,

> Mr. Kennedy stood within a few feet of the wall at Checkpoint Charlie. At the Brandenburg Gate, a viewing stand was erected for him about 50 yards from the wall. The wall is about six feet high at this point and without barbed wire along its upper edge. The President's approach to the wall were moments charged with drama, but so was almost every other move he made in Berlin today.¹³

Kennedy reportedly told his staff to stay on the ground while he climbed to the top of the wall to peer over. On the other side the streets were cleared. Three women had their windows open waving handkerchiefs at him. He turned to

General James Polke, the American commander in the city, and asked if that was dangerous. He replied, "Yes it is." Hugh Sidey, the writer for *Time* magazine, commented, as Kennedy slowly climbed down: "He looks like a man who just glimpsed Hell."[14]

The motorcade made its way to city hall, where there was a high platform built. Kennedy made his way up to the podium to address the 150,000 people who squeezed themselves into the square. Leaning on the podium as the wind pushed the tapestry and flowers around, Kennedy started by thanking Mayor Willy Brandt for letting him speak. Ted Sorensen looked on as Kennedy gave a speech that he wrote. He started his speech saying, "Two thousand years ago the proudest boast was 'civis Romanus sum.' Today, in the world of freedom, the proudest boast is 'Ich bin ein Berliner.'" The crowd roared in agreement with Kennedy. After the applause he went on to say, "There are many people in the world who really don't understand, or say they don't, what is the great issue between the free world and the Communist world." He pounded on the podium with each of the next six syllables: "Let them come to Berlin." His thick Boston accent was evidence of the emotion he felt being in front of those people, who he claimed were on the front lines. There was no way he could hide the feelings he had in front of people he stood up for on many occasions.

The emotion was palpable on both sides of the podium. People were cheering and waving their hands in agreement. "There are some who say that communism is the wave of the future. Let them come to Berlin." Each time Kennedy said, "Let them come to Berlin," he emphasized it with his gesture on the podium. He went on slowly, saying, "And there are even a few who say that it is true that communism is an evil system, but it permits us to make economic progress. Lass' sic nach Berlin kommen. Let them come to Berlin." Using the German language added to the emotion of the event and the meaning in his words, fostering solidarity between these two nations. Sorensen played a major role in a successful statement of Kennedy's resoluteness in Europe as well as his empathy toward the Berlin cause.

Kennedy went to great lengths in this speech, not only to demonstrate his unwillingness to give up Berlin, but also to show the world that, while he wanted peace, he was also able to meet confrontation. He addressed the wall, which he climbed, looking over to see those three women waving: "Freedom has many difficulties and democracy is not perfect, but we have never had to put a wall up to keep our people in, to prevent them from leaving us." He said that he wanted to extend the thanks of all Americans for what West Berliners had been doing the past few years. "I know of no town, no city, that has been besieged for 18 years," he said, "that still lives with the vitality and the force, and the hope and the determination of the city of West Berlin." With each adjective, he stressed the importance. This speech was largely a success not only because of Sorensen's words, but also the passion and zeal with which Kennedy gave the speech.

As the wind tussled his thick, wavy hair Kennedy commented further on the wall, saying:

> While the wall is the most obvious and vivid demonstration of the failures of the Communist system, for all the world to see, we take no satisfaction in it, for it is, as your Mayor has said, an offense not only against history but an offense against humanity, separating families, dividing husbands and wives and brothers and sisters, and dividing a people who wish to be joined together.

On the heels of the "peace speech," this was a serious detour and an embrace of Cold War rhetoric. Indeed, using imagery that linked lost family members and associating the Berlin Wall with the failures of communism could potentially hurt the test ban treaty as well as other means for peace. In fact, Sorensen and Bundy were worried that these words could hamper any peace arrangement with the Soviets and tailored the subsequent speech at the Free University of Berlin to tone down the message.

Invoking John Donne, Kennedy told the crowd at city hall, "You live in a defended island of freedom, but your life is part of the main." He went on:

> So let me ask you, as I close, to lift your eyes beyond the dangers of today, to the hopes of tomorrow, beyond the freedom merely of this city of Berlin, or your country of Germany, to the advance of freedom everywhere, beyond the wall to the day of peace with justice, beyond yourselves and ourselves to all mankind.

Kennedy was slow and methodical. He pronounced his words, stressing their importance. It was a great speech, worthy of the attention it gets from historians not only for its message, but also its delivery. "Freedom is indivisible," he said, "and when one man is enslaved, all are not free." He went on to say that the people of West Berlin would take pride when the day came that Berlin was a part of the rest of the free world in that they were on the front lines. He finished by saying, "All free men, wherever they may live, are citizens of Berlin." He paused, looked up and said, "Therefore, as a free man, I take pride in the words 'Ich bin ein Berliner.'"[15] Kennedy took his speech, shoving it in his pocket and turned to leave the stage in dramatic fashion. He looked out at the crowd and smiled, putting his hand in his coat.

"We'll never have another day like this one, as long as we live."

While the speech and the trip were successful, it did not do much to strengthen his relationship with the Soviets, and the French were still a thorn in the side of the United States. Regardless, it was a trip that Kennedy needed in order to see that he had come into his own with his foreign policy. Khrushchev did not beat on him, as he did in Vienna, nor was he considered the man who accompanied Jackie Kennedy to France. He was the president of the United States who gave a stirring speech in West Berlin, the symbol of the Western push against communism. When he boarded the plane to fly to Ireland, he commented to Sorensen: "We'll never have another day like this one, as long as we live."[16] Indeed, it was a momentous speech that would be lauded by many as showing Kennedy's determination to keep Berlin free.

The *New York Times* wrote an editorial the next day: "President Kennedy strode up to the Berlin wall, peered over it into drab communist ruled territory and denounced the barricade as a symbol of communism's failure and offense against history and humanity." The editorial asserted, "Defense, vital as it is, is only one aspect of Mr. Kennedy's 'strategy of peace,' which he also carried to and over the wall." The *Times*, like Kennedy, saw a strong stance against communism as an important factor for peace. "But the winds of change," the editorial stated, "are unmistakably blowing across the Iron Curtain, undermining the anachronistic police state and creating a new climate which will some day permit the reunification of peoples." The editorial went on to say that Kennedy reminded Americans how strong the allure of the West was to the East. It concluded by saying that Kennedy left "to Berlin, Germany and all of Europe — East and West — a message of hope and caution." It went on, "Premier Khrushchev, who is now rushing to Berlin, may dispute the course of history, but even he cannot dispute the President's peaceful intent."[17] The editors of the *New York Times* saw this speech as complementary to American University speech. They even went as far to cite the phrase "strategy of peace" from that speech when characterizing this Berlin speech.

Tom Wicker of the *New York Times* wrote, "President Kennedy saw the miracle and the tragedy of West Berlin today as the city turned out to greet him and applaud his country. The reception was one of the largest and most emotional Mr. Kennedy has ever received." Indeed, Berlin was literally and symbolically the front line in the Cold War. Kennedy had staked a good deal of his presidency on the well-being of Berlin. In 1961, he had nearly gone to war with Khrushchev. In 1962, he had avoided using Berlin as bargaining chip to assure American security. "The West Berliners," Wicker wrote, "leaped and screamed along the curbs, waved their handkerchiefs and a variety of flags, threw flowers and broke through police barriers to run aside Mr. Kennedy's car. Some succeeded in shaking his hand. Twice he caught bouquets."[18] Emotion ruled the day and Kennedy was at the center.

TASS, the official Soviet press, reported, "Kennedy's visit to the Berlin wall 'heated the atmosphere in the front-line city to the limit.'" The agency went on to state that Kennedy's "speech at City Hall had 'further whipped up anti-communist hysteria, fanned these days by the West Berlin advocates of the cold war.'"[19] Indeed, some of Kennedy's advisors had felt similarly, in that they wanted to foster the notion of peace and the provocative language did not help that endeavor. Later in the day, at the Free University of Berlin, Kennedy said,

> As I said this morning, I am not impressed by the opportunities open to popular fronts throughout the world. I do not believe that any democrat can successfully ride that tiger. But I do believe in the necessity of great powers working together to preserve the human race, or otherwise we can be destroyed.[20]

This was a clear overture to Khrushchev, saying that the two powers must "work together" to "preserve the human race." Arthur Krock of the *Times* argued, "Working with the communists is precisely what the United States has been trying to do." Krock went on to write,

> The spokesmen to the press of the White House and the State Department who are accompanying Mr. Kennedy will have no difficulty in explaining how a policy "of working together" with the Soviet Union can be pursued when anyone when anyone has only to come to Berlin to understand that to "work with the communists" is an utter impossibility.[21]

Kennedy was throwing off the ghosts of the past. Berlin was the cathartic speech he needed to hopefully reassure his alliance with Western Europe while ushering in a period of peace and prosperity in the world. There were many, however, who did not want peace. Unfortunately, they were the ones to shape the Cold War after 1963, not President Kennedy.

Peace President

John Kennedy wanted peace, not war. His American University speech can be seen as a doctrine, outlining how he planned to bring the world away from the brink of war. Sorensen's words combined with Kennedy's delivery gave the president two speeches that have been remembered for decades. The American University speech stands as the call for world peace. The Berlin speech complements this doctrine, sending a message about how the U.S. could achieve peace, but not at the expense of prestige or its allies. The test ban treaty lay at the heart of the commencement address, while fostering better relations with Europe were behind the strong rhetoric at Berlin. Indeed, both speeches were foreign policy achievements that laid the groundwork for future generations.

Ted Sorensen was Kennedy's scribe who crafted his public voice. While JFK collaborated with his advisor, it was Sorensen's deliberate language that sent a message to the Soviets and the world. He captivated the world on many occasions, helping them see Kennedy's full vision. After the Cuban Missile Crisis, Kennedy and Khrushchev attempted to communicate peaceful ideas. Their endeavor at this back-channel correspondence, once again, is evidence of this effort. It seemed their brush with nuclear war shaped these new attitudes. In addition, it may have warmed some in their governments as well. Clearly, there was a small window to achieve a substantial peace agreement. While the test ban treaty did not guarantee a world without nuclear war — indeed the provisions in it were limited — it did demonstrate that there was some goodwill on both sides. Despite the fact that the Chinese were challenging Khrushchev and the French were always reluctant allies of the United States, this act gave hope to the rest of the world. Hope was at the heart of both speeches.

While Kennedy and Khrushchev continued their discourse on disarmament, JFK's reliance on unusual channels for diplomacy also paved the way to a deeper understanding between the United States and the Soviet Union. Norman Cousins' advice, after a meeting with Khrushchev, had an effect on Kennedy. Cousins' insistence that Kennedy should proclaim such a statement on world peace gave him the final ingredient needed to do so. Moreover, Kennedy's decision to do this without consulting his advisors, as Sorensen wrote, is evidence that his confidence in foreign affairs had changed since the start of his administration. All of his challenges brought him to the realization that the world needed a leader in peace, not war. There were few times in history that the world had experienced such leadership. Kennedy was trying to foster such a period. His death, however, made it impossible.

Ted Sorensen's rules for speech writing had governed his actions with every speech. These basic tenets sent a public message, not only to Khrushchev, but also to the world. It was not limited to foreign policy. This approach would also guide the nation at dangerous times in the civil rights struggle. Indeed, his last point, that "if ideas are great, the speech will be great," dictated the premises of both the American University speech and the Berlin speech. What greater ideas were there at that time than world peace and self-determination? Sorensen's pen sent the world a message from the young president that after three years in office he was just getting warmed up.

Kennedy's insistence that Americans must reexamine their attitudes was contrary to American ideology. From Americans' perspective democracy and freedom were right and communism was wrong. Clearly, the evidence examined in this study suggests that Kennedy did not abide by the established way of thinking. His intent had always been to usher in a new age of peace. Pressure from the military and world events beyond his control led him to embrace nuclear testing, counter-insurgency, and other less peaceful means to confront the Soviet Union. This speech was Kennedy and Sorensen's vision for the world, and defined the role America would play in that vision. Moreover, they hoped that more nations would embrace this vision. Kennedy has commented to Khrushchev that they were the only ones to understand what it meant to bring one's country to the brink of war in the nuclear age. Much as in the inaugural address, Kennedy emphasized time and sacrifice to the American people. In his speech, he asked Americans, once again, to look inward and examine their own attitudes and how those ideas had shaped America. He also asked the world to embrace his "strategy of peace." Many argue that the American University speech was Kennedy's greatest success. Berlin, however, is another speech that has withstood time and is considered equally important.

When Kennedy went to Europe in June 1963, it was to foster a greater relationship with Europe. His four days in Germany would give the world a vision of a young, vibrant Cold Warrior refusing to give in to communist aggression. After the American University speech, Kennedy's words in Germany demonstrated that the path to peace was not laden with naiveté. He was realistic, in a Rooseveltian sense, that without a clear opposition to communism he could not foster self-determination, which was paramount in his vision of peace. His point of view was not limited to the Berlin speech. The speeches and press conference prior to that statement shaped the tone of his trip. The speech was a culminating, climactic event, defining America's role in the world. Sorensen and Bundy were a part of Kennedy's entourage. Unlike the first trip to Europe, this excursion had seasoned veterans crafting Kennedy's message. Each time JFK spoke, he had clear objectives. This is a clear example of how Kennedy learned to work with his advisors and they, in turn, learned to work with him.

The Berlin speech was given with such drama and deliberateness that Khrushchev could not misconstrue Kennedy's message. The solidarity that Sorensen hoped to convey worked brilliantly. Much like the American University speech, it was lauded as a major triumph. The speech, at the outset, seemed a truculent, defying move in the wake of a speech outlining a peaceful doctrine. The Berlin speech and the American University speech acutely defined American foreign policy for the world. Kennedy wanted peace, but was unwilling to compromise American values and allies in the process. These two speeches show the world that Kennedy was able to lead in peace and war — a quality that few leaders had. Unfortunately, he would not live to act on his vision of peace.

Epilogue

John Kennedy evolved from a young, ambitious senator in 1960 to a learned statesman in 1963. That growth did not come without travails and triumphs. The Bay of Pigs was a defining moment for his presidency. It demonstrated to the world and the United States that JFK still had much to learn, but was willing to take the blame and move on. The instance led Kennedy to second-guess his military advisors and establish a better system of advisement that involved people he trusted. This kitchen cabinet helped him establish his foreign policy. Kennedy's subsequent performance at Vienna only brought more apprehension and foreboding from members of his administration and abroad. Indeed, Kennedy faltered for much of 1961.

The Berlin crisis in 1961 was another turning point for Kennedy. He relied on back-channel overtures, not the usual diplomatic course, to stave off crisis. From then on Kennedy surrounded himself with people who would shape his vision and not act on their own personal agendas. Robert Kennedy, Maxwell Taylor, Robert McNamara, McGeorge Bundy and Theodore Sorensen were people to whom Kennedy confided ideas and aspirations. While it was not unprecedented for a president to have such relationships, recognizing this instance helps see how JFK moved from a leader who stumbled out of the gates to one with conviction, vision and the tools to implement those ideas. Kennedy did not have a chief of staff and relied on these chosen few to advise him on every matter. While they all contributed, it seemed that after the Bay of Pigs, Robert Kennedy took the lead. JFK valued relationship and saw his ability to foster these relationships as a method to gain direction and guidance from those whom he trusted. Kennedy's personality lent itself to creating rapport with people and establishing long lasting relationships. Those were the elements necessary to confront Soviet aggression.

As the decade moved on, the Cold War went from a focus on Berlin and Cuba to Southeast Asia. Vietnam became a source of tension and trepidation in those final months of 1963. After the Taylor mission, Kennedy was reluctant to send in a great many U.S. troops. George Herring comments, "American officials had long agreed that Diem's repressive and inefficient government constituted a major obstacle to defeating the insurgency."[1] Herring states, "The number of American 'advisors' was increased from 3,205 in December 1961 to more than 9,000 by the end of 1962."[2] Veterans of both World War II and Korea helped the Vietnamese in their efforts with the Vietcong. While this improved South Vietnamese morale, the insurgents quickly adapted and would regain the initiative in late 1962.[3] Herring argues, "Throughout the spring of 1963, optimism and uncertainty coexisted uneasily in both Saigon and Washington."[4] Indeed that summer Buddhists, in protest of the Diem regime, staged an uprising in Saigon that led to an elder monk's setting himself ablaze for the world to see. Diem's government slowly collapsed. At one point Robert Kennedy suggested that the United States leave the region.[5] Diem faced a great deal of scrutiny. By early November a coup would topple his government and kill its leaders. This act ushered in a new phase in American foreign policy.

Kennedy was unable to refocus his efforts in Vietnam. So much was unknown because he chose to focus on Russia instead of Southeast Asia. Vietnam was something he hoped to tackle in the next few months and into 1964. On 22 November 1963 Lee Harvey Oswald's bullets put an end to the Kennedy era. His doctrine of peace and the New Frontier vision were laid to waste at Dealey Plaza. The subsequent issues pervading Vietnam muffled some of those grand ideas. His brother's campaign in 1968 sought to reignite those ideas, but was dashed when he was also assassinated. Lyndon Johnson's shift in foreign policy focused on increasing American involvement in Vietnam, straying away from the mutual tolerance and self-determination that Kennedy invoked in the last year of his life. John Kennedy had much to deal with in his three years in office. He was fortunate to promote strong, lasting ideas. The men who helped him shape those ideas were as much responsible for that vision as JFK. The difference, however, was that Kennedy was the linchpin that kept those notions alive and a part of the discourse.

Chapter Notes

Preface

1. *New York Times* (New York), March 5, 1961.

Introduction

1. Sergei Khrushchev, "How My Father and President Kennedy Saved the World," *American Heritage* 53, no. 5 (2002): 75.
2. George Kennan, letter to President John F. Kennedy, October 22, 1963, President's Office Files, Special Corr—Kennan, G—10/22–2/8/63, Box 31, John F. Kennedy Library, Boston, MA.
3. Ibid.
4. President John F. Kennedy, letter to George Kennan, October 28, 1963, President's Office Files, Special Corr—Kennan, G—10/22–2/8/63, Box 31, John F. Kennedy Library, Boston, MA.
5. *New York Times* (New York), March 5, 1961.

Chapter 1

1. Thomas Paterson, *Kennedy's Quest for Victory: American Foreign Policy, 1961–1963* (New York: Oxford University Press, 1989), 5.
2. Arthur Schlesinger, Jr., *A Thousand Days: John F. Kennedy in the White House* (Boston: Riverside Press, Cambridge, 1965), 117.
3. David Halberstam, *Best and the Brightest* (New York: Ballantine Books, 1992), 38.
4. Anna Kasten Nelson, "President Kennedy's National Security Policy: A Reconsideration," *Reviews in American History* 19, no. 1 (March 1991): 2.
5. Michael Beschloss, *The Crisis Years: Kennedy and Khrushchev 1960–1963* (New York: Edward Burlingame Books, 1991), 11.
6. Robert Dallek, *An Unfinished Life: John F. Kennedy 1917–1963* (Boston: Little, Brown, 2003), 309.
7. Ibid., 315.
8. Halberstam, *Best and Brightest*, 28.
9. Ibid., 31.
10. Ibid., 36.
11. Dallek, 38.
12. Ibid., 64.
13. Dallek, *Unfinished Life*, 49.
14. Ibid., 51.
15. Halberstam, *Best and Brightest*, 43.
16. Ibid., 49–50.
17. Ibid., 55.
18. Ibid., 56.
19. Ibid., 59.
20. Ibid.
21. Beschloss, *Crisis Years*, 4.
22. Ibid.
23. Ibid., 50.
24. Ibid., 51.
25. Ibid., 49.
26. Ibid., 50.
27. *Foreign Relations of the United States 1961–1963* (hereafter FRUS), volume 5, *Soviet Union* (Washington: United States Government Printing Office, 1998), 15.
28. Ibid.
29. Ibid.
30. Beschloss, *Crisis Years*, 37.
31. Ibid., 42.
32. Ibid.
33. Nikita Khrushchev, *Khrushchev Remembers* (New York: Little, Brown, 1970), 505.
34. William Taubman, *Khrushchev: The Man and His Era* (New York: W.W. Norton), 484.
35. Ibid., 485.
36. Beschloss, 42.
37. William Taubman, "Khruschev vs. Mao: A Preliminary Sketch of the Role of Personality in the Sino-Soviet Split," *Cold War International Project Bulletin,* Winter, 1996/1997, issues 8–9, 243.
38. Hope Harrison, *Driving the Soviets up the Wall* (New Jersey: Princeton University, 2003), 78.
39. Gordon Chang, "JFK, China, and the Bomb," *The Journal of American History* 74, no. 4 (March 1988): 1287.

40. Ibid., 1289.
41. Beschloss, *Crisis Years*, 47.
42. Ibid., 58.
43. Richard Reeves, *President Kennedy: Profile of Power* (New York: Touchstone, 1993), 37.
44. Ibid., 41.
45. Llewellyn Thompson, telegram to President John F. Kennedy, January 19, 1961, President's Office Files, USSR — SEC 1/61–5/61, Box 125a, John F. Kennedy Library, Boston, MA.
46. Ibid.
47. FRUS 5:39.
48. Ibid., 42.
49. Llewellyn Thompson, telegram to President John F. Kennedy, January 21, 1961, President's Office Files, USSR — SEC 1/61–5/61, Box 125a, John F. Kennedy Library, Boston, MA.
50. Ibid.
51. FRUS 5:32.
52. Ibid., 31.
53. Ibid., 33.
54. Ibid., 33.
55. Ibid., 34–35.
56. Rusk's papers are not accessible at the JFK Library as of the writing of this manuscript. If they were available, the role he played in decision-making might be much clearer. However, it is clear that Rusk's advice may have been off the record on many occasions.
57. Harrison, *Driving the Soviets*, 47.
58. Ibid., 48.
59. Ibid.
60. Ibid., 94.
61. Ibid., 95.
62. Llewellyn Thompson, telegram to President John F. Kennedy, February 4, 1961, President's Office Files, USSR — SEC 1/61–5/61 Box 125a, John F. Kennedy Library, Boston, MA.
63. Ibid.
64. Ibid.
65. Ibid.
66. Ibid.
67. McGeorge Bundy, memorandum to President John F. Kennedy, February 13, 1961, National Security Files, Chronological File 1/61–3/61, Box 398, John F. Kennedy Library (hereafter JFKL), Boston, MA.
68. Ibid.
69. Marc Trachtenberg, *A Constructed Peace: The Making of the European Settlement* (New Jersey: Princeton University Press), 285.
70. McGeorge Bundy, memorandum to President John F. Kennedy, February 13, 1961, JFKL, National Security Files, Chronological File 1/61–3/61, Box 398.
71. Ibid.
72. Beschloss, *Crisis Years*, 70.

Chapter 2

1. McGeorge Bundy, memorandum to President John F. Kennedy, February 27, 1961, National Security Files, Chronological File 1/61–3/61, Box 398, JFKL.
2. McGeorge Bundy, memorandum to Pierre Salinger, February 28, 1961, National Security Files, Chronological File 1/61–3/61, Box 398, JFKL.
3. McGeorge Bundy, memorandum to Director of CIA Allen Dulles, March 10, 1961, National Security Files, Chronological File 1/61–3/61, Box 398, JFKL.
4. McGeorge Bundy, NSAM, March 11, 1961, National Security Files, Chronological File 1/61–3/61, Box 398, JFKL.
5. Ibid.
6. FRUS vol. 14, *Berlin Crisis, 1961–1962* (Washington: United States Government Printing Office, 1993), 9.
7. Ibid.
8. Frank Costigliola, "The Pursuit of the Atlantic Community: Nuclear Arms, Dollars, and Berlin," in Paterson, *Quest for Victory*, 38.
9. Ibid.
10. Ibid.
11. Ibid., 27.
12. Ibid., 39.
13. Ibid.
14. FRUS 14:18–19.
15. Ibid., 19.
16. Ibid.
17. Taubman, *Khrushchev*, 485.
18. FRUS 14:20.
19. Ibid., 24.
20. Ibid.
21. Ibid., 24.
22. Ibid., 27.
23. Ibid., 29.
24. Ibid.
25. Ibid., 30–31.
26. Ibid., 32.
27. Ibid., 35.
28. Ibid.
29. Ibid., 36–37.
30. Ibid., 37.
31. Ibid.
32. Ibid.
33. Ibid.
34. Ibid.
35. Ibid., 46.
36. Richard Reeves, *President Kennedy: Profile of Power* (New York: Touchstone, 1993), 93.
37. Arthur Schlesinger, Jr., *Robert Kennedy and His Times* (New York: Houghton Mifflin, 2002), 443.
38. McGeorge Bundy, memorandum to General Maxwell Taylor, May 4, 1961, National Security Files, Chronological File 1/61–3/61, Box 398, JFKL.

39. Ibid.
40. Ibid.
41. Ibid.
42. Ibid.

Chapter 3

1. FRUS vol. 6, *Kennedy-Khrushchev Exchanges* (Washington: United States Government Printing Office, 1998), 6.
2. Ibid.
3. Beschloss, *Crisis Years*, 80.
4. Ibid.
5. FRUS 5:93.
6. Ibid.
7. Beschloss, *Crisis Years*, pg 150.
8. Taubman, *Khrushchev*, 493.
9. Ibid.
10. FRUS 5:131.
11. Ibid., 131–132.
12. Ibid., 132.
13. FRUS 6:18.
14. Ibid., 19.
15. Ibid.
16. Dallek, *Unfinished Life*, 367.
17. Beschloss, *Crisis Years*, 152.
18. Ibid., 153.
19. Ibid.
20. Evan Thomas, *Robert Kennedy: His Life* (New York: Touchstone, 2000), 133.
21. Schlesinger, *Robert Kennedy*, 500.
22. Ibid., as quoted in a recorded interview by John Barlow Martin, March 1, 1964, I, 40, 47, JFKL oral history program.
23. Beschloss, *Crisis Years*, 156.
24. See Beschloss, *Crisis Years*, 157; Thomas, *His Life*, 135.
25. Thomas, *His Life*, 134.
26. Ibid., 135.
27. McGeorge Bundy, memorandum to President John F. Kennedy, May 16, 1961, National Security Files, Chronological File 5/16–5/31, Box 398, JFKL.
28. Ibid.
29. Ibid.
30. Ibid.
31. Ibid.
32. Ibid.
33. Ibid.
34. McGeorge Bundy, memorandum to President John F. Kennedy, May 26, 1961, National Security Files, Chronological File 5/16–5/31, Box 398, JFKL.
35. Ibid.
36. McGeorge Bundy, memorandum to President John F. Kennedy, May 27, 1961, National Security Files, Chronological File 5/16–5/31, Box 398, JFKL.
37. FRUS 5:163.
38. Ibid.
39. FRUS 5:169–170.
40. Ibid.
41. Ibid.
42. Dallek, *Unfinished Life*, 402–403.
43. Ibid., 402.
44. Thomas Paterson, "John F. Kennedy's Quest for Victory and Global Crisis," in Paterson, *Quest for Victory*, 7.
45. Ibid., 9.
46. Ibid., 14.
47. FRUS 5:139.
48. Ibid.
49. Ibid., 140.
50. Ibid.
51. Ibid., 141–142.
52. Ibid., 144.
53. Ibid., 144–145.
54. Ibid., 146.
55. Ibid., 147.
56. Ibid., 154.
57. Ibid., 155.
58. Ibid.
59. Ibid., 156–157.
60. Dallek, *Unfinished Life*, 416.

Chapter 4

1. Footage provided by the JFKL, Audiovisual Archives, TNC: 233 & FON:19.
2. Reeves, *President Kennedy*, 159; Dallek, *Unfinished Life*, 404.
3. Footage provided by the JFKL, Audiovisual Archives, TNC: 233 & FON:19.
4. Beschloss, *Crisis Years*, 193.
5. FRUS 5:172.
6. Ibid., 173.
7. Beschloss, *Crisis Years*, 186.
8. Reeves, *President Kennedy*, 160.
9. FRUS 5:175.
10. Ibid., 177.
11. Ibid.
12. Ibid., 178.
13. Reeves, *President Kennedy*, 160–161.
14. Ibid., 161.
15. Ibid., 162.
16. Taubman, *Khrushchev*, 495–496.
17. Reeves, *President Kennedy*, 162; Dallek, *Unfinished Life*, 406; Beschloss, *Crisis Years*, 197.
18. Dallek, *Unfinished Life*, 406.
19. Ibid.
20. FRUS 5:183.
21. Ibid.
22. Ibid., 184.
23. Dean Rusk, memorandum to Acting Secretary of State, June 4, 1961, JFKL, National Security Files, Countries—USSR—K Talks, Vol. I, Box 187a.
24. FRUS 5:184.
25. Dallek, *Unfinished Life*, 406.

26. Reeves, *President Kennedy,* 166; Dallek, *Unfinished Life,* 408.
27. Dallek, *Unfinished Life,* 408.
28. Ibid., 409.
29. Beschloss, *Crisis Years,* 209.
30. Ibid.
31. FRUS 5:206–207.
32. Ibid., 207.
33. Ibid., 208.
34. Ibid.
35. Beschloss, *Crisis Years,* 213.
36. FRUS 5:213.
37. Ibid., 216–217.
38. Ibid., 218.
39. Beschloss, *Crisis Years,* 217.
40. Ibid., 220.
41. FRUS 5:229.
42. Ibid., 230.
43. Beschloss, *Crisis Years,* 224.
44. Ibid.
45. Ibid.

Chapter 5

1. Beschloss, *Crisis Years,* 227.
2. Ibid., 229.
3. FRUS 14:107.
4. Ibid., 108.
5. Ibid.
6. Ibid.
7. Ibid.
8. Ibid.
9. FRUS 14:119.
10. Ibid.
11. Frank Costigliola, "Kennedy, the European Allies, and the Failure to Consult," *Political Science Quarterly* 110, no. 1 (Spring 1995): 107.
12. FRUS 14:119–120.
13. Ibid., 120.
14. Ibid.
15. Ibid.
16. Ibid.
17. FRUS 14:139.
18. Ibid., 140.
19. Ibid., 142.
20. Ibid.
21. Ibid., 162.
22. Ibid., 163.
23. Ibid.
24. Arthur Schlesinger, memorandum to President John F. Kennedy, July 7, 1961, National Security Files, Germany, Security 7/61, Folder 6, Box 117, JFKL.
25. Ibid.
26. Ibid.
27. Schlesinger, *Robert Kennedy,* 430.
28. Arthur Schlesinger, memorandum to President John F. Kennedy, July 7, 1961, National Security Files, Germany, Security 7/61, Folder 6, Box 117, JFKL.
29. Ibid.
30. McGeorge Bundy, memorandum of meeting on Berlin, July 17, 1961, National Security Files, Germany Security 7/61, Folder 6, Box 117, JFKL.
31. Ibid.
32. Ibid.
33. Ibid.
34. FRUS 14:218.
35. Maxwell Taylor, memorandum to President John F. Kennedy, July 19, 1961, National Security Files, USSR Security 6/61–8/61, JFKL.
36. FRUS 14:217.
37. Ibid.
38. Ibid.
39. Ibid., 217–218.
40. Beschloss, *Crisis Years,* 258.
41. FRUS 14:219.
42. Ibid.
43. Ibid.
44. Ibid., 220.
45. Ibid.
46. Ibid.
47. Ibid.
48. Ibid.

Chapter 6

1. Walt Rostow, memorandum to President John F. Kennedy, July 22, 1961, President's Office Files, Box 125a, JFKL.
2. Ibid.
3. Ibid.
4. Ibid.
5. Ibid.
6. Dallek, *Unfinished Life,* 423.
7. FRUS 14:226.
8. Dallek, *Unfinished Life,* 423.
9. JFKL.
10. Taubman, *Khrushchev,* 502; Beschloss, *Crisis Years,* 262–263.
11. Ibid.
12. FRUS 14:229.
13. Ibid., 235.
14. Ibid., 241.
15. Taubman, *Khrushchev,* 505.
16. Ibid., 502.
17. FRUS 14:243.
18. Ibid.
19. FRUS 14:259–260.
20. Ibid.
21. Ibid.
22. FRUS 14:262.
23. Ibid.
24. Ibid., 264.
25. Beschloss, *Crisis Years,* 265.
26. Ibid., 271.
27. Ibid., 272.
28. Ibid., 273.
29. Dallek, *Unfinished Life,* 426.

30. Ibid.
31. FRUS 14:330–331.
32. Ibid., 332.
33. Ibid., 347.
34. Ibid., 359–360.
35. For a good account of Kennedy's reaction see Beschloss, *Crisis Years*, 291.
36. Beschloss, *Crisis Years*, 293.
37. Ibid., 296.
38. Ibid.
39. Ibid., 316.
40. Schlesinger, *Robert Kennedy*, 502.
41. Beschloss, *Crisis Years*, 319.
42. Ibid.
43. FRUS 6:25.
44. Ibid., 25–26.
45. Ibid., 35.
46. Beschloss, *Crisis Years*, 319.
47. Ibid., 320.
48. FRUS 6:38.
49. Ibid., 42.
50. FRUS 14:460–461.
51. FRUS 6:44.
52. Taubman, *Khrushchev*, 538.
53. Beschloss, *Crisis Years*, 334.
54. Ibid., 335.

Chapter 7

1. Schlesinger, *Robert Kennedy*, 97.
2. Ibid., 600.
3. Robert F. Kennedy, recorded interview by John Bartlow Martin, p. 56, 3/1/1964, John F. Kennedy Oral History Project of the JFKL.
4. Robert F. Kennedy, recorded interview by John Bartlow Martin, p. 16, 2/29/1964, John F. Kennedy Oral History Project of the JFKL.
5. Ibid., 17.
6. Ibid., 16.
7. Ibid., 18.
8. Ibid., p. 22.
9. Ibid., 21.
10. Ibid., 21–22.
11. Thomas, *Robert Kennedy*, 18.
12. Ibid., 126.
13. Schlesinger, *Robert Kennedy*, 433.
14. Ibid., 417.
15. Ibid., 449.
16. Ibid., 430.
17. Robert F. Kennedy, recorded interview by John Bartlow Martin, p. 83, 3/1/1964, John F. Kennedy Oral History Project of the JFKL.
18. Schlesinger, *Robert Kennedy*, 428.
19. Robert F. Kennedy, recorded interview by John Bartlow Martin, p. 20, 2/29/1964, John F. Kennedy Oral History Project of the JFKL.
20. Schlesinger, *Robert Kennedy*, 429.
21. Robert F. Kennedy, recorded interview by John Bartlow Martin, p. 36, 2/29/1964, John F. Kennedy Oral History Project of the JFKL.
22. Ibid.
23. Schlesinger, *Robert Kennedy*, 429–430.
24. Ibid., 433.
25. Ibid., 439.
26. Ibid.
27. JFK, speech to the American Foreign Service, July 2, 1962, John T. Woolley and Gerhard Peters, *The American Presidency Project* (Santa Barbara, CA: University of California [hosted], Gerhard Peters [database]), http://www.presidency.ucsb.edu/ws/?pid=8753.
28. Schlesinger, *Robert Kennedy*, 599.
29. Ibid.
30. Ibid., 443.
31. Ibid.
32. Ibid., 444–445.
33. Ibid., 445.
34. Ibid., 446.
35. Ibid., 447.
36. Robert F. Kennedy, recorded interview by John Bartlow Martin, p. 50, 3/1/1964, John F. Kennedy Oral History Project of the JFKL.
37. Lawrence Freedman, *Kennedy's Wars: Berlin Cuba, Laos and Vietnam* (New York: Oxford University Press, 2000), 19.
38. Robert F. Kennedy, recorded interview by John Bartlow Martin, p. 97, 3/1/1964, John F. Kennedy Oral History Project of the JFKL.
39. Ibid., 51.
40. Ibid., 47.
41. Ibid., 52.
42. Ibid., 53.
43. Ibid., 50.
44. Schlesinger, *Robert Kennedy*, 452.
45. Ibid., 458.
46. FRUS 8:110.
47. Ibid.
48. Ibid., 113.
49. Schlesinger, *Robert Kennedy*, 459.
50. FRUS 10:719.
51. Ibid.
52. Ibid.
53. Ibid., 720.
54. Ibid.
55. Robert F. Kennedy, recorded interview by John Bartlow Martin, p. 65, 3/1/1964, John F. Kennedy Oral History Project of the JFKL.
56. Ibid.
57. Ibid., 99.
58. Ibid.
59. Ibid., 66.
60. Robert F. Kennedy, recorded interview by John Bartlow Martin, p. 109, 4/13/1964, John F. Kennedy Oral History Project of the JFKL.
61. Ibid.
62. Ibid.
63. Robert F. Kennedy, recorded interview by John Bartlow Martin, p. 66, 3/1/1964, John F. Kennedy Oral History Project of the JFKL.
64. Ibid., 68.
65. Ibid., 69.

66. Ibid.
67. Schlesinger, *Robert Kennedy*, 574.
68. Ibid.
69. Ibid.
70. *New York Times* (New York), February 23, 1962.
71. Ibid.
72. Ibid.

Chapter 8

1. Robert F. Kennedy, recorded interview by John Bartlow Martin, p. 111, 4/13/1964, John F. Kennedy Oral History Project of the JFKL.
2. Robert F. Kennedy, recorded interview by John Bartlow Martin, p. 62, 3/1/1964, John F. Kennedy Oral History Project of the JFKL.
3. Ibid., 61.
4. Ibid.
5. Schlesinger, *Robert F. Kennedy*, 463.
6. Robert F. Kennedy, recorded interview by John Bartlow Martin, p. 112, 4/13/1964, John F. Kennedy Oral History Project of the JFKL.
7. Ibid., 123.
8. Schlesinger, *Robert Kennedy*, 492.
9. JFK, University of Washington Centennial Speech, Nov. 16, 1961, Woolley and Peters, *American Presidency Project*, http://www.presidency.ucsb.edu/ws/?pid=8448.
10. Schlesinger, *Robert Kennedy*, 493.
11. Ibid., 476.
12. Ibid., 477.
13. Ibid., 475.
14. FRUS 10:702.
15. Ibid., 703.
16. Robert F. Kennedy, recorded interview by John Bartlow Martin, p. 163, 4/13/1964, John F. Kennedy Oral History Project of the JFKL.
17. FRUS 10:688.
18. Ibid., 745.
19. Ibid., 746.
20. Ibid.
21. Ibid.
22. Ibid., 767–768.
23. Ibid., 771n.
24. Ibid.
25. Ibid., 824.
26. Ibid.
27. Aleksandr Fursenko and Timothy Naftali, *"One Hell of a Gamble": Khrushchev, Castro, and Kennedy 1958–1964* (New York: W.W. Norton, 1997), 158.
28. FRUS 10:850.
29. Ibid.
30. Robert F. Kennedy, recorded interview by Arthur M. Schlesinger, Jr., p. 609, 2/27/1965, John F. Kennedy Oral History Project of the JFKL.

Chapter 9

1. Robert S. McNamara with Brian VanDeMark, *In Retrospect: The Tragedy and Lessons of Vietnam* (New York: Random House, 1995), 26–27.
2. Robert S. McNamara, recorded interview by Arthur M. Schlesinger, Jr., p. 1, 4/4/1964, John F. Kennedy Oral History Project of the JFKL.
3. Ibid.
4. Ibid.
5. Ibid., 2.
6. Ibid.
7. Ibid., 3.
8. Ibid.
9. Ibid., 5.
10. Ibid., 13.
11. Maxwell Taylor, *Swords and Plowshares* (New York: W.W. Norton, 1972), 180.
12. Ibid., 181.
13. Ibid., 182.
14. Ibid., 184.
15. Ibid., 184–185.
16. Ibid., 195.
17. Ibid., 197.
18. Ibid., 198.
19. Ibid.
20. Ibid.
21. Ibid., 199.
22. Ibid., 200.
23. Ibid., 201.
24. McNamara, *In Retrospect*, 30.
25. Ibid., 31.
26. Ibid., 39.
27. Taylor, *Swords and Plowshares*, 202.
28. Ibid.
29. George C. Herring, *America's Longest War: The United States and Vietnam 1950–1975*. Second edition (New York: McGraw-Hill, 1986), 55.
30. Ibid., 75.
31. Freedman, 322.
32. Ibid., 288.
33. Taylor, *Swords and Plowshares*, 225.
34. Ibid.
35. Ibid., 226.
36. Ibid., 229.
37. Ibid., 228.
38. Ibid., 244.
39. FRUS vol. 1, *Vietnam* (Washington: United States Government Printing Office, 1988), 479.
40. Ibid., 480.
41. Freedman, 330.
42. FRUS 1:559.
43. Ibid., 560.
44. Ibid.
45. McNamara, *In Retrospect*, 38–39.
46. Ibid., 39.
47. FRUS 1:574.
48. Schlesinger, *A Thousand Days*, 547.
49. Ibid., 548.

Chapter 10

1. David Talbot, *Brothers: The Hidden History of the Kennedy Years* (New York: Free Press, 2007), 51.
2. Ibid.
3. H.R. McMaster, *Dereliction of Duty: Lyndon Johnson, Robert McNamara, the Joint Chiefs of Staff, and the Lies That Led to Vietnam* (New York: HarperPerennial, 1998), 15.
4. Mark J. White, ed., *The Kennedys and Cuba: The Declassified Documentary History* (Chicago: Ivan R. Dee, 1999), 112.
5. Ibid., 113.
6. Ibid., 114.
7. Talbot, 107.
8. Ibid., 108.
9. Taylor, 252.
10. Ibid.
11. John T. Woolley and Gerhard Peters, *The American Presidency Project* [online]. Santa Barbara: University of California (hosted), Gerhard Peters (Database). Available at: http://www.presidency.uscb.edu/ws/?pid=869J.
12. Ibid., 253.
13. Ibid., 259.
14. Ibid., 261.
15. Ernst May and Philip Zelikow, eds., *The Kennedy Tapes: Inside the White House During the Cuban Missile Crisis* (Cambridge: Harvard University Press, 1998), 6.
16. Talbot, 66.
17. Ibid., 67.
18. May and Zelikow, *Kennedy Tapes*, 6.
19. Reeves, 182.
20. Ibid., 222.
21. Schlesinger, *A Thousand Days*, 912.
22. Schlesinger, *Robert Kennedy*, 450.
23. James McPherson, *Tried by War: Abraham Lincoln as Commander in Chief* (New York: Penguin Group, 2008), 6–7.
24. Taylor, *Swords and Plowshares*, 253.
25. Ibid., 253–254.
26. Talbot, 107.
27. McNamara, *In Retrospect*, 47.

Chapter 11

1. FRUS 10:944.
2. Ibid.
3. Ibid., 947–948.
4. Ibid.
5. Ibid.
6. White, *The Kennedys and Cuba*, 141–142.
7. Ibid., 143–144.
8. FRUS 10:1002–1003.
9. White, 151.
10. Ibid.
11. Ibid., 153.
12. Fursenko and Naftali, "*One Hell of a Gamble*," 179.
13. White, *The Kennedys and Cuba*, 153–154.
14. Ibid., 155.
15. Ibid., 156.
16. FRUS 6:158.
17. Ibid., 159.
18. Ibid., 159–160.
19. FRUS vol. 11, *Cuban Missile Crisis and Aftermath* (Washington: United States Government Printing Office, 1996), 6–7.
20. Ibid., 12.
21. Ibid., 14.
22. Ibid.
23. Ibid., 15.
24. White, 166.
25. Ibid. n16.
26. Robert Kennedy, *Thirteen Days: A Memoir of the Cuban Missile Crisis* (New York: W.W. Norton, 1971), 19.
27. Ibid., 20.
28. Schlesinger, *Robert Kennedy*, 507.
29. Robert Kennedy, *Thirteen Days*, 29–30.
30. Theodore Sorensen, *Counselor: A Life at the Edge of History* (New York: HarperCollins, 2008), 285.
31. Robert Kennedy, *Thirteen Days*, 25.
32. Michael Dobbs, *One Minute to Midnight: Kennedy, Khrushchev, and Castro on the Brink of Nuclear War* (New York: Alfred A. Knopf, 2008), 3–4.
33. May and Zelikow, *The Kennedy Tapes*, 49.
34. Ibid., 51.
35. Ibid., 54.
36. Ibid., 56.
37. Ibid., 58–59.
38. Ibid., 62.
39. Ibid., 63.
40. Ibid., 68.
41. Ibid., 69–70.
42. FRUS 11:46.
43. May and Zelikow, *The Kennedy Tapes*, 85.
44. Ibid., 86.
45. Ibid., 87.
46. Ibid., 88.
47. Ibid., 89.
48. Ibid., 90.
49. Ibid., 92.
50. Ibid., 96–97.
51. Ibid., 97–98.
52. Ibid., 102.
53. Ibid., 112.
54. Ibid., 113–114.

Chapter 12

1. May and Zelikow, *The Kennedy Tapes*, 133.
2. Ibid.
3. Ibid., 135.

4. Ibid., 137.
5. Ibid., 142–143.
6. Ibid., 144.
7. Ibid., 149.
8. FRUS 11:114.
9. May and Zelikow, *The Kennedy Tapes*, 169.
10. Theodore Sorensen, *Kennedy* (New York: Konecky and Konecky, 1965), 691.
11. George W. Ball, recorded interview by Joseph Kraft, p. 63–64, 4/16/1965, John F. Kennedy Oral History Project of the JFKL.
12. May and Zelikow, *Kennedy Tapes*, 172.
13. Ibid., 175–176.
14. Ibid., 178.
15. Ibid., 182; see also Michael Dobbs, *One Minute to Midnight*, 22.
16. May and Zelikow, *Kennedy Tapes*, 188.
17. Ibid., 192.
18. FRUS 11:128.
19. Ibid.
20. Ibid., 129.
21. Ibid., 130–131.
22. Ibid., 131–132.
23. Ibid.
24. May and Zelikow, *Kennedy Tapes*, 203.
25. Ibid., 258–259.
26. Ibid., 264.
27. Ibid., 264–265.
28. Ibid., 271.
29. Ibid., 275.
30. Sorenson, *Kennedy*, 702–703.
31. Dallek, *Unfinished Life*, 557–558.
32. Kenneth P. O'Donell and David Powers, *Oh Johnny We Hardly Knew Ye* (Boston: Little, Brown, 1970), 328.
33. Beschloss, *Crisis Years*, 481.
34. May and Zelikow, *Kennedy Tapes*, 283.
35. Ibid., 285–286.
36. Ibid., 287.
37. FRUS 6:167.
38. Aleksandr Fursenko and Timothy Naftali, *Khrushchev's Cold War: The Inside Story of an American Adversary* (New York: W.W. Norton, 2006), 477.
39. Robert F. Kennedy, *Thirteen Days*, 51.
40. Dallek, 561.
41. Ibid., 54.
42. Beschloss, *Crisis Years*, 498; see also Dallek, 562.
43. Dallek, 505–506.
44. Dallek, 565.
45. May and Zelikow, *Kennedy Tapes*, 483.
46. FRUS 6:173.
47. Dallek, 565–566.
48. FRUS 6:174.
49. FRUS 6:176.
50. FRUS 6:177.
51. Ibid.
52. FRUS 6:179.
53. Dallek, 567.
54. May and Zelikow, *Kennedy Tapes*, 509.
55. Ibid., 510–511.
56. Ibid., 554.
57. Ibid., 557.
58. Schlesinger, *Robert Kennedy*, 519.
59. May and Zelikow, *Kennedy Tapes*, 606.
60. Schlesinger, *Robert Kennedy*, 520.
61. FRUS 11:270–271.
62. Fursenko and Naftali, *Khrushchev's Cold War*, 481.
63. FRUS 11:270–271.
64. Fursenko and Naftali, *Khrushchev's Cold War*, 491.
65. Ibid., 489–490.

Chapter 13

1. FRUS 6:226.
2. Ibid., 227.
3. Ibid., 228.
4. Ibid., 230.
5. Ibid., 232.
6. Ibid., 233.
7. Ibid.
8. Ibid., 234–235.
9. Ibid., 236.
10. Ibid.
11. Ibid., 238.
12. Ibid.
13. Ibid., 240.
14. Fursenko and Naftali, *Khrushchev's Cold War*, 507.
15. Ibid., 508–509.
16. FRUS vol. 7, *Arms Control and Disarmament* (Washington: United States Government Printing Office, 1995), 645.
17. Sorensen, *Kennedy*, 729.
18. Ibid., 730.
19. Reeves, 510.
20. Ibid., 511.
21. Ibid.
22. Sorensen, *Counselor*, 138.
23. Ibid., 139.
24. Ibid., 141.
25. Ibid.
26. Woolley and Peters, *The American Presidency Project,* http://www.presidency.ucsb.edu/ws/?pid=9266.
27. *The New York Times* (New York), June 11, 1963.
28. Ibid.
29. Ibid.
30. Ibid.
31. Ibid.
32. Beschloss, 599–600.
33. Naftali and Fursenko, *One Hell of a Gamble*, 337–338.
34. Beschloss, 623–624.
35. Sorensen, *Counselor*, 327.
36. Ibid., 326.

Chapter 14

1. Costigliola, "The Pursuit of the Atlantic Community," in Paterson, ed., *Kennedy's Quest for Victory*, 53.
2. Reeves, *Profile of Power*, 534.
3. Ibid.
4. FRUS vol. 15, *Berlin Crisis 1962–1963* (Washington: United States Government Printing Office, 1994), 525.
5. Ibid., 525–526.
6. Reeves, 534.
7. Wooley and Peters, *The American Presidency Project*, http://www.presidency.ucsb.edu/ws/?pid=9289.
8. Wooley and Peters, *The American Presidency Project*, http://www.presidency.ucsb.edu/ws/?pid=9291.
9. Woolley and Peters, *The American Presidency Project*, http://www.presidency.ucsb.edu/ws/?pid=9297.
10. Ibid.
11. Ibid.
12. Ibid.
13. *The New York Times* (New York), June 27, 1963.
14. Reeves, 535.
15. Woolley and Peters, http://www.presidency.ucsb.edu/ws/?pid=9307.
16. Reeves, 537.
17. *The New York Times* (New York), June 27, 1963.
18. Ibid.
19. Ibid.
20. Woolley and Peters, http://www.presidency.ucsb.edu/ws/?pid=9310.
21. *The New York Times* (New York), June 27, 1963.

Epilogue

1. Herring, 84.
2. Ibid., 86.
3. Ibid., 87–88.
4. Ibid.
5. Ibid., 100.

Bibliography

Primary Sources

Audiovisual Files, National Security Files, and President's Office Files. John F. Kennedy Presidential Library, Boston, Massachusetts.

Ball, George W., recorded interview. John F. Kennedy Oral History Project of the John F. Kennedy Presidential Library.

Foreign Relations of the United States 1961–1963. Volume 1, *Vietnam.* Washington: United States Government Printing Office, 1988.

Foreign Relations of the United States 1961–1963. Volume 5, *Soviet Union.* Washington: United States Government Printing Office, 1998.

Foreign Relations of the United States 1961–1963. Volume 6, *Kennedy-Khrushchev Exchanges.* Washington: United States Government Printing Office, 1996.

Foreign Relations of the United States 1961–1963. Volume 7, *Arms Control and Disarmament.* Washington: United States Government Printing Office, 1995.

Foreign Relations of the United States 1961–1963. Volume 8, *National Security Policy.* Washington: United States Government Printing Office, 1995.

Foreign Relations of the United States 1961–1963. Volume 10, *Cuba.* Washington: United States Government Printing Office, 1997.

Foreign Relations of the United States 1961–1963. Volume 11, *Cuban Missile Crisis and Aftermath.* Washington: United States Government Printing Office, 1996.

Foreign Relations of the United States 1961–1963. Volume 14, *Berlin Crisis, 1961–1962.* Washington: United States Government Printing Office, 1993.

Foreign Relations of the United States 1961–1963. Volume 15, *Berlin Crisis, 1962–1963.* Washington: United States Government Printing Office, 1994.

Kennedy, Robert F., recorded interviews. John F. Kennedy Oral History Project of the John F. Kennedy Presidential Library.

McNamara, Robert S., recorded interviews. John F. Kennedy Oral History Project of the John F. Kennedy Presidential Library.

Woolley, John T., and Gerhard Peters. *The American Presidency Project.* Santa Barbara: University of California (hosted), Gerhard Peters (database), http://www.presidency.ucsb.edu/ws.

Secondary Sources

Beschloss, Michael. *The Crisis Years: Kennedy and Khrushchev 1960–1963.* New York: Edward Burlingame Books, 1991.

Dallek, Robert. *An Unfinished Life: John F. Kennedy 1917–1963.* Boston: Little, Brown, 2003.

Dobbs, Michael. *One Minute to Midnight: Kennedy, Khrushchev, and Castro on the Brink of Nuclear War.* New York: Alfred A. Knopf, 2008.

Fursenko, Alexsandr, and Timothy Naftali. *Khrushchev's Cold War: The Inside Story of an American Adversary.* New York: W.W. Norton, 2006.

———. *"One Hell of a Gamble": Khrushchev, Castro, and Kennedy 1958–1964.* New York: W.W. Norton, 1997.

Freedman, Lawrence. *Kennedy's Wars: Berlin Cuba, Laos and Vietnam.* New York: Oxford University Press, 2000.

Halberstam, David. *The Best and the Brightest.* New York: Ballantine Books, 1992.

Harrison, Hope. *Driving the Soviets up the Wall: Soviet–East German Relations, 1953–1961.* Princeton, N.J.: Princeton University Press, 2003.

Herring, George C. *America's Longest War: The United States and Vietnam 1950–1975.* Second edition. New York: McGraw-Hill, 1986.

Kennedy, Robert. *Thirteen Days: A Memoir of the Cuban Missile Crisis.* New York: W.W. Norton, 1971.

Khrushchev, Nikita. *Khrushchev Remembers.* New York: Little, Brown, 1970.

May, Ernest, and Philip Zelikow, eds. *The Kennedy Tapes: Inside the White House During the Cuban Missile Crisis.* Cambridge, Mass.: Harvard University Press, 1998.

McMaster, H. R. *Dereliction of Duty: Lyndon Johnson, Robert McNamara, the Joint Chiefs of Staff, and the Lies That Led to Vietnam.* New York: HarperPerennial, 1998.

McNamara, Robert S., with Brian VanDeMark. *In Retrospect: The Tragedy and Lessons of Vietnam.* New York: Random House, 1995.

McPherson, James. *Tried by War: Abraham Lincoln as Commander in Chief.* New York: Penguin Group, 2008.

O'Donell, Kenneth P., and David Powers. *Oh Johnny We Hardly Knew Ye.* Boston: Little, Brown, 1970.

Paterson, Thomas, ed. *Kennedy's Quest for Victory: American Foreign Policy, 1961–1963.* New York: Oxford University Press, 1989.

Reeves, Richard. *President Kennedy: Profile of Power.* New York: Touchstone, 1993.

Schlesinger, Arthur, Jr. *Robert Kennedy and His Times.* New York: Houghton Mifflin, 2002.

———. *A Thousand Days: John F. Kennedy in the White House.* Boston: Riverside Press, 1965.

Sorensen, Theodore. *Counselor: A Life at the Edge of History.* New York: HarperCollins, 2008.

Sorensen, Theodore. *Kennedy.* New York: Konecky and Konecky, 1965.

Talbot, David. *Brothers: The Hidden History of the Kennedy Years.* New York: Free Press, 2007.

Taubman, William. *Khrushchev: The Man and His Era.* New York: W.W. Norton, 2003.

Taylor, Maxwell. *Swords and Plowshares.* New York: W.W. Norton, 1972.

Thomas, Evan. *Robert Kennedy: His Life.* New York: Touchstone, 2000.

Trachtenberg, Marc. *A Constructed Peace: The Making of the European Settlement.* Princeton, N.J.: Princeton University Press, 1999.

White, Mark J., ed. *The Kennedys and Cuba: The Declassified Documentary History.* Chicago: Ivan R. Dee, 1999.

Journal Articles

Chang, Gordon. "JFK, China, and the Bomb." *The Journal of American History* 74, no. 4 (March 1988): 1287–1310.

Costigliola, Frank. "Kennedy, the European Allies, and the Failure to Consult." *Political Science Quarterly* 110, no. 1 (Spring 1995).

Khrushchev, Sergei. "How My Father and President Kennedy Saved the World." *American Heritage* 53, no. 5 (2002): 66–75.

Nelson, Anna Kasten. "President Kennedy's National Security: A Reconsideration." *Reviews in American History* 10, no. 1 (March 1991): 1–14.

Taubman, William. "Khrushchev vs. Mao: A Preliminary Sketch of the Role of Personality in the Sino-Soviet Split." *Cold War International History Project,* Winter 1996/1997, issues 8–9: 243–248.

Index

Acheson, Dean 31–33, 72–79, 81–83, 86, 88, 90, 91, 101, 179, 195, 196
Adenauer, Konrad 28–29, 32–33, 71, 85, 213
Adzhubei, Aleksei 43
Africa 137
Akolovsky, Alexander 55, 56
Alsop, Joe 70
American University 198; Kennedy's "peace speech" at 9, 202, 205–210, 212, 214, 220, 221, 222
"Appeasement at Munich" 14

Ball, George 179, 212, 213
Bay of Pigs 2, 3, 6, 7, 33, 35, 37, 41, 42, 45, 46, 50, 74, 76, 77, 87, 102, 108, 112, 113, 119, 125–129, 134, 143, 145, 148, 151, 166, 176, 184, 187, 202, 223
Berlin 23, 27, 32, 52, 62, 63, 67, 70–74, 78, 80, 85, 87–91, 93, 95–100, 116, 117, 143, 162, 165, 169, 173, 177, 178, 180, 183, 185, 187, 199, 200, 213; Kennedy's speech at 216–218, 221, 222
Berlin Crisis (1961) 72, 79, 92–103, 109, 187, 223
Berlin Wall 92, 102, 118, 216–217
Bissell, Richard 111, 122
Bohlen, Charles 15, 55, 94
Bolshakov, Georgi 43, 44, 51, 61, 65, 95, 102, 116, 194
Brandt, Willy 30, 117, 217
Bundy, McGeorge 2, 7, 14–16, 24–27, 31, 33–37, 45, 46, 47, 65, 66, 70–72, 75, 79, 81, 82, 84, 86, 89–94, 97, 99, 100, 107, 135, 158–161, 164, 166, 167, 170, 171, 172, 173, 174, 176, 177, 178, 179, 189, 191, 194–196, 211, 222, 223
Burke, Adm. Arleigh 33, 135
Bush, George W. 1, 2, 4

Castro, Fidel 58, 111, 125, 146, 160–163, 166, 183, 190, 194
Central Intelligence Agency (CIA) 27, 32, 109, 113, 114, 125, 126, 129, 165
Checkpoint Charlie 99, 115, 216
Cheney, Richard 1
China 17–18, 48, 59, 202, 212

Choate 6, 14
Clifton, Gen. Chester 92
Cousins, Norman 201–203
Cronkite, Walter 187
Cuba 27, 33, 44, 58, 60, 112, 113, 115, 124, 146, 148, 158–196, 199, 200
Cuban Missile Crisis (1962) 8, 73, 124, 143, 158–196, 198, 200, 206, 210–211, 213, 220

de Gaulle, Charles 28, 49, 66, 85, 212
Diem, Ngo Dinh 138–144, 223–224
disarmament 221
Dobrynin, Anatoly 162, 174, 179, 188, 192–194
Dulles, Allen 26, 114
Dulles, John Foster 56, 114

East Berlin 102, 216
East Germany 28, 50, 93
Eisenhower, Dwight D. 46, 47, 56, 109, 132, 148, 166, 194, 210
England 86
Erhard, Ludwig 213
Europe, Kennedy's 1963 trip to 212–218
EXCOMM 103, 168, 172, 174, 181, 188, 190, 191, 204

Federal Republic of Germany (FRG) 23, 28–29, 32–33, 52, 212, 213, 215
Fomin, Alexander 190, 191
Forrestal, Michael 107
France 83, 86
Frankel, Max 210
Fulbright, J. William 184, 186

German Democratic Republic (GDR) 18, 22, 23, 28–29, 32, 52, 80
Germany 26–31, 52, 59, 83 Soviet peace treaty with 62
Gilpatric, Roswell 141
Goldwater, Barry 210
Goodwin, Richard 121
Gromyko, Andrei 40–41, 99, 163, 179, 181

Harriman, Averell 17, 24, 49, 66, 210, 211
Harvard University 6

Index

Hilter, Adolf 62, 207, 215
Holeman, Frank 43
Houston, Lawrence 121
Hyman, Sidney 2, 9

ICBM sites in Cuba 181

Jacobson, Dr. Max 54, 59
Johnson, Lyndon B. 120 , 132, 135, 224
Johnson, U. Alexis 122, 126, 159
Joint Chiefs of Staff 3, 7, 34, 80, 109, 113, 114, 120, 125, 126, 141, 144–156, 158, 168, 169, 170, 173, 174, 176, 177, 180–184, 195

Kennan, George 6, 18, 48, 49, 66, 139
Kennedy, Caroline 168
Kennedy, Edward M. 117
Kennedy, John F. 79, 121, 136, 137, 160, 171, 188–196; Addison's disease and 67; American University Speech and 205–209; Berlin Crisis 92–100; Berlin discussion at Vienna and 62–63; Berlin speech of 217–218; Berlin Wall visit 216–217; Choate and Harvard and 14; communication with Khrushchev after the Cuban Missile Crisis 198–201; Congressional leadership during Cuban Missile Crisis and 184–186; Cuba buildup 159–164; Curtis LeMay and 151; Joint Chiefs during Cuban Missile Crisis and 180–184; the Joint Chiefs of Staff and 146–154; Khrushchev letters to 97–100; Khrushchev meeting at Vienna with 54–57; missiles in Cuba and 165–175; Operation Mongoose and 124–125; Prime Minister Macmillan during Cuban Missile Crisis and 187; reaction to the Bay of Pigs 33; relationship with Bundy 15–16; replying to Khrushchev pre-presidency 17–18; RFK and 106–111; the Vienna Summit preparation and 40–50; the Vienna Summit proposal and 40; wars of liberation speech and 19
Kennedy, Robert 2, 3, 8, 33, 43, 44, 61, 65, 79, 93, 94, 95, 100, 106–130, 137, 152, 156, 158–160, 165, 167, 168, 171, 172, 176, 177, 179, 181, 183, 188, 191–196, 223, 224
"Kennedy Doctrine" 198, 210, 220
Khrushchev, Nikita 16–20, 23–25, 28–29, 36, 40, 42, 48, 50, 51, 54–64, 76, 78, 86–89, 95–100, 108, 120, 136, 162, 163, 164, 166, 172, 173, 177, 178, 188, 189, 190, 192–194, 198–203, 207, 219–221
Khrushchev, Sergei 5
Kissinger, Henry 31–32, 70, 72, 101
Korea 145
Krock, Arthur 220

Lansdale, Gen. Edward 114, 115, 122, 123, 124, 125, 129, 138, 159
Laos 60, 62
Latin America 137, 145, 210
LeMay, Gen. Curtis 119, 150, 151, 180–183, 195

Lemnitzer, Gen. Lyman 3, 36, 109, 119, 136, 145, 146, 147, 151, 153, 159
Lincoln, Abraham 70, 152, 198
Lippman, Walter 70–72
Lovett, Robert 179

Macmillan, Harold 30–31, 70, 85, 186–187, 189, 192
Mao Zedong 20
McCloy, John 87–89
McCone, John 122, 123, 127, 159, 160, 165, 166, 167, 175, 182, 184, 195
McNamara, Robert 2, 3, 8, 79, 81, 83, 84, 108, 109, 110, 111, 119, 122, 132–134, 136, 137, 139, 141, 142, 146, 147, 150–156, 158–160, 165, 168–179, 181, 182, 184, 185, 191, 195, 202, 211, 223
Menshikov, Mikhail 17, 42
Minh, Ho Chi 138, 139, 143, 155
Monroe Doctrine 161, 163
Morris, Errol 3
MRBM sites in Cuba 159, 166, 167, 170, 173, 181, 195
Murrow, Edward R. 110

National Security Council 27, 76, 77, 85, 86, 128, 166, 181
NATO (North Atlantic Treaty Organization) 47, 65, 147, 160, 170, 178, 190–192, 196
"New Frontier" 1, 127, 133
New York Times 2, 9, 209, 210, 219, 220
Nitze, Paul 122
Nixon, Richard 47
Nuclear Test Ban Treaty 51, 61, 198, 212; see also Test ban treaty
Nuclear War 1

O'Donnell, Kenneth 55, 58, 78, 92, 107, 186
Operation Mongoose 115, 122, 124–126, 129, 147, 159, 165, 172, 181
Operation Northwoods 146, 147, 166, 194
Oswald, Lee Harvey 224

Powell, Colin 1

RB-47 flyers 25, 27, 36
Roosevelt, Franklin D. 9, 14, 17, 42, 57, 59
Rostow, Walt 85–86, 92, 101, 138, 141, 142, 155
Rusk, Dean 13, 14, 16, 21–22, 27, 35–36, 48, 55, 80, 82, 83, 89, 90, 92–94, 97, 99, 101, 108, 112, 142, 159, 169, 171, 172, 189, 211
Russell, Richard 184–186

Salinger, Pierre 26, 95, 161
Scali, John 190
Schlesinger, Arthur, Jr. 3, 12, 27, 78–80, 101, 106, 110, 113, 143, 168
SEATO 139, 143
Sino-Soviet Relations 17–18, 48, 124, 139, 200
Sorensen, Theodore 2–4, 9, 87, 107, 162, 168, 179, 182, 186, 192, 198, 202–204, 207, 209, 211, 217, 220–223

Southeast Asia 133, 137–144, 148, 155, 165, 223–224
Soviet-American relations 53, 60, 76, 198
Soviet Union (USSR) 50, 51, 53, 56, 58, 59, 63, 96, 137, 178, 191–194, 198, 201, 202, 206–209, 221
Stalin, Joseph 22, 57, 210
State Department, U.S 50–53, 66, 90, 192, 213
Stevenson, Adlai 16, 183, 189
Szulc, Ted 121

TASS 219
Taylor, Gen. Maxwell 2, 3, 8, 37, 81, 91, 108, 109, 112, 114, 119, 120, 122, 123, 126, 129, 134–144, 146, 147, 149, 151–155, 165, 168, 170, 172, 174, 176, 179, 180, 182, 183, 194–196, 223
Test ban treaty 51, 61, 199, 202, 220; *see also* Nuclear Test Ban Treaty
Thompson, Llewellyn 7, 15, 16, 19–21, 23, 29–30, 33, 36, 40–42, 44, 48, 49, 65, 66, 88, 89, 177, 178, 186, 189, 191, 195, 196
Truman, Harry S. 46, 196
Tuchman, Barbara 58
Turkey 161, 183, 190–193, 196

U-2 Spy Plane 167, 192
Udall, Stewart 162, 163, 194
Ulbrict, Walter 20, 22, 193
United Nations 93, 162, 189
United States Information Agency (USIA) 60

Vienna Summit 6, 7, 46, 47, 48, 76, 99–100, 184, 189, 198
Viet Cong 137, 140, 142
Vietnam 132, 137–145, 223–224

Wars of Liberation speech 19, 133
Washington, George 2
West Berlin 29, 71, 93, 99, 102, 117, 208, 217, 218
West Germany 86
Western Europe 208, 215
Why England Slept 14
Wicker, Tom 216, 219

Zhukov, Georgi 43
Zorin, Valerian 189

www.ingramcontent.com/pod-product-compliance
Lightning Source LLC
Chambersburg PA
CBHW051218300426
44116CB00006B/629